In Praise of *Projecting Enthusiasm*

Engaging and written in an easy-to-read style, this is an invaluable handbook. This book should be essential reading for both new and experienced teachers and presenters.

—*Maureen Bennett, Retired Teacher, Head Teacher,*
and OFSTED Inspector, England

Tauber's *Projecting Enthusiasm* offers evidenced-based techniques to put more oomph in your presentations, whether at work, a conference, or in the classroom. Great book!

—*Eric W. Corty, Director, School of Humanities and*
Social Sciences, Penn State University, The Behrend College

I had discovered the usefulness of many of the topics discussed in this book during the many decades of collegiate teaching and presentations. How much easier things would have been, for me and my audiences, if I had this book when I started my career. This book should be required reading for anyone who has to give presentations.

—*George J. Dudas, Lecturer in Computer Science and*
Software Engineering, Penn State University, The Behrend College

In his breezy, informative style, Dr. Tauber shows just how easy it is to infuse your talks with enthusiasm and spellbind your audience. Don't lend it to your colleagues or they'll finally learn how to match your ratings on the podium!

—*Ian Harper, Dean, Melbourne School of Management*

This has been the first book about teaching theory that I have enjoyed reading. I loved the tips and the quotations, and the enthusiasm and the joy of teaching was palpable.

—*Elizabeth Kennedy, GP and Medical Student Teacher, Australia*

Tauber's approach to effective presentations is dead-on, both in its rationale and in the mechanics of making it work. Extremely readable while being authoritative, and enthusiastically—even passionately—encouraging.

—*James A. Kurre, PhD, Director Emeritus and*
Senior Research Associate, Economic Research Institute of Erie

Tauber has not only identified some of the main components of enthusiasm, but he also very explicitly shows how these can be successfully learnt. This book will be of immense value to anyone keen to improve their presentation skills.

—*Ramon Lewis, Professor Emeritus, Education,*
Latrobe University, Melbourne, Australia

Projecting Enthusiasm is a captivating and enjoyable book that contains a gold mine of information for both seasoned and novice presenters. *Projecting Enthusiasm* belongs on every presenter's shelf!

—*Marilyn Livosky, Professor of Psychology, Mercyhurst University*

The ideas of many intelligent, informed people literally "fall on deaf ears" when not presented with the enthusiasm that should reveal their passion for their subject matter. Readers in a wide variety of professional fields will find the material comprehensible and immediately useful.

—*Cathy Sargent Mester, Chair, Department of*
Communication (retired), Penn State University, The Behrend College

This book covers the gamut of strategies for increasing audience engagement, making it a valuable tool for presenters from all professions and with a wide range of personal styles. The degree of specificity, such as in animation techniques, is exceptional. As a faculty developer, professor, and conference presenter, I will definitely make use of some of the tools contained in the book.

—*Carolyn Spies, Associate Vice President for Academic Affairs, Dean of*
Graduate Studies, and Professor of Psychology, Bloomfield College

It is a practical guide urgently needed and a must-read in order to enlighten presentations, to grab the immediate attention of the audience, and to hold that attention so ultimate retention and learning will occur.

—*Joseph Vergona, EdD, Adjunct Instructor,*
Graduate School of Education, Gannon University;
Director of Elementary Education, Principal, Classroom Teacher

Projecting Enthusiasm

THE KEY TO DYNAMIC PRESENTATIONS FOR PROFESSIONALS

Robert T. Tauber, PhD

PRAEGER®

An Imprint of ABC-CLIO, LLC
Santa Barbara, California • Denver, Colorado

Library of Congress Cataloging-in-Publication Data

Names: Tauber, Robert T., author.
Title: Projecting enthusiasm : the key to dynamic presentations for
    professionals / Robert T. Tauber.
Description: Santa Barbara, CA : ABC-CLIO, [2019] | Includes bibliographical
    references and index.
Identifiers: LCCN 2019010135 (print) | LCCN 2019020373 (ebook) | ISBN
    9781440872631 (eBook) | ISBN 9781440872624 (print : alk. paper)
Subjects: LCSH: Business presentations. | Enthusiasm. | Psychology,
    Industrial.
Classification: LCC HF5718.22 (ebook) | LCC HF5718.22 .T38 2019 (print) | DDC
    658.4/52—dc23
LC record available at https://lccn.loc.gov/2019010135

ISBN: 978-1-4408-7262-4 (print)
      978-1-4408-7263-1 (ebook)

23 22 21 20 19   1 2 3 4 5

This book is also available as an eBook.

Praeger
An Imprint of ABC-CLIO, LLC

ABC-CLIO, LLC
147 Castilian Drive
Santa Barbara, California 93117
www.abc-clio.com

This book is printed on acid-free paper ∞

Manufactured in the United States of America

Learn the proven dynamic delivery skills that award-winning presenters use to engage, excite, enlighten, inform, persuade, and motivate an audience. Let this book be your "coach" to great presenting.

Contents

Preface xv

Acknowledgments xix

PART I: The Key to Being a Dynamic Presenter: Feel It! Project It!

CHAPTER 1
Pedagogical Training That Works! *3*
    Introduction *3*
    The Importance of Pedagogy *3*
    What's in It for Me? *4*
    Two Weights on Your Shoulders *5*
    Summary *6*

CHAPTER 2
To Present Is to Teach; To Teach Is to Present *7*
    Introduction *7*
    A Rose by Any Other Name . . . *8*
    Sharing *"Ah, Ha"* Experiences *9*
    Conversational Writing Style *9*
    Learning is *Fun*(damental) *10*
    Telling Quotations *10*
    Presentation Is Everything! *11*
    Summary *11*

CHAPTER 3
The Case for Presentations, Lectures, Spiels, and Other
Talks *12*
 Introduction *12*
 What Do Audiences Think? *12*
 Let's Hear It for *Good* Lectures and Presentations *13*
 What's in a Name? *14*
 Presenting It Live *14*
 Should *"You"* Lecture or Present? *15*
 TED Talks *16*
 Summary *17*

CHAPTER 4
Enthusiasm: A Presentation Necessity *18*
 Introduction *18*
 Enthusiasm: A Presentation Necessity *18*
 Enthusiasm: Useful Synonyms *19*
 Enthusiasm: Its Relationship to Pedagogy *20*
 Wanted! More "Oomph" *21*
 It Can't Be That Simple, Can It? *22*
 Passion: "Let's Kick It Up a Notch!" *22*
 Enthusiasm: Can Too Much Be Too Much? *23*
 Presenter Evaluations *24*
 Enthusiasm and Subject-Matter Matrix *25*
 Summary *26*

CHAPTER 5
Parallel between Acting, Teaching, and Presenting *27*
 Introduction *27*
 "Act" Your Age *28*
 Teaching Is Teaching; Presenting Is Presenting *29*
 A Yorkshire Story *30*
 Power of Expectations: It Works Both Ways *30*
 Summary *31*

CHAPTER 6
Educational Foundations: Presenters as Actors *33*
 Introduction *33*
 Sound Theory and Effective Practice *34*
 Educational Foundations for Enthusiasm *34*
 Theorists Speak; Let's Listen *35*

You Don't Need to Be an Einstein *35*
Award-Winning Presenters Speak; Let's Listen *36*
The Profession's Response, or Lack Thereof *37*
Summary *38*

PART II: Enthusiasm-Generating Skills!
Introduction *41*
Might as Well Be Hanged for a Sheep as for a Lamb *42*
Yul Brynner: Row G, Seat 6 *42*

CHAPTER 7
A Craftsperson's Toolbox *43*
Introduction *43*
Tools for Boosting Presenter Enthusiasm *44*
Creating Your Teacher- or Presenter-Self *44*
A Craftsperson's Toolbox *45*
A Craftsperson's Knowledge *46*
A Craftsperson's Top-Tray Delivery Tools *46*
A Craftsperson's Other Delivery Tools *47*
Enthusiasm Rating Chart *48*
Summary *49*

CHAPTER 8
Animation in Body: A "Top-Tray" Tool *50*
Introduction *50*
We Are Designed to Move *50*
Value of Animation in Body *51*
Raise Your Left Hand *52*
How a Simple Change Made a Difference *52*
TED Talks *53*
Categories of Movement *54*
    Do Nothing, but Do It Well *54*
    Plan Where You Step *55*
    Gestures *55*
    Facial Expression *58*
    Eye Contact *59*
    Smiling *61*
    Posture *62*
Behaviors to Avoid *63*
True Story? Maybe, Maybe Not! *65*
Summary *65*

CHAPTER 9
Animation in Voice: A "Top-Tray" Tool 66
    Introduction 66
    Great Orators 67
    Hurl Your Words 68
    How Do You Sound to Others? 69
    Vocal Fitness 69
    Paralanguage 70
    Spontaneous Voice Variations 71
    Deliberate Voice Variations 71
        Volume and Projection 72
        Whispering 72
        Rate 73
        Tone 73
        Pitch 75
        Quality 75
        Cadence and Inflection 76
        Pauses 76
    Dreaded "Ums" 77
    Creating Characters 77
    Laryngitis and Sore Throats 78
    Summary 78

CHAPTER 10
Humor: A "Top-Tray" Tool 79
    Introduction 79
    Is Humor Too "Mickey Mouse"? 80
    Competent and Confident 80
    Benefits of Humor 81
    Humor: Its Impact on Audiences 83
    Categories of Humor 84
    Self-Deprecating Humor 86
    Lettermen's *Top Ten Reasons* 87
    Brainstorm Humorous Sentence Endings 88
    Humor in Patients' Hospital Charts 88
    What You Say May Not Be What They Hear 89
    Cartoons: A Safe First Step into Humor 90
    Using Humor: A Gaggle of Ideas 92
    Possible Unexpected Benefits of Humor 93
    Summary 94

CHAPTER 11
Suspense, Surprise, and Storytelling 96
  Introduction 96
  Creating Suspense and Surprise 97
  Ignorance 101! 99
  Storytelling 100
  Relationship to Other Performance Skills 103
  Surprise! Don't Talk 104
  Using Suspense and Surprise 104
  Summary 109

CHAPTER 12
Role-Playing 111
  Introduction 111
  Dr. Eakin: Great Scientists Speak 111
  Playing a Role 113
  Creating a Character 114
  Dead Poets Society 114
  Meeting of Minds 115
  The Role-Play Process 116
  Skinner versus Rogers 118
  The Actual Debate 118
  Storytelling: Here It Is Again 120
  Mime 121
  Summary 121

CHAPTER 13
Use of Props 122
  Introduction 122
  Picture Props 123
  Sound Props 124
  Music, Movies, and Television Props 124
  Alex Trebek's *Jeopardy!* 125
  "Imagine": A John Lennon Prop 126
  "The Raven": Edgar Allan Poe Prop 128
  Spandex Reveals All 129
  Presenter Props 130
  Puppets as Props 131
  Selected Medical Props 132
  Using the Audience as Props 133

Prop Box *134*
Guidelines for Using Props *135*
Technology Props Invade *136*
PowerPoint *137*
Notes as Props *137*
Summary *138*

CHAPTER 14
Space Utilization *139*
Introduction *139*
Lectern Lingering *140*
Proxemics *141*
Space and Its Limitations *141*
Blocking *142*
Venue Seating *143*
Where Audiences Choose to Sit *144*
Spontaneous Use of Space *145*
Summary *146*

CHAPTER 15
Creative Entrances and Exits *147*
Introduction *147*
Entrances and Exits *148*
Using "Hooks" *148*
Using Law Quotations as "Hooks" *149*
Ethics of Playing Musical Chairs *149*
Physical Entrances *150*
Verbal Entrances *151*
Musical Entrances *153*
Mister Rogers' Neighborhood *154*
What's in a Name or Title? *155*
Crafting a Title *157*
For the Love of Three *158*
Entrance Rituals *158*
Entrance Pageantry *159*
A Presenter's Marquee *160*
Ending on a High Note *160*
Stage Fright *161*
Showtime! *163*
Summary *164*

CHAPTER 16

Behind the Scenes *165*

    Introduction *165*

    Work behind the Scenes *165*

    Behind the Scenes Suggestions *166*

    Summary *168*

PART III: Engage Master Presenters

CHAPTER 17

Engage the Masters: Learn from Them *171*

    Introduction *171*

    No Serious Challenge to This Book's Premise *172*

    Knock on Their Doors; Pick Up Your Phone *173*

    They Have Walked in Your Shoes *173*

    Humility and Curiousness *174*

    "Objection, Your Honor" *174*

    Stop Spinning Your Wheels *174*

    What Else Can You Do? Lots! *175*

CHAPTER 18

Conclusion *178*

    Introduction *178*

    Willingness and Courage *179*

    A Presenter's Manner and Method *179*

    The Curtain Comes Down *180*

    Ferris Bueller's Day Off *180*

Appendix: Enthusiasm Rating Chart *181*

References *183*

Index *191*

Preface

My thought was to start this book by making an exhaustive list of the professions, and hence, the professionals who as part of their job present. I began the list, but it seemed to go on and on. I then decided that instead of listing all the professionals who need to deliver dynamic presentations, I would list all professionals who do not need to deliver presentations. This list was much shorter. In fact, this list was zero!

All professionals at one time or another are called upon to present. There is no escaping this fact. When presenting, the primary thing presenters do is communicate. They communicate with superiors, colleagues, and subordinates, and with patients, families, clients, board members, voters, workers, customers, and others. They perform, they act, and they play a role.

Their communication takes the form of engaging, enlightening, informing, persuading, motivating, and, dare I say, sometimes even entertaining an audience. The goals, then, for all presenters are similar, if not the same. Further, the tools used to attain these goals are the same. Because communication is communication, *dynamic* communication ought to be the aim of all presenters!

Presenters have still one more thing in common—all presenters teach. The presenter is cast in the role of the "teacher" and the audience is cast in the role of "students." Here are just a few examples of where effective teaching and presenting skills are required of professionals.

In medicine, the word *doctor* comes from the Latin *docere*, meaning to teach or instruct. Being a physician, therefore, means being a teacher. An attending physician conducts rounds, a doctor presents a diagnosis to a patient, department chairs run meetings, interns instruct med-students, nurses teach and monitor staff, academic faculty present papers at professional conferences, and medical educators give in-house talks to colleagues. We seem to be drawn to the *drama* surrounding the world of medicine. The skills offered in this book will help you to have audiences drawn to your presentations.

In the field of law, lawyers are called upon to sway juries—clearly where honed presentation skills are required. Witnesses need to be prepped. Legal options need to be presented. They respond to media and other requests to be interviewed about the law in general or a single case in particular. Their "closing arguments" are actually just enthusiastic closing presentations. Like medicine, the world of law often seems so dramatic that lawyers, themselves, could be actors operating on a stage—a courtroom. In fact, "the best lawyers understand that every trial is inherently dramatic" (Havener 2005, 1).

All politicians stump for votes, rallying those already on their side of an issue and trying to influence or persuade those on the other side. This involves presenting. Periodic press briefings demand skilled, often improvisational, presentations. Like doctors and lawyers, politicians respond to media and other requests for interviews and debates. Effective presentation skills can be a matter of political life or death.

Leaders in business, from salespersons to CEOs, must communicate with stockholders, the media, boards, customers, employees, and government representatives. In other words, they must effectively teach and present. No doubt, these successful presenters have used many of the presentation skills that are offered in Part II of this book. Keep in mind a recent *Harvard Business Review* publication titled "The Best Leaders Are Great Teachers" (Finkelstein 2018, 1). So, teaching is everywhere; presenting is everywhere.

This book provides relatively low-tech, easily mastered, proven presentation skills that can be used to deliver any desired message effectively and dynamically. These skills find their roots in the world of the theater where they too engage, enlighten, inform, persuade, and entertain audiences. The difference is that in the theater, actors and actresses receive training in *how* to dynamically engage their audiences. This book enables presenters, like you, to "catch up" with and master these same proven performance-based skills as you move toward becoming a more dynamic presenter.

You will find little stories woven in the text of this book with the goal of highlighting selected presentation skills. Here are just a few. Why does ice float—it shouldn't? Why don't baby sea turtles have any fun? Should we play musical chairs so everyone wins? Is using humor too Mickey Mouse for you? You will also find endless ideas for putting the described enthusiastic delivery skills into action.

The importance of *projecting* enthusiasm, and then using the proven dynamic presentation skills offered in this book to do so, applies to *all* communication no matter the venue. Many of the examples presented in this book are generic to the craft of presenting. Others reflect my academic disciplines of physics and teacher preparation. Finally, still other examples come from colleagues in other disciplines, including significant contributions from Dr. Rebecca Sivarajah, MD. All these examples reinforce the need for presenters to project enthusiasm no matter the discipline or venue. I am confident that readers can make the transfer from any and all these examples to their own content specialty.

Acknowledgments

I want to thank all those presenters who, over the years, have had the courage to step up and deliver presentations without any real training to do so. For many, it was trial and error, sink or swim. I offer special thanks to my wife, Cecelia, for putting up with me when I repeatedly asked, "What do you think about including such and such?" Her responses helped provide focus to this book; her overall editing helped make the book be more readable.

I want to thank Dr. Rebecca Sivarajah, whose spark regarding the need to project enthusiasm motivated me to start this project in the first place. Her concrete examples helped justify that this book's message applies to any and all presenting venues. Finally, I want to thank all the authors across many disciplines who wrote articles highlighting the importance of enthusiastically and passionately delivering presentations. I tried to build upon their work.

I wish to offer special acknowledgment to my wife, Cecelia; my son, David; my daughter, Becky; and to my five grandchildren, Sebastian, Olivia, Ethan, Noah, and Henry. Collectively, they are my best presentation yet!

A special thanks to Cathy Sargent Mester, a valued colleague, who helped pioneer many of the ideas presented in this book.

PART I

The Key to Being a Dynamic Presenter: Feel It! Project It!

Assuming that you know your subject matter, the *key* to being a dynamic presenter is being *enthusiastic* on the inside and *projecting* it on the outside! This book defends the importance of presenter *enthusiasm* and then addresses *how* to best *project* it.

1

Pedagogical Training That Works!

INTRODUCTION

According to Tompkins (1990, 655), "teaching (i.e., presenting) was exactly like sex for me—something you weren't supposed to talk about or focus on in any way, but you were supposed to be able to do it properly when the time came." Although we willingly talk a lot about *what* we are supposed to present, we seem embarrassed or afraid to ask *how* we are to present it (Charles 2015). Yet, we still just expect the untrained to go in there and present dynamically.

Surely you have heard someone exclaim, "So and so is a born presenter." It is true; some lucky presenters have had a head start with higher intelligence, verbal fluency, patience, good looks (yep, it helps), a pleasant-speaking voice capable of great variation, charm, a mind for detail, and a good memory. Luckily, for the rest of us, dynamic presenting depends upon mastering a set of skills that can be learned. The world of theater has known this forever.

THE IMPORTANCE OF PEDAGOGY

As a professional, just when you thought your learning and training were over, the powers-to-be remind you that your job also entails teaching and presenting. A class must be taught. A conference presentation must be delivered. A witness must be prepped. Participation in a live television interview is required. New company guidelines urgently need to be shared with all staff. An argument for additional funding must be made. Yet, presenters are only rarely taught *how* to teach and present. Most professionals who are required to present possess little or no formal training in pedagogy—how to dynamically "deliver the goods!"

Some institutions and companies are beginning to see the importance of educating presenters on how to effectively deliver their message, but basic delivery techniques (which are offered in this book) aren't always stressed with new, more "glossy" and "innovative" delivery formats taking the front seat. Everyone seems to be seeking that "silver bullet" for great presenting when the skills to accomplish this goal are right in front of them.

When providing pedagogical assistance, time is always of essence. Therefore, the training that is offered must be specific, easily mastered, and immediately useful to those required to teach or present. This book offers such proven, easy-to-master presentation skills.

Of course, many presenters are excellent at it. But, often, that is by coincidence rather than by design. If presenters had to pick up their dynamic presentation skills along the way, one might expect that it would take some time, if ever, for them to become accomplished presenters. Experience, perhaps doing the same thing wrongly due to lack of training, is not the best teacher. Neither is trial and error. No one wants to be the recipient of "error" teaching—perhaps negatively influencing one's financial or other critical life circumstances.

Given that most professionals have assigned to them a teaching or presenting responsibility greater than "just a bit of their schedule," it would behoove them to seek help with pedagogy. The research is clear that the majority of new, as well as seasoned, presenters feel apprehensive when called upon to present. It is not that they don't want to present well; they do.

WHAT'S IN IT FOR ME?

To teach is to learn twice.
—Joseph Joubert

One possible reason why presenters receive so little training is the disparaging comment: "He who can, does. He who cannot, teaches." The depressing point is that there is a possible third part of this maxim that reads "Those who can't teach, teach others to teach." I suppose that this refers to your author. Apparently, he is at the very bottom of the pecking order. Perhaps institutions and companies conclude that it is just not worth expending precious resources on presenter training. They are wrong.

Teaching was not, nor is it today in many circles, a prestigious position. But the fact remains that most presenters really want to make their presentations better. If institutions want quality presenting, no matter the discipline or venue, then they must recognize its importance and provide support for presenter training.

Shields (2010) offers reasons why institutions may not be providing presenters with quality pedagogical training. She suggests that it may hinge on those around the presenters. It could be that administrators and other superiors, themselves, do not feel all that confident about presenting, at least not confident enough to instruct others how to do it. At best, the advice they might offer is "Here is what I did; why don't you try it?" At worst, they may feel that adequate subject-matter knowledge is enough preparation to teach or present.

Specifically, what's in it for you? As Elizabeth Barrett Browning wrote in Sonnet 43, "Let me count the ways." One of the most convincing sets of reasons for teaching and presenting was written by Herrell (2016), who sees presenting just as much as a giving experience as it is a selfish one. Presenting gives you an opportunity to discover your knowledge deficits, to practice repetition (an educationally sound learning principle) of what you do know, and a chance to grow in confidence and eloquence—yes, eloquence!

TWO WEIGHTS ON YOUR SHOULDERS

> *Passion is energy. Feel the power that comes from focusing on*
> *what excites you.*
> —Oprah Winfrey

Professionals carry two weights on their shoulders. On one shoulder, they carry the burden of knowing their subject area. On the other shoulder, they carry the responsibility of being dynamic teachers or presenters.

Unfortunately, if presenters stumble or falter, they face the real prospect of "being blamed but not trained," and this is unfair. Having the qualifications in a field (e.g., degrees and experience) does not necessarily equate to one's competence to present that field effectively.

Presenter training may often be overlooked or avoided because of reluctance or ignorance. With reluctance, one is opposed to providing it. With ignorance, one isn't opposed to providing it; one just hasn't done it for some reason. I favor the "ignorance" reason because this book, by introducing proven dynamic pedagogical presenter skills, can easily overcome that hurdle.

Most presenter training, if offered at all, is not subject specific, and it need not be. The *how*, presented in Part II of this book, to engage, inform, and motivate an audience, any audience, consists of the same presenter delivery behaviors. Engaging is engaging. Informing is informing. Motivating is motivating.

SUMMARY

Does good coaching make a difference? Of course, it does! Observe any winning team, and, in addition to having some "star" players, you will find "star" coaches. My "coaching" goal is to convince you that you can be a winner in any and all presentation venues if I do my part and equip you with the necessary delivery skills. Part II of this book presents these specific delivery skills that, when properly executed, can contribute to dynamic presentations.

A colleague noted how impressed she was regarding TED talks (described in chapter 3). She stated:

> Clearly the speakers all have been coached on how to deliver an effective talk—they use the stage, they use pauses well, and they use their arms to gesture. I am certain that they were not all great speakers before they were coached. Not only are they generally delivering compelling lectures on interesting topics, but they speak clearly and pace the talk well and use interspersed stories. (Lewis 2018)

If we recognize the value of good "coaching" in every other field of endeavor, then we simply must recognize its value in delivering dynamic presentations, sales pitches, and talks in any and all other communication venues. This book is a type of "coach."

2

To Present Is to Teach;
To Teach Is to Present

INTRODUCTION

Good teaching (i.e., presenting) is one-fourth preparation
and three-fourths theater.
—Gail Godwin

To present is to teach—defined as "to show or tell somebody something." We spend our lives "showing" and "telling" people things, and they, in turn, reciprocate by doing the same thing to us. We jump back and forth from being the teacher or presenter to being the student or audience member.

A successful teacher can engage, enlighten, challenge, inform, persuade, and motivate students. This is exactly what dynamic presenters, lecturers, and deliverers of spiels and other talks do. Their audience might be called clients, customers, committees, investors, juries, patients, parishioners, voters, or citizens, but they are really students—at least for the time that they are under the presenter's tutelage.

Just last week I contacted my accountant, met with a real estate agent, inquired as to the market for single-family dwelling in my area, called my IRA representative, contacted a plumber for advice on a leaking faucet, and sought advice from my physician. In each case, although possessing a

PhD, I was the student and the professional sought out for advice was my teacher. These "teachers" informed me, influenced me, and motivated me to act. They were presenters. This is how the world works.

For those readers who did not necessarily choose to pursue a career in teaching, thinking that teaching is something done only in elementary and secondary schools (and perhaps, college), boy do I have a surprise for you. When you were not looking, you probably woke up one morning only to find that your schedule for that day involved doing some teaching or presenting, because all professions, without exception, demand of its members that they "present." This book, and the skills that it offers, can help you deliver dynamic presentations!

A ROSE BY ANY OTHER NAME . . .

Shakespeare, in the play *Romeo and Juliet*, captures the point I want to make. It doesn't matter what we call it when we communicate with others: "presenting," "lecturing," "delivering an address, spiel, or speech," or simply giving a "pep talk" (as in what a coach does before and at half-time of a big game). They are synonyms for each other; the words are interchangeable. For the bulk of this text, I will use the terms "teach" or "present." The key is not what we call it but that we deliver it dynamically!

How scary is it for even well-prepared speakers and presenters to face an audience? It can be very scary! Consider the claim, attributed to Seinfeld, that when someone is given the choice at a funeral to either be the person in the coffin or the person delivering the eulogy, for a moment or two one often is tempted to choose the former.

This book recognizes the need for anyone doing anything well to be trained to do that thing. That includes stepping in front of an audience to present. I never cease to be amazed how some presenters consider themselves prepared to present by self-proclamation despite having had no formal training to do so. To declare it so, does not make it so!

Whether we are referring to your specific profession or to those in the children's hand-clapping nursery rhyme, *Rich Man, Poor Man, Beggar Man, Thief, Doctor, Lawyer, Merchant, Chief*, the fact remains that there are well-tested and researched pedagogies that can make the teaching or presenting aspect of your job more dynamic, successful, and rewarding for both you and your audience.

I assume that you will not take at face value anything that I say. Who would blame you? Give this book a chance. Evaluate the arguments it presents, and then consider how you might incorporate many of the proven pedagogical delivery skills presented in Part II. Early reviews of the ideas presented in this book state that "This book is amazing" and "It should be required reading for all individuals aspiring to be great teachers (or presenters)."

SHARING "AH, HA" EXPERIENCES

As frightening as teaching or presenting might be for some professionals, this part of your job can be a welcome relief from your primary responsibilities. There is a great deal of satisfaction that can come from sharing the "Ah, ha" experiences of your audience. You get to see their "light bulbs of comprehension" illuminate. And, because there often is not a prescribed method of engaging an audience, you have a real chance to be creative in this part of your job. Go for it. And if there is any thought that "teaching" somehow might distract you from your real job, keep in mind that when you are presenting, you, too, are learning.

The direction this book takes, first, is to convince you that there is one overriding characteristic that all dynamic presenters share. No *ifs*, *ands*, or *buts* about it. The book then introduces a set of proven pedagogical skills, flowing from the world of theater, guaranteed to help you put this important characteristic into play. The result is that you will be able to use these skills over and over in any and all teaching or presenting situations.

As the Aussies say, "No worries!" Don't worry, I am not trying to turn you into an actor but, the truth be told, from the moment you awake until the moment you fall asleep, you act. Thus, we ought to "act" well, especially when we are presenting.

You may recognize some of the presentation skills that follow in Part II because they are basic communication skills that we use every day. My goal is to get you to specifically plan for and then incorporate the best of these skills, often in a more frequent and exaggerated form than you might normally do, into your presenting. Nothing more. But, then again, that is a lot!

Finally, I am aware that I have not yet identified that "special" presenter characteristic. This was done on purpose. I am whetting your appetite; I am teasing you a bit. I want your curiosity heightened. I want you to experience some suspense in your mind—one of my soon-to-be highlighted delivery skills. But, rest assured, the characteristic will soon be unveiled, and then, in Part II, I will deliver on *how* to make it happen.

CONVERSATIONAL WRITING STYLE

This book is not written as, nor was it intended to be, primarily a piece of scientific literature, complete with an Abstract, Methods, Subjects,

Results, and Conclusions. You will be spared all those elaborate and seeming endless charts and graphs that often accompany scientific articles. These charts and graphs may have value, but just not for my aim of making you a more dynamic presenter.

LEARNING IS *FUN*(DAMENTAL)

The day we stop playing is the day we stop learning.
—William Glasser

At times, it may appear that I do not take myself all that seriously because I insert a bit of humor here and there. But I am deadly serious about the value of dynamic presenting. I also like to have fun. I will offer tongue-in-cheek statements, a few cartoons, a pun or two, and some pithy quotations. I hope that you have a bit of fun while reading (and using) this book. After all, fun is nature's reward for learning.

William Glasser, MD (1999) identifies *fun* as one of five basic human needs, the others being *survival, love, power,* and *freedom,* shared by all human beings. Just wait until the chapter titled "Suspense and Surprise" when I explain why sea turtles just do not have any fun in their lives.

At the end of the day, good teaching (and dynamic presenting) is about having fun, experiencing pleasure, and enjoying intrinsic rewards. It is like locking eyes with someone in the back row and seeing the synapses and neurons connecting, thoughts being formed, and finally a smile cracking across a face as learning suddenly occurs (Leblanc 2010).

Having fun is not something that has to be delayed until one is off work or on vacation. In fact, if you enthusiastically introduce fun into your presenting experience, you may no longer think of what you are doing as "work"!

TELLING QUOTATIONS

If a picture is worth a thousand words, then a good quotation must be worth at least as much. I have included some great quotations. Think about them as they apply to great teaching and presenting. Here is just one of those quotations to get you thinking about delivering a dynamic performance: "If they like you, they didn't applaud—they just let you live!" (Bob Hope).

I hope that you never have to play a gig that is this demanding!

PRESENTATION IS EVERYTHING!

Preparing to teach or present requires several prerequisites. Of course, one must know the subject matter. This is a given. Next, one must create (and convey to an audience) objectives, goals, and expectations for what will be expected from them. Last, is the focus of this book—how to best present and deliver one's message.

We have all heard the saying, "Presentation is everything!" My wife and I recently went to Key West for several days. We have a favorite pub that has incredible (e.g., low price, high quality, and large quantity) appetizers during happy hour. We ordered a heaping half pound of peel-and-eat shrimp. Normally such an order is delivered in a disposable, flimsy paper bowl of some sort with paper napkins. Our order, placed and eaten at the bar, came out with cloth napkins, in a china bowl, on a china plate, and garnished with arugula and cherry tomatoes! *Presentation, presentation, presentation.* Did this presentation make the shrimp taste any better? Maybe, maybe not. Notice, though, that I am still talking about the experience—and, perhaps more important, we will be going back for more! Isn't this what you want your audiences to do?

Of course, "presentation is *not* everything," but it can go a long way toward enhancing the delivery experience for both a presenter and an audience.

SUMMARY

There is no doubt that as a professional your job demands that you present effectively. You may not have considered that you would end up having to do so much presenting, but here you are being called upon to do it regularly. The skills in this book can help you do it well!

Note: If your appetite has been whetted, literally, feel free to email me (Robert T. Tauber at rtt1453@comcast.net) and I would be happy to share the name of the Key West restaurant.

3

The Case for Presentations, Lectures, Spiels, and Other Talks

INTRODUCTION

The decrying of wholesale lecturing is certainly justified. The wholesale decrying of lectures is just as certainly not justified!
—George Cameron and Michael Manogue

For the foreseeable future, presentations will be with us. As you read this chapter, keep in mind that although the words "lecture" and "presentation" are most often used, I could have just as easily substituted the words "speech," "address," "sermon," "pitch," "spiel," "oration," or simply a good old "pep talk" by coaches (e.g., as in "win one for the Gipper"). The bottom line is that if you ever have been, or suspect you ever will be, called upon to deliver something via any of these delivery formats, then this chapter should be of interest to you.

WHAT DO AUDIENCES THINK?

It's not that audiences dislike presentations, they just dislike bad or boring ones. Who could blame them? But presentations are not inherently "always" good or bad. Their quality depends upon the talents of the designer and the skills of the deliverer. These factors are under our control.

Any discussion of lectures cannot overlook the comment in B. F. Skinner's 1948 novel, *Walden Two*. "The lecture became obsolete with the invention of printing. It survives only in our universities and a few other backward institutions" (cited in Taylor 2007, 128). Well, the date of the invention of the printing press has come and gone, and lecturing and presenting are still here.

We also cannot overlook Charles Eliot's 1869 inaugural address as president of Harvard College where he said, "The lecturer pumps laboriously into sieves. The water may be wholesome, but it runs through. A mind must work to grow." I agree! Exercising mental faculties is crucial for its growth. But I take issue with his inference that minds cannot be stretched in a good lecture or presentation. "Despite vilification, the lecture is still alive and well" (Turner, Palazzi, and Ward 2008, 133). For the foreseeable future, *good* lecturing and *good* presenting will still be with us.

LET'S HEAR IT FOR *GOOD* LECTURES AND PRESENTATIONS

> *Be sincere, be brief, be seated.*
> —Franklin D. Roosevelt

Dubrow and Wilkinson (1984, 25) more than adequately defend a place for lectures and presentations.

> To hear a good lecture is an inspiring experience. We leave with our imagination broadened and our interest piqued; we find ourselves entertained, prodded, and illuminated in turn. What evokes our response is an intricate blend of qualities. The lecture must have enough intellectual content to challenge us . . . like a dramatic monologue, it engages our emotions and keeps them in play, thanks to frequent shifts in mood and intensity. It mixes humor and erudition and gives us a sense of the personal involvement of the lecturer.

The key to success is not lecturing and presenting, per se, but "good" lecturing or presenting. This is where the need for pedagogical training comes in. Lectures and presentations are probably here to stay, and, due to expectations of the audience, they sometimes are just preferred. Two examples would be presentations at professional conferences and "over lunch" mini-talks.

First, lecturing is the primary way information is disseminated to attendees at most professional conferences. Attendees want to be educated and provided with a framework to understand the information, but often would rather learn in their seats by a dynamic, engaging presenter (while drinking their morning cup of coffee) than have to participate in more involved active learning techniques. Second, attendees often squeeze in mini-lectures during their lunch hour where taking a break can be paired with hearing an informed enthusiastic presenter, which actively uses their minds but otherwise lets them "rest."

The bottom line is that presenters need to be trained in *how* to deliver dynamic presentations. "What you say is important, how you say things is often just as crucial, if not more so" (Oleniczak 2015, 1). Before we dismiss the value of good, even great, presentations, let's train presenters to deliver them in an engaging, informative, and memorable manner.

All delivery methods that have the presenter involved in any capacity rely on the same set of skills that are introduced in Part II of this book, and they can make a delivery great. There are no exceptions. These skills are the "only game in town" in all venues where someone is called upon to communicate.

WHAT'S IN A NAME?

> *You say tomato, I say tomahto.*
> —Adapted from Gershwin's 1937 song
> "Let's Call the Whole Thing Off"

What's in a name? Everything. In the South, an unpopular home invasive insect is called both a Palmetto Bug and a cockroach. Same bug. But which name would have you phoning the local exterminator most quickly?

You say teaching, I say presenting! Or maybe you simply call it delivering an informative or persuasive speech. You could also call it a stirring address, a moving sermon, a provocative spiel, or an interesting talk. The fact is that presenting covers a very wide swatch when referring to people communicating with each other. Call them what you like, lectures are "more or less continuous periods of expositions by a speaker who wants an audience to learn something" (Bligh 2000, 4). Don't get hung up on a name.

PRESENTING IT LIVE

> *A good friend is someone who visits you when you are in prison. But a really good friend is someone who comes to hear your lectures.*
> —Malcolm Bradbury

Presenting can have the benefit of a real presenter and a real audience, small or large. We have real people communicating with real people. The presenter can read the audience, and, in turn, they can read him or her. A relationship, a chemistry, between the presenter and the audience can develop. An audience can be informed, they can be inspired, and they can be challenged. They can be left wanting more. They can be left possessing the desire to seek out that more.

I recently joined my wife in attending the production of *The Phantom of the Opera* in London. We didn't just attend the production, we experienced it. We were enthralled by it. We both tingled and had goose bumps. Later, at dinner, we talked and talked about it, we critiqued it, we tried to relive the experience. And, afterward, we told other people all about it. We just could not contain ourselves.

Apparently, the play has had this same effect on a lot of people because it has been presented about 12,000 times over thirty years at Her Majesty's Theatre. Would reading a book about *The Phantom of the Opera* have had the same impact? Probably not. Would listening to a CD of the sound track have had the same impact? Perhaps, just a bit. But nothing compares to being there and experiencing a great production in person.

Your presentation venue can be your own shared theater. Theater performers, and make no doubt about it when "on stage" you are a performer, use a relatively small set of skills to engage an audience, not just for ten or fifteen minutes, but perhaps for hours. If they can do it, you can do it!

Is lecturing and presenting likely to disappear soon? As a means of communication, they have existed since the beginning of time. Cavemen, as presenters, sat around a fire where elders "presented" the history of the clan, shared visions of the spirit world, and conveyed other folklore. I use campfire stories to captivate my grandchildren in much the same way. Even without having read this book, cavemen's "presenting" incorporated most of the delivery skills (e.g., voice inflection, gesturing, suspense, surprise) offered in Part II of this book.

A presentation can be formal with a speaker presenting to a large audience. It can be less formal where a seminar is the format. It can be a stirring closing argument. It can be a one-to-one scheduled or impromptu meeting. It can be a provocative discussion moderator. It can be an integral part of doing rounds in a hospital. Don't waste your time fighting it. Accept the fact that we all present and move on to acquiring the Part II dynamic delivery skills.

SHOULD *"YOU"* LECTURE OR PRESENT?

> *When audiences come to see us authors lecture, it is largely in the hope that we'll be funnier to look at than to read.*
> —Sinclair Lewis

Today it seems more popular to move from "sage on the stage," a term coined by Allison King (1993), to "guide on the side." But King herself saw a need for incorporating the latter into the former, not substituting one for the other. Detractors have co-opted the term "sage on the stage" for their own purposes, but there can be immense value in presenting, and it must not be written off as boring and ineffective (Walthausen 2013).

Examine your own life. More than likely you have sat through endless lectures and presentations, from grade school through to the present. Were they all great? Probably not. But they *could* have been great. Good, or not so good, these presentations have contributed heavily to what you are, who you are, what you know, and what you might become in the future. You owe a lot to lectures and presentations—especially the good ones.

Can we, through training, create dynamic presenters? Probably. Can we create lots of them? I don't see why not. Presentations offer an opportunity for presenters to introduce and deal with new, perhaps confounding, research or procedures right in front of a live audience. The audience gets to see how the presenter, now as a learner right along with the audience, grapples with this newness and problem solving. The master gets to experience, once again, the thrill of discovery that probably dominated his or her early career and gets a chance to recall just what it was like to be a student—just like those in the audience. It sounds exciting because it is exciting!

A final point: "It takes two to tango," and thus, not only are presenters expected to present well but also an audience is expected to listen well. Both need to sharpen their respective skills of communication. Learning is too important to be left to an "I dare you to teach me" attitude by an audience or a "take it or leave it attitude" by a presenter.

TED TALKS

> *Most people think entertainment is having a nice laugh.*
> *But you can be entertained by a lecture.*
> —Ron Howard

If lecturing or presenting is no longer p.c. (pedagogically correct), then someone should inform the TED talks folks. A nonprofit started in the early 1980s devoted to spreading ideas, initially in Technology, Entertainment, and Design, TED talks has almost 3,000 TED talks posted as of 2018 with videos viewed over fifty million times. A great variety of topics are covered. Not only are the topics interesting, they are presented well! It is clear that presenters have been coached in using one or more of the dynamic presentation skills that are offered in Part II of this book.

We could profit from viewing TED talks in order to improve our own dynamic presentations. TED talks are made freely available on the TED talks website. Watch and listen to *how* their messages are delivered.

Selected TED talks include:

"Alice Dreger: Is Anatomy Destiny?"

"Vivek Maru: How to Put the Power of Law in People's Hands"

"Robin Steinberg: What If We Ended the Injustice of Bail?"

"William Li: Can We Eat to Starve Cancer?"

"Brett Hennig: What If We Replaced Politicians with Randomly Selected People?"

SUMMARY

In the eulogy for Julius Caesar (Shakespeare, *Julius Caesar*, Act 3, Scene 2), Antony says: "The evil that men do lives after them; the good is oft interred with their bones." Although it seems popular today to treat presenting as some sort of evil pedagogy, used at the right time for the right purpose and delivered by a skilled dynamic presenter, it still can be good pedagogy—in fact, it can be great pedagogy.

I started this chapter with an uplifting quotation by Dubrow and Wilkinson (1984). I'll end by offering another uplifting comment with a quotation from Toth (1997, 90):

> Ms. Mentor happens to enjoy the theatrical side of teaching . . . for it makes use of her native grandiosity. . . . She can lecture with equal brilliance to one hundred and fifty or to one poor advice seeker. . . . It is far easier to lecture than to try to wrest any kind of discussion from recalcitrant or puzzled or very large audiences. A lecturer can write on the board, or pace, gesture, dramatize, grimace, snicker. She can use her voice as an expressive tool . . . sometimes burst into a song.

4

Enthusiasm: A Presentation Necessity

INTRODUCTION

If you are not fired with enthusiasm, you will be fired with enthusiasm.
—Vince Lombardi

Vince Lombardi, renowned coach of the Green Bay Packers, hit the nail on the head with this quotation. Uninspiring and unenthusiastic presenters, too, may be "fired" via audiences tuning them out mentally or downright physically ignoring them. Unfortunately, the value of enthusiasm has not been widely recognized, especially by those who could profit most from its use. "A presenter's thoughtful preparation may be wasted, or at least undermined, if content is delivered poorly" (Goulden 1991, 1). This chapter plans to remedy this situation.

ENTHUSIASM: A PRESENTATION NECESSITY

There is real magic in enthusiasm. It spells the difference between mediocrity and accomplishment.
—Norman Vincent Peale

According to Benjamin Franklin, "nothing can be said to be certain, except death and taxes." He was only partially correct. There exists another certainty in life, and that is, "All great presenters *are* enthusiastic." Inside, presenters need to *be* enthusiastic; outside they need to show their audience that they *are* enthusiastic! Presenters who are unable to project enthusiasm for their subject or topic, even though they may feel it inwardly, labor under a great handicap. Audiences are unwilling to accept presenters who cannot transmit to them something of the excitement of their field. Lombardi's quotation confirms the value and reality of enthusiasm.

When any audience, any time, any place is asked how they would characterize a great teacher or presenter, the number one response is "He/she is Enthusiastic!" Let me reiterate their response. "He/she is Enthusiastic!" Now and then it will share the number one spot with "Knowledge of Subject Matter." Only occasionally, does the trait of enthusiasm fall to number two. One would think that the importance of projected enthusiasm would be highlighted in any and all presenter training programs. Wrong!

Dynamic presenting requires both mastery of subject matter and the ability to project enthusiasm. If you are standing in front of an audience, it is assumed that you possess subject mastery. Thus, half the battle is won. You then can focus your attention to your dynamic delivery.

One of the great benefits to a presenter of being enthusiastic, curious, and open to new or challenging views, is that he or she, not just the students, learns. Sir William Osler (1913, 326), one of the founders of Johns Hopkins Medical Center, said it best, "No man can teach successfully who is not at the same time a student." As a dynamic presenter, plan on being a "student" for the rest of your career.

That Holy Grail that so many seek is within your grasp. It is called "enthusiasm." Other people might refer to it by another word. A list of synonyms for enthusiasm, and it is a long and exciting one, follows. Are you ready? Pretend fireworks are going off and church bells are loudly ringing.

ENTHUSIASM: USEFUL SYNONYMS

Nothing great was ever achieved without enthusiasm!
—Ralph Waldo Emerson

Shields (2010) identified sixty positive personal qualities of successful teachers and presenters. At the very top of the list was enthusiasm. Synonyms for the word "enthusiasm" follow:

zest, passion, excitement, exuberance, animation, ardor, fire, gusto, fervor, intensity, vigor, exhilaration, craze, liveliness, vim, drive, frenzy, oomph, pep, zealousness, zip, flame, dash, ecstasy, initiative, vitality, glow, inspiration, joy, push, fury, spiritedness, thirst, craving, determination, effervescence, elation, fascination, friskiness, snappiness, and rapture

If you could describe some of your best teachers from kindergarten through the present, would more than a few of these enthusiastic synonyms apply? Most assuredly. If you could describe some of your worst teachers, professors and presenters, would these synonyms be missing? Probably.

If you could look at yourself while presenting, would you use one or more of these words to describe your delivery? Would your audience describe your delivery using any of these words? When presenters are more enthusiastic, audiences pay better attention and learn more. It is win-win for everyone.

As a dynamic presenter, it really doesn't matter what you call *it*, you simply must possess *it*, and you must project *it*. Of course, just because you were to teach or present with enthusiasm, there is no guarantee that sunshine and smiling faces would forever greet you, but you increase the odds of presenting more effectively and having audiences learn more (Urban 2008). I will take "increased odds" anytime!

The rest of this chapter is dedicated to convincing you of the importance of *projected* enthusiasm. It is hoped that by the end of this chapter you will be overwhelmingly, no-buts-about-it, convinced that projected enthusiasm leads to presenter greatness. At that point, you will be "enthusiastically" ready to learn the enthusiastic-generating skills presented in Part II.

ENTHUSIASM: ITS RELATIONSHIP TO PEDAGOGY

> *To waken interest and kindle enthusiasm is the sure way*
> *to teach easily and successfully.*
> —Tryon Edwards

It is Wednesday morning, 9:00 a.m. Attendees have gathered for an in-house presentation. Some have a cup of coffee; others have coffee and a doughnut. The stage is set. The presenter welcomes participants, then asks them silently to read a series of quotations handwritten on poster board that she tapes, one at a time, to the walls of the room. Participants also are asked to determine the message that is common among the displayed quotations. The task is not difficult, but it is enlightening!

Among the quotations hung on the wall are:

- Presenter *enthusiasm* is a core factor leading to effective presenting (Hooda and Annu 2017).

- The most valuable asset . . . is the inspired presenter with that indefinable something that arouses the interest and *enthusiasm* of an audience (Sutkin et al. 2008).

- Enthusiasm is generally recognized as one of the most essential qualities of effective presenters . . . the more *enthusiastic* presenters were, the more engaged the audience became (Zhang 2014).

- A great presenter—as opposed to scholar or ethical exemplar or authority figure—has intensity and communicates it *enthusiastically* (Hanning 1984).
- *Enthusiastic* presenters are authentically passionate about both their subject matter and teaching (Dudas and Bannister 2014).
- Effective presenting presupposes a command of the material. . . . But most of all it supposes *enthusiasm* (Rossetti and Fox 2009).
- A presenter's most valuable trait is inspiration and *enthusiasm* (Strang 2014).
- The top three desirable qualities of an effective presenter are knowledge of subject matter, communication, and *enthusiasm* (Simerjit et al. 2013).

Did you figure it out? Were you able to glean the common message in all these citations? Basically, "enthusiasm" is good, and by inference, "lack of presenter enthusiasm" is bad.

As you can see, evidence prevails in the case for presenters, across the board, projecting enthusiasm. After reviewing these citations, we hope that you feel like scratching your head, slamming your hands on the table, and screaming, "Why hasn't the importance of this one crucial delivery tool been made known to us as presenters? Why haven't we been trained in *how* to be enthusiastic?"

A great presenter isn't simply a scholar—one who knows a lot—although knowing a lot about one's field certainly can contribute to greatness. What a presenter knows must be communicated. Jordan (1982, 124) reminds us, "The Teacher as Scholar is *important*, the Teacher as Person is *crucial*, and the Teacher as Communicator is *indispensable*." Projected enthusiasm is fundamental to effective communication. Researchers document it; practitioners testify to it.

Another point that emerges from these quotations is that projected enthusiasm is a quality associated with effective presenting across *all* disciplines and venues. Presenter enthusiasm is as important in Medicine as it is in Engineering, as important in Business as it is in Law, as important in Politics as it is in Physics, and as important in Economics as it is in Mathematics.

WANTED! MORE "OOMPH"

> *Enthusiasm is contagious. Be a carrier.*
> —Susan Rabin

There is no one characteristic that is more important in delivering a message than a presenter's enthusiasm. Audiences want more "oomph," more enthusiasm, from their presenters. Enthusiasm is compelling and, happily, infectious. Lack of enthusiasm is also infectious, but too often, deadly.

Projected enthusiasm plays a critical role in heightening an audience's attention, generating greater interest, and developing a more positive attitude toward the presenter's message. These are all crucial ingredients to effective deliveries.

Presenter enthusiasm has a reciprocal effect. That is, not only does it positively affect the audience, but the resulting heightened level of audience attention, interest, and motivation that occurs likely impacts presenter enthusiasm, as well (Keller, Neumann, and Fischer 2013). Thus, an ever-ending circle of satisfaction and achievement by both presenters and audiences can begin. The fire of curiosity and learning is stoked as we build on one another's enthusiasm and passion. Can you feel the heat?

IT CAN'T BE THAT SIMPLE, CAN IT?

I believe that education is all about being excited about something. Seeing passion and enthusiasm helps push an educational message.
—Steve Irwin

At this point in discussions about the importance of *projected* enthusiasm, audiences often exclaim, "It can't be that simple, it just can't!" Well, it is that simple. If you are convinced that projected enthusiasm is where you want to place your bets, but are not exactly sure how to do it, continue reading. I can't tell you where best to invest your money—in the stock market, bonds, or under your mattress—but I can direct you toward investing your time and energy in heightening your projected presenter enthusiasm.

PASSION: "LET'S KICK IT UP A NOTCH!"

Passion takes a teacher (or presenter) from being merely good to great.
—Adrian Furnham

Let's ratchet it up, for a moment, from enthusiasm to passion! Feeling enthusiastic is an emotion that can come and go . . . she was enthusiastic about going sailing on Saturday. Passion, often, is ongoing, even lifelong . . . she has been passionate, almost devoted, to sailing since she was a little girl.

When we think about passion, immediately our mind conjures up people who have inspired us in our life. Long after forgetting specifically what was taught or delivered, a presenter's passionate delivery will be remembered. It is because of Mr. John Sabol, my high school physics teacher, that I majored in physics. To this day, I remember the passion Mr. Sabol displayed for his subject area and for teaching. Passion is one of the greatest human assets that allow some to lead, teach, and influence the lives of others (Villarroel 2015).

Perhaps Chef Emeril has it right when he says to his audience, "Let's kick it up a notch!" Maybe presenter enthusiasm is not enough; perhaps we should hold out for presenter passion. According to Day (2004), passion should be center stage for good presenting. Our passion, in turn, can help audiences to share our passion. This notion has been affirmed and confirmed since ancient times.

We find it in the writings of the ancient philosopher Plutarch, who wrote, "The mind is not a vessel to be filled, but a fire to be ignited." We find it in the quotation, "A person without passion has no more value than a candle without a flame" (Hansbury 2009, 192). Exceptional presenters are passionate, and they are not afraid to show it (Peterson 2017). The delivery skills in Part II of this book will help you to "project" this passion.

Passion is not something that is reserved for the young, those just entering professions idealistic and ready to make their mark. Passion also is something for the seasoned presenter. McTaggart (2003), after forty-two years of teaching, reports in her book *From the Teacher's Desk* that for her teaching is not simply a profession, it is a passion! She autographs her books, "A teacher has a profession; a good teacher has a passion. Be passionate!"

In addition to reading about and then mastering the skills in this text, readers can enhance their passion for presenting by watching passionate teachers teach, passionate presenters present, passionate preachers preach, passionate politicians stump, and passionate sales people sell. What is it that they do? How do they use their voices, their bodies, and their environs to convey their passion?

If you are a presenter, you should err on the side of passionate presenting. A passionate presenter teaches with his heart, inspires passion in others, energizes them, and helps them reach their goals.

ENTHUSIASM: CAN TOO MUCH BE TOO MUCH?

People who never get carried away should be!
—Malcolm Forbes

We offer a caution regarding presenter enthusiasm and passion. A colleague of mine is a particularly passionate presenter. He is loud, moves rapidly around the room, and sometimes "invades" an audience's personal space; he is, by any definition, zealous. What is the result? Most of the audience find his enthusiasm and passion to be contagious; most cite him as one of the best presenters they have had in their program. Many say that for the first time they have experienced a presenter who makes the subject matter interesting and engaging. The audience clearly does not doze off in his presentations.

But. Yes, there is a "but." Some in the audience are intimidated, put off, and slowly gravitate to the safety of the back of the room. These people stop participating, commenting that the presenter's excessive exuberance intimidates them. Apparently, they were turned off by the very presenter enthusiasm and passion that most others found motivating.

What does the future hold for those who gravitated to the rear of the room? Many of them as soon-to-be professionals, themselves, in just a few years will be standing up in front of an audience of some sort presenting as part of their job description. There will be no slinking to the back of the room to hide then.

Brookfield and Preskill (1999) caution overenthusiastic presenters to balance their enthusiasm with periods of calm. This is good advice because too much of a good thing can be counterproductive. The "at times over-the-top" passionate presenter has gone so far as to pass out paper fans (the kind that they hand out in non-air-conditioned churches) during class to several students that say, "Dr. So-and-So, you are yelling!" These students, strategically seated throughout the audience, use these to signal him to rein in his passionate actions a notch or two. When students wave their fans, the professor gets the message and gets it in a humorous way.

PRESENTER EVALUATIONS

*Nothing is as important as passion. No matter what you want
to do with your life, be passionate.*
—Jon Bon Jovi

It is possible for the opening night of a play to be the last night of that play. It also is possible for the production to run months or years. It often depends upon the reviews of the play and, in particular, the reviews the actors and actresses receive. Savvy consumers read these reviews and then act accordingly. Consumers vote with their feet and with their pocketbook.

Presenters are reviewed and rated, too. Sometimes, an audience may well evaluate or "vote with their feet" choosing not to attend "poor" and "uninspired" lectures, presentations, talks, or addresses. In addition to the informal word-of-mouth evaluations, sometimes reviewers use standardized forms. One of the most common categories evaluated on such forms is that of "enthusiasm." Typically, the category falls under a broader label of Professional Skills. Sample category wordings include "Shows enthusiasm" or "Demonstrates enthusiasm for the subject and learner." The reviewer checks off the degree—Observable Strength / Satisfactory / Needs Improvement—to which enthusiasm has been observed.

Recall the boring economics teacher (played by Ben Stein) from the classic movie *Ferris Bueller's Day Off* who had his students almost asleep even before he finished taking attendance! Now it may be possible for Ben Stein to have a career by being (playing) a monotoned boring teacher, but this persona probably will not work for most of us, especially if we are aspiring to be dynamic presenters.

The evidence is clear: enthusiastic teachers and dynamic presenters, those who are expressive in their manner and method and who demonstrate mastery of their subject matter, do earn higher audience evaluations. These presenters deliver the goods—the requisite content! More important, audiences are "buying" the goods.

ENTHUSIASM AND SUBJECT-MATTER MATRIX

> *True enthusiasm is a fine feeling whose flash I admire wherever I see it.*
> —Charlotte Brontë

In teaching and presenting, we have two forces operating—delivery and subject matter knowledge. These can be combined in a two-by-two matrix, generating only four possible combinations.

(1) A presenter can lack enthusiasm (e.g., be boring) and not know the subject matter.

(2) A presenter can lack enthusiasm (e.g., be boring) and know the subject matter.

(3) A presenter can be enthusiastic and not know the subject matter.

(4) A presenter can be enthusiastic and know the subject matter.

Which of these four combinations would you choose for yourself if you were an audience member? I believe that the pedagogical literature clearly supports the last choice.

Patricia Graham, former Dean of Harvard Graduate School of Education, agrees. She asserts "You can have academic mastery with no passion, and that is not effective . . . it is extremely rare to have passion for an academic subject and not have a degree of mastery" (Graham 1999, 2005, personal communication).

SUMMARY

Enthusiasm is the most important thing in life.
—Tennessee Williams

There is an overwhelming pedagogical case for teachers and presenters *being* enthusiastic and *projecting* that enthusiasm. The basis for *how* to project enthusiasm follows in Part II of this text. Your job will be to brainstorm how you can best use each performance skill to project *your* enthusiasm.

When thinking about the term "enthusiasm," other "e" words come to mind. Among them are expressing, exhilarating, exciting, enlightening, enthralling, and, for that matter, even entertaining. A stage production or movie described this way would signal a dramatic or cinematic success. It would be a credit to the actors. A presentation, speech, or lecture characterized this way, similarly, would be a "hit" and a credit to the presenter. Exactly *how* presenters are supposed to convey their enthusiasm—their passion—is the emphasis of the book you are reading.

When surveyed, audiences often point out that "worst teachers or presenters" share a common characteristic—they are boring! Although not a "betting person," I would wager that on more than one occasion you have described a lecturer, speaker, boss, or presenter as boring. One student recently has sued Oxford University (England) for one million pounds alleging that the "hopelessly bad," "appalling," and "boring" teaching that he received resulted in him getting a second-class degree that led to loss of earnings later in his career as a lawyer (Mortimer 2018).

Clearly, those who are aspiring to be judged as one of the "best presenters" should work, and work hard, at not being boring. Given the physics principle that two things cannot occupy the same place at the same time, one cannot be perceived as enthusiastic and, at the same time, be perceived as boring.

This book is all about boosting presenter enthusiasm. For those who may believe that enthusiastic teaching somehow sacrifices truth and scholarship, consider what Kenneth Eble has to say. "I have never encountered any evidence that a dull and stodgy presentation necessarily carries with it an extra measure of truth and virtue" (cited in Showalter 2003, 16). I dare anyone to prove him wrong!

5

Parallel between Acting, Teaching, and Presenting

INTRODUCTION

Color in a picture is like enthusiasm in life.
—Vincent Van Gogh

As a presenter, being convinced of the need to project enthusiasm is only half the battle. Now you must let your valuing of projecting enthusiasm "spill out"! You need to *act* on your newfound recognition of the value of projected enthusiasm. As the quotation states, you need to convey your enthusiasm to your audience. Actions speak louder than words; actions convey commitment more than words.

Urbanowicz (2000, 1) asserts that when he began university teaching, he believed that there was a "fine thin line between teaching and acting." He has come to change his opinion. "There is NO fine thin line, for we act (or 'perform') as we teach." Genard (2015, 1) states that actors and presenters "so often take part in the same activities—engaging, influencing and moving audiences, and that sometimes it's difficult to see daylight between the two." I agree!

All of us recognize an enthusiastic presenter when we see one. But, defining an enthusiastic presenter can for some be a bit like Justice Potter Stewart's 1964 comment regarding obscenity—"I know it when I see it" even if I can't define it. Too many presenters know it when they see it but they "do not know *HOW* it is actually done" (Sutkin et al. 2008, 453).

One of the reasons is that the "performance aspect of the job (e.g., teaching and presenting) is rarely emphasized or taught" (Schwartz 2013, 1). When you finish reading this book, you not only will be able to recognize presenter enthusiasm but also will be able to recognize, define, and use the performance skills likely to enhance it.

"*ACT*" YOUR AGE

If academics are indeed "performers," then the one branch of performance they are actually connected to most closely is stand-up comedy: only the teacher and the stand-up comedian rely on the continuous interaction between themselves and the people in front of them.
—Kenneth E. Eble

Did your parents ever tell you to "act your age"? Sometimes, for extra emphasis, did they say, "For Heaven's sake, act your age?" Has your dad ever said, "You're supposed to be the big brother, act like it"? Did your mom ever remind you to act like a gentleman when taking Suzie from down the street to the dance? It seems as if the deliverers of these messages really don't want us to be something we aren't; they only want us to "act" like that something.

Each of the messages has you on the receiving end; you are the one who is supposed to "act." Now, examine how often you have been the deliverer of such messages. What specifically did you want the receivers of your messages to do? What is clear in these messages is that we can "turn on" and "turn off" our "acting our age," our "acting like a big brother," our "acting like a gentleman," or our acting like anything else, including a great teacher or dynamic presenter. When you act, you play a role just like actors do in a theater. You are likely to act one way in the courtroom, another way in the conference room, another way at a staff meeting, another way when presenting, and still another way at the local watering hole after a long, trying day.

I want to make it perfectly clear that, as reinforced by Mozes (2007), I am not trying to turn you into an actor. I am not trying to get you a "gig" on *SNL*. What I do want is for you to learn and then apply many of the engagement skills that are being taught and effectively used in the theater. It is all communication in which the shared behaviors of actors and presenters include, among other things, eye contact, vocal inflection, body language, and overall expressiveness. These can make the difference between success and failure. But, make no mistake about it, teachers and presenters are actors and they deliver performances (Stone 2010). All presentations are performances.

Felman, in her book *Never a Dull Moment: Teaching and the Art of Performance*, insists, "There is a difference between performance for the sake of entertainment and performance that is integral to the process of learning." Further, she believes, "Performative teaching allows the presentation venue to become a truly dynamic and dramatic space" (2001, 15).

Many professionals mistakenly believe "acting" is all about pretending to be what you are not. This makes them resistant to approaches that seem to transfer acting techniques to the world of presenting (McCrory 2018, personal communication). "The suspicion against presenters as performers is an ancient one" (Eble 1988, 12). Eble further responds to those who believe that the skills offered in this book to project enthusiasm are just phony, trashy, unsound, deceptive, or showy by stating that he is "less appalled by flashy deception than by undisguised dullness." Hopefully, this book is neither.

When you read Part II of this book and learn the specific acting or delivery skills that can successfully transfer to any and all presentation venues, you will be able to elevate your presentations to something well above "pretending." With practice, your newly acquired skills will be, part-and-parcel, you.

TEACHING IS TEACHING; PRESENTING IS PRESENTING

No professor should be blind to the intelligence and knowledge that goes into an effective teaching performance.
—Kenneth E. Eble

As you may recall, the title of chapter 2 was "To Present Is to Teach; To Teach Is to Present." They are one and the same. I would like to expand this claim by saying that "teaching is teaching" and "presenting is presenting."

A surprising realization to me was when it dawned upon me that I had never read a disclaimer of any kind that, in effect, said that there is one set of skills for presenting doctors, one set for presenting lawyers, one set for politicians, one set for businessmen and women, and one set each for all other presenters. Teaching is teaching! Presenting is presenting! The main reason the same skills are used by all these communicators is that they are all trying to engage, inform, stimulate, persuade, and, sometimes, entertain their audience.

The same presentation skills used by actors (animation in voice, animation in body, humor, role-playing, use of props, suspense and surprise, space utilization, and creative entrances and exits) are, or should be, used by all teachers and dynamic presenters. Some use them better than others because they have learned the powerful connection between using these skills and the projected presenter enthusiasm that is likely to follow.

A YORKSHIRE STORY

Enthusiasm is excitement with inspiration, motivation,
and a pinch of creativity.
—Bo Bennett

Enthusiasm and passion do not have to take one single form, and it does not always include being loud, having grand hand gestures, and running around the venue jumping up on tables. But it does require that presenters raise their awareness of their own way of being enthusiastic about their message and then grafting it into their delivery persona (Carroll 2002). And, on those days when you don't feel all that excited about the material that you are presenting, at least *act* like you are excited. Put on your best performance! Surely actors delivering the same lines in afternoon and evening performances for months on end occasionally do not always feel at their best when going on stage. But, as professionals, they know the show must go on. The audience deserves the actor's or presenter's best delivery.

O'Donnell (2005) learned the power of acting skills in his medical practice by having accompanied his father, a GP in Yorkshire, England, on his visits to sick patients. O'Donnell noted that when the car stopped at a patient's home, his dad, assuming various persona, became a performer—kindly wise, cool assessor, or sympathetic counselor, as the situation demanded. Just as quickly when returning to the car, his dad dropped out of character. He simply became "dad" once again. He watched his dad play the right doctor role at the right time for the right purpose.

POWER OF EXPECTATIONS: IT WORKS BOTH WAYS

We act as though comfort and luxury were the chief requirements
of life, when all that we need to make us really happy is
something to be enthusiastic about.
—Charles Kingsley

It is clear that a presenter's projected enthusiasm can rub off on an audience. There is no disputing this fact. When a presenter's enthusiasm rubs off, audiences pay greater attention, are more interested, and have a more positive attitude, among other pedagogically desired outcomes. Hence, they learn more, and the presenter feels more satisfied. What is not so obvious is that audience enthusiasm rubs off on teachers and presenters, too! Projected enthusiasm is a two-way street. Just as audiences who perceive a presenter's projected enthusiasm are likely to get "turned on," audience enthusiasm can "turn on" (or turn up) a presenter's enthusiasm.

When we expect someone to achieve, that person generally will. When audiences expect presenters to be great, they are likely to be rewarded with presenter greatness. That is just how human nature works. Expect it and you increase the odds of getting it. What happens is that if an audience expects greatness, they will display all the outward signs and behaviors of someone expecting greatness—arrive early, sit closer to the presenter, lean a bit forward in their seat, be more attentive, convey more interest, and so on. The presenter (you), in turn, picks up on these audience behaviors and up goes your enthusiasm level. It would not be surprising for audiences to leave such a venue saying, "I told you she was going to give a great presentation."

Who cares who initiated the positive expectations as long as they are initiated! The sooner, the better. And, because first impressions are lasting impressions, the rest of the presentations throughout the term or rotation are likely to be equally impressive and well received. Why? One, the presenter, having picked up on the positive expectations of the audience, is likely to do an even better job of preparing for the next presentation so as not to disappoint his or her audience. Two, the audience, having observed what appeared to be a pretty good presentation, are energized to better prepare for the next presentation.

Suffice it to say at this point, an audience will take no more than sixty seconds to form their first impression of you. That's it, just sixty seconds! That is just about the same amount of time that you will take to form your first impressions of them. And, because "first impressions are lasting impressions," you'd better hope that their first impressions of you and your enthusiasm level are positive. Better still, don't just hope so, use the skills in this book to make it so.

SUMMARY

Enthusiasm is the greatest asset in the world.
It beats money, power and influence.
—Henry Chester

Actors, teachers, and presenters share the same goal—the goal of communication. They often even share what sounds like a similar physical world. For instance, in the world of medicine, the terminology "operating theater" has existed for centuries. These amphitheaters, often tiered, were used by onlookers to observe surgeons performing operations. Everyone wanted a good seat. Theaters, today, from a Mountain Playhouse to the Globe Theatre in London, are designed for onlookers, the audience, to observe the production.

In the world of law, a courtroom, often full of drama, has an audience, and displays accoutrements or trappings that would compete with the props and scenery for any stage play. Judges in robes and wigs, sometimes joined by barristers with the same regalia, richly paneled walls, along with "taking an oath," complete the theatrical stage.

Politicians, sometimes holding a potential voter's infant (e.g., a prop) for dramatic effect, make sure that the scenery behind them helps convey their message. President Reagan's famous, "Mr. Gorbachev. Tear down this wall" speech carried greater impact because it was delivered standing directly in front of the Berlin Wall. To help secure the conservative or liberal vote, politicians choose dress (e.g., outfits or costumes) appropriate for the message.

Business folks, although they may lounge in jeans and a T-shirt around the house, adopt the expected three-piece suit or tailored dress while at work. Unless you are fabulously wealthy, like Mark Zuckerberg or the late Steve Jobs, wearing these expected outfits at work signals the role you play in the company—boss. Actors and other performers reinforce their roles by adorning themselves with costumes—a toga or operating gown, a tunic or a white coat of various lengths conveying one's station.

Actors, teachers, and presenters share an exhilarating game of wits. Shields (2010, 3) says, "I am constantly thinking of my next phrase, question, and gesture, adjusting and readjusting my tone, gaze, and intensity. I am in contact with my feelings about my audience's response and my response to them." Finally, to not act is to act—there is no escaping the fact that human beings in all walks of their life, act! We may as well act well.

6

Educational Foundations:
Presenters as Actors

INTRODUCTION

All the world's a stage,
And all the men and women merely players:
They have their exits and their entrances;
And one man in his time plays many parts.
—Shakespeare, *As You Like It*

The world may *not* actually be a stage but acting is part and parcel of everyday life. Everyone plays a role; in fact, many roles: parent, child, sibling, customer, client, investor, boss, subordinate, judge, jury, colleague, coach, neighbor, or friend. "If you teach (e.g., present), you are acting" (Cavanagh 2017, 1).

Many readers may be more interested in the *how-to* chapters that immediately follow in Part II. But, little of what follows would be of any use if what is presented was not based upon firm pedagogical grounds. Presenters are held accountable today more and more for their actions. Being accountable means, at a bare minimum, understanding why one uses the presentation strategies one does and being able to defend one's actions if challenged.

SOUND THEORY AND EFFECTIVE PRACTICE

> *Try not to have a good time. . . . This is supposed to be educational!*
> —Charles Schultz

Presenters, no matter the discipline or specialty, need both sound theory and effective practice. One without the other is not enough. Knowing theory but being unable to effectively apply it leaves the job half done. Being able to present something but not knowing the "whys" and "wherefores" behind what one is presenting and *how* one should present it leaves the presenter, at best, vulnerable. This book has the theory and the practice to back up my claim regarding *what* contributes to great presenting. Further, it delivers proven pedagogical specific skills for *how* to get this job done.

EDUCATIONAL FOUNDATIONS FOR ENTHUSIASM

> *In a completely rational society, the best of us would be teachers*
> *and the rest of us would have to settle for something less.*
> —Lee Iacocca

It is not good enough simply to use presentation techniques that work; one must also know *why* they work. Without understanding *why*, presenters stop being professionals. This chapter is designed briefly to review the educational foundations for the use of theatrical devices in effective teaching and dynamic presenting.

When we think of theater, we think of acting and the goals of entertainment; whereas, in teaching and presenting, we think of the goals of informing or persuading. Because these two goals are often deemed incompatible, entertainment has been a dirty word to many presenters. More than once we have overheard a presenter, with a scowling face, proclaim with some vehemence:

- "I'm paid to educate them, not entertain them!"
- "I will not 'Oprah' my presentation, no matter what you say."
- "I'm not going to sacrifice scholarship by entertaining the audience."
- "Presenters who entertain students are just trying to get higher ratings."
- "I see entertaining as just pandering to an audience!"

The fact that these presenters fail to realize is that if they expect to impact an audience, they must, in some form or another, first attract and hold their attention—just as actors must do with an audience. Skeptics may claim that they are not really entertainers, but they are! All lectures and presentations are performances.

THEORISTS SPEAK; LET'S LISTEN

Very simple was my explanation, and plausible enough . . .
as almost all wrong theories are!
—H. G. Wells

All presenters want their audiences to value what is presented. According to the dated, but still relevant, taxonomy for the affective domain of learning (Krathwohl, Bloom, and Masia 1956), *receiving* is a prerequisite to *valuing*. Therefore, before audiences can possibly have a commitment to something (value it), they must first be willing to give controlled or selected attention to it, both physically and mentally. If we expect audiences to absorb the material presented, we must cultivate their attention by offering the material in an interesting and captivating way.

According to Jerome Bruner (1960), a renowned cognitive psychologist, such attention and interest can be generated by using "dramatizing devices," including the development of a dramatic personality on the part of the teacher or presenter. We have known this for some time. These strategies support the fourth major theme in his *The Process of Education* (1960), the consideration of how an audience's interest can be stimulated.

Similarly, Albert Bandura (1986), a name synonymous with the study of modeling, notes that securing someone's attention is first among four important elements involved in observational learning. Whether one is demonstrating a process or lab technique, elaborating upon a Shakespearian play, or exploring the impact of global warming, little or no learning will take place unless the presenter is able to secure and hold an audience's attention. Therefore, the first thing a successful presenter must do is to get an audience to attend to important material (Dembo 1988). Dembo's thirty-year-old assertion is just as true today.

YOU DON'T NEED TO BE AN EINSTEIN

I never really thought of myself as an actor, but . . .
—Trudy Steuernagel

A recent conference presentation by one of my contributors, Dr. Rebecca Sivarajah, highlights just how easy it can be to deliver a more enthusiastic, engaging, and memorable presentation. Her presentation, titled "I Can See Clearly Now: Breast Ultrasound Optimization Tips and Tricks," was scheduled second to last at a conference and, as such, one might expect the audience to be a bit less attentive. Not so in her case.

Here are representative audience comments:

Great talk, Excellent, Very informative, Great lecture, Outstanding, Very good lecture, Excellent explanations, One of the best presenters, She should come back next time (note, the audience was asked to select two people who they would like to hear at a future date).

Dr. Sivarajah realized that her topic could be a bit "dry," so she incorporated several acting or performance skills that are presented in this book. She used storytelling, lots of visual props, a surprise beginning, a catchy ending, animation in body, animation in voice, space utilization, and some role-playing.

For instance, she showed a picture of her son in his last year's Halloween outfit (Einstein) and noted that you don't have to be an Einstein to understand breast imaging. The audience gave a quick chuckle, was made to feel more at ease, and the stage was set for the rest of her presentation.

She showed a picture of Prince Harry and Meghan Markle at their wedding where they are sitting listening to the song, "Stand by me." This "hook" of a picture highlighted the concept of lateral resolution in breast imaging. A picture of a couple on a tandem bicycle highlighted the concept of axial resolution. A series of several pictures of her son's soccer team, where the brightness was "too bright or too dark" were used in a discussion of "gain." She made sure to leave the lectern and "work the crowd." Finally, she supplied a creative exit to her breast ultrasound presentation by playing a portion of the song, "I Can See Clearly Now."

Dr. Sivarajah's use of various acting or performance skills contributed to her success as a presenter. The addition of these engaging acting or performance strategies took just minutes to prepare and took very little time away from the presentation, itself. In fact, the use of these acting and performance strategies made the presentation more memorable!

AWARD-WINNING PRESENTERS SPEAK; LET'S LISTEN

When contacted, what do award-winning presenters have to say about their use of acting or performance skills? Their comments might not be from each reader's specific career specialty, but their message is clear, and it is transferable! The following excerpts are from testimonials contributed for the book *Acting Lessons for Teachers: Using Performance Skills in the Classroom* (Tauber and Mester 2007). The perceptions are still true today.

An English teacher, V. S. Carroll, agrees that acting skills can be useful in engaging audiences and focusing their attention on the major ideas or problems of a discipline. Another presenter readily attests to the usefulness of acting skills as an "aid in maintaining both the vibrancy and quality of learning" (C. L. Harrison, cited in Tauber and Mester 2007, 195).

K. A. Grimnes, although admitting that she has had no formal training in acting techniques, has become increasingly aware of the importance of acting skills to the quality and effectiveness of her presenting. While instruction is never simply entertainment, nonetheless, to learn how to work an audience should not be downplayed. Another contributor claims, "Good teaching sweeps people away. . . . It is the ability to involve an audience that a presenter must master if he/she is to be completely successful in teaching" (D. Light, cited in Tauber and Mester 2007, 198).

W. M. Mahoney comments that his development of acting skills and the awareness of the classroom as a stage enable him to combine aspects of the lecturer and the performer. He has learned how to act and how to teach on the same stage.

A telecommunications professor acknowledges that the real challenge is to present "that material each time as if it's the first time. Every 'performance' must retain the excitement of opening night" (M. Rogers, cited in Tauber and Mester 2007, 204). In a response typical of those received from award-winning presenters, a presenter starts off her testimony with "I never thought of myself as an actor or the classroom as a stage" (T. Steuernagel, cited in Tauber and Mester 2007, 207), and then goes on to enumerate presentation techniques that she believes she shares with fellow "performers."

Award-winning presenters, among other common elements, compare their presenting to a theatrical performance. They report that they "come alive" when they step in front of an audience. At this point, they feel they are "on stage." When one takes on a presenter role, he or she can speak with a sense of confidence and enthusiasm that energizes both themselves and their audience.

THE PROFESSION'S RESPONSE, OR LACK THEREOF

A good education should leave much to be desired!
—Alan Gregg

Although there are strong educational foundations for presenters using acting skills, too few presenters are prepared to do so. It is not their fault. They should not be blamed because they have not been trained.

Tompkins, on her early years of presenting, reflects, "I'm amazed that my fellow PhDs and I were let loose in the classroom with virtually no preparation for what we would encounter. . . . If only I'd known, if someone I respected had talked to me honestly about teaching, I might have been saved from a lot of pain" (Showalter 2003, 5–6). Most professors "picked up teaching through painful experience, doing unto others as was done to [them]" (Showalter 2003, 4).

Norman Maclean (1975), author of *A River Runs Through It* and three-time winner of the University of Chicago award for teaching excellence, in an essay "On Changing Neckties: A Few Remarks on the Art of Teaching," writes that the only advice he ever received was to wear a different suit every day of the week. He couldn't afford that many suits, so he wore a different necktie every day instead.

Even where institutions do provide presenter training, such training seems to overlook two crucial areas of skill development associated with presenter success—speech communication and drama. Although not the specific focus of this book, many speech communication skills parallel those found useful in drama: animated voice, animated body, and space utilization. It is astonishing that teachers in training typically are required to take only one speech course, usually the same course that students majoring in agriculture, accounting, engineering, and liberal arts schedule. One would think that potential teachers being prepared for a field so reliant upon speaking and presenting would be required to schedule more than one speech course. Such is not the case.

The second overlooked skill is drama. The situation for teachers in training, and for presenters already in their profession, is even worse when it comes to receiving training in drama. Typically, teacher majors are required to schedule *no* acting or drama courses. Yet Hanning (1984, 33) claims that teachers regularly "must give a performance, of sorts, in order to communicate effectively with students." Where are teachers and presenters supposed to learn how to perform or present?

Why the reluctance to incorporate acting skill development in presenter training programs? The answer is either an ignorance of the importance of communication and acting skills, or downright fear of them! Yes, fear, fear of speech communication and drama (acting skills). It should not be surprising that these two fears are shared more broadly among professionals than might be expected. What are we to do?

For some, even the thought of everyone in a room suddenly focusing on them makes their face turn red. They feel that they are not a "natural" lecturer or presenter. I would ask these folks to persevere because the dynamic presentation skills presented in Part II, easily mastered one small step at a time, will help overcome this anxiety. I guarantee it.

SUMMARY

In Part I of this book, I have offered an informative Preface; claimed that lectures, presentations, and other such delivery methods are not dead yet (if well done); acknowledged presenter enthusiasm as a legitimate catalyst for learning; pointed out the parallel between acting, teaching, and presenting; and offered educational foundations (both research and award-winning practitioner testimonials) for using acting or performance skills to better engage and inform an audience.

Part II will present these long-awaited specific acting or performance skills. From now on, your *act*ions have the potential to propel you toward becoming a great presenter.

PART II

Enthusiasm-Generating Skills!

INTRODUCTION

A good teacher, like a good entertainer, first must hold his audience's
attention, then he can teach his lesson.
—John Hendrik Clarke

Assuming one knows his or her subject matter, the *key* to great teaching and dynamic presenting is being *enthusiastic* on the inside and *projecting* it on the outside! In Part I of this book, I tried to convince you of this assertion. In Part II, I'll provide the skills that are designed to help you "project" that enthusiasm.

Think about how you normally prepare to deliver a talk, lecture, or presentation. You probably spend much of that time and energy preparing *what* you are going to say. After reading this book, you might consider spending more time preparing *how* you are going to deliver your subject matter. Tell you what. Why don't we strike a deal? Let's concentrate on both!

Part II presents specific behaviors that, if incorporated into your delivery, will have an audience seeing you as more enthusiastic—the number one characteristic of a great presenter. I recommend that you don't try to master and incorporate all the following presenter strategies at one time.

Work at becoming proficient at one skill, then another, then another. As you are successful, the adage "Nothing breeds success like success" will kick in. Your confidence tackling each new skill, then, will build upon those mastered earlier.

Finally, as you venture along this path of learning and using enthusiastic-generating behaviors, consider involving your audience. Tell them:

> I really care about how well I present. Therefore, I will be using some behaviors (e.g., gestures, humor, surprise) that I believe can make a difference in the quality of my delivery. Some are a bit new to me. Like any skill, I may not be perfect at it at first. I would appreciate your help. Let me know what is working and what isn't. I'm open to suggestions. Keep in mind that in just a few years you may well be standing in front of an audience presenting. Thank you.

MIGHT AS WELL BE HANGED FOR A SHEEP AS FOR A LAMB

Think for a moment how disastrous it would be if you had worked years to master your subject matter, then expended time, talent, and energy creating appropriate objectives, goals, and expectations, only to fall short of offering an enthusiastic, engaging, dynamic, and memorable presentation—all because you had not been trained. Yet, this happens far more often than need be.

As you examine each of the acting and performance skills presented in Part II, consider "going for broke." Consider using each of them with exaggerated gusto in your delivery. "You can always cut back, but it's difficult to add on" (Burns and Woods 1992, 97). If using a bit of these skills is seen as a little "gutsy," why not be seen as a lot "gutsy"?

If you feel prepared to take a little risk, why not consider taking a larger pedagogical risk? The ability to accept risk is a key characteristic of a true professional and a successful presenter. What do you have to lose?

YUL BRYNNER: ROW G, SEAT 6

Yul Brynner delivered his King of Siam performance in *The King and I* approximately 4,500 times over the course of thirty years. When asked how he kept his delivery so fresh he responded, "I follow the Row G, Seat 6 rule." At the beginning of the play, he would look directly at the man (or woman) in Row G, Seat 6, and remind himself that for this theatergoer this was probably his or her first time experiencing the play.

7

A Craftsperson's Toolbox

INTRODUCTION

> *It is not who you are but what you do*
> *that conveys enthusiasm.*
> —Anonymous

Craftspersons craft things and they use the tools of their trade to do it. Without their tools they are lost. Aspiring apprentices are introduced to and instructed in the proper use of the tools of their trade by master craftsmen or journeymen. The process is the same whether one is talking about masons, plumbers, and electricians, or actors, actresses, teachers, and presenters, or doctors, lawyers, and politicians. It is the skilled use of one's tools that separates the master from the apprentice.

Different craftspersons, such as masons and carpenters, might use the same tool (e.g., using a level to plumb a wall). Likewise, actors, teachers, and presenters share many of the same tools even though their ultimate goals may differ. The title of Eble's often cited book *The Craft of Teaching* (1988) reinforces that presenters and actors share a craft. Actors and presenters both use the "tools" of body and vocal animation, humor, and the rest of the skills that follow in Part II. These tools, and their effective use, address the *how* of projecting enthusiasm.

TOOLS FOR BOOSTING PRESENTER ENTHUSIASM

In real life . . . no one cares if you're boring.
On stage you cannot afford to be boring.
—Stella Adler

The point of the prior section was that more enthusiastic presenters are perceived as more effective presenters. Presenter enthusiasm (and the perceived competence that it conveys), in turn, often leads to more audience interest, positive attitude, and greater achievement. The question now is how can presenters become more enthusiastic? As the quotation at the beginning of this chapter says, "It is not *who* you are but *what* you do that conveys enthusiasm." It should also say "how skillfully you do what you do!" To be of value, enthusiasm and passion must be illuminated by knowledge. That knowledge follows in the acting and performance skills that are presented in Part II of this book.

Years ago, I supervised senior interns. Prior to beginning their role as professionals, many of them had bouts of severe anxiety—they had the actor's version of stage fright. To calm their nerves, I reassuringly offered this profound statement: "Don't worry. Just go in there and be yourself." In hindsight, this was terrible advice because many of them were, truth be told, less than enthusiastic people. If they "remained themselves," they would have been less than enthusiastic presenters. I can't imagine a director telling stage-frightened actors to just go on stage and "be themselves."

This story continues in that later after observing these interns present, it was clear that many of them were not projecting enthusiasm, and it showed. Their audience seemed bored to tears. To help, I met later with them and offered still more profound advice. I said, "You need to be more enthusiastic." The interns nodded their heads in agreement and off they went. Two weeks later, I again observed the same interns, presenting. Surprise, surprise, they were just as unenthusiastic as they had been before! I was tempted to scream, "Didn't I tell you to be more enthusiastic?" It wasn't until years later when researching the power of enthusiasm that I realized I had neglected to tell the interns *how* to be more enthusiastic. Shame on me!

I believe that a "performance" is required of presenters because the enthusiasm that is so highly valued does not simply "ooze" out. I said it earlier and it bears repeating. Presenters not only need to *be* enthusiastic about the subject matter, they must *project* that enthusiasm.

CREATING YOUR TEACHER- OR PRESENTER-SELF

We all struggle to form a self. Great teaching . . . involves taking this
struggle and engaging in it with others.
—Spencer Robins

According to Hanning (1984, 33), "You don't have a 'self' when you start out as a teacher; that is, you don't have a teacher-self. You have to develop one, and you do that by acting a part, by performing a role . . . as you would in a theatre." Hanning (2005) stands by his 1984 proclamation. Every teacher or presenter needs to create and then master a "presenter persona."

At first glance, performing a role—acting a part—may sound phony and appear out of place to professionals. It shouldn't. In both cases, a group of persons (audiences) perceive themselves as relatively passive (in body but, hopefully, not in mind) participants in an interaction led by a dominant other. Successful presenting is a performance, and the sooner we make peace with that fact the better (Carroll 2002). Luckily for us, the techniques of performing, although not innate, can be taught, can be learned, and can be mastered (Ramani 2006). Presenting is not unlike acting on the stage or in the cinema. In both the theater and the presentation venue, the character on stage must hold the attention of the listeners by using a variety of captivating devices.

Despite the parallel between the two professions, very little has been written about how presenters might employ techniques used by actors to develop Hanning's concept of presenter-self. Nor has much been written about theatrical or acting devices for holding the audience's attention that might be suited to that same goal in the lecture hall, stockholder meeting, or political rally.

One need only look at the world of drama in order to see people regularly acting as someone they most often are not in real life. Actors constantly are developing their acting-selves in a manner like Hanning's recommendation that presenters develop their presenter-selves. Actors use acting skills. More successful actors more successfully use these skills. Presenters, too, can—and should—use these same skills. If for no other reason, they are the only skills available.

A CRAFTSPERSON'S TOOLBOX

Knowledge is power, and enthusiasm pulls the switch.
—Steve Droke

I envision a presenter's dynamic delivery skills as analogous to the tools carried by any professional craftsperson, including actors. This analogy is supported by Rubin (1985, 15) when he explains that the artistry part of presenting consists of "master craftsmanship." This presenting toolbox contains a set of skills or tools. According to Elaine Showalter (2003), these skills should, among other things, address developing a speaking voice that has range, force, and direction; a presence that uses the dynamics of physical movement to lend conviction to inner strengths and imagination; and the dramatic abilities that can fashion scenes and build climaxes.

In the craftsperson's toolbox, there are two categories of tools. Some tools are used more frequently and so are kept ever handy in the top tray. Other tools, used less frequently, are stored in the bottom of the craftsperson's toolbox. Such an organization of tools enables the knowledgeable professional craftsperson to have the right tool handy to accomplish the desired task. Without the right tools, always kept sharp, and the knowledge of how to use them, a craftsperson would be limited in his or her effectiveness. The same holds true for presenters.

A CRAFTSPERSON'S KNOWLEDGE

Although having the right tool for the job helps, a prerequisite to this is the possessing of the knowledge to use that tool in the first place. Tools do not operate themselves. But, even prior to knowing *how* to use a tool, one needs to know *what* tool from those available should be used in each situation. It reminds me of trying to solve problems in a physics course. The mathematics used in physics, normally, is not the stumbling block. The real difficulty is deciding (knowing) what formula, of the many available, best applies to the circumstances of the problem. It takes knowledge to make these intelligent decisions.

Actors must know their lines before they can expect to deliver them effectively. Presenters must know their subject matter before they can expect to present it effectively. One of the major conclusions from Bain (2004) is that outstanding presenters know their subjects extremely well. Subject Matter Mastery is the first acting or presenting skill that I will address. Because even the anticipation of having to deliver subject matter to an audience can create feelings of anxiety, I agree with Burns and Woods (1992) when they say that the best advice for nervous actors is to overprepare! Presenters should start their overpreparing with a goal of mastering their subject matter.

In my craftsperson analogy, Subject Matter Mastery is not something viewed as a single tool to be carried in the toolbox. Subject Matter Mastery is carried in the craftsperson's head—always ready, constantly used. Without the proper mastery of content knowledge, the delivery, no matter how dynamic, becomes as Shakespeare wrote "full of sound and fury, signifying nothing" (*Macbeth*, Act 5, Scene 5).

A CRAFTSPERSON'S TOP-TRAY DELIVERY TOOLS

Through both research and interviews with award-winning presenters, I have identified three delivery skills that, because of their routine use by effective and dynamic presenters, can be visualized as "top-tray" tools. They include:

- Chapter 8: Animation in Body
- Chapter 9: Animation in Voice
- Chapter 10: Humor

Why these three? No successful actor could, or would, overlook the importance of physical animation. The power of body language, perhaps even more convincing than verbal language, is not lost on the successful actor. Imagine the absurdity of actors standing still like telephone poles and delivering their lines. The lack of purposeful actor movement would get old real fast. Presenters, too, should be sensitive to their stage presence.

In a like manner, it would be unheard of for actors to ignore the importance of vocal animation (e.g., pitch, volume, voice quality, and rate) in their attempt to hold an audience's attention and to get their message across. Should presenters be any less concerned about their effective use of their voice? Actors take voice lessons and practice-practice-practice this skill. Should presenters, too, work at improving the impact of such a resource? Of course!

Finally, other than body and vocal animation, no other presentation tool under the *direct control* of a presenter has more potential for engaging and holding the attention of an audience than humor. Whereas the value of the first two tools, physical and vocal animation, are probably obvious to the reader because he or she uses both daily, humor too often is seen as something received rather than delivered. Humor isn't something most of us think about using purposefully as a powerful dynamic presentation tool. Start thinking about it!

A CRAFTSPERSON'S OTHER DELIVERY TOOLS

There are five other skills that are used less routinely by presenters. They normally are carried in the toolbox, but beneath the top tray. These skills include:

- Chapter 11: Suspense, Surprise, and Storytelling
- Chapter 12: Role-Playing
- Chapter 13: Use of Props
- Chapter 14: Space Utilization
- Chapter 15: Creative Entrances and Exits

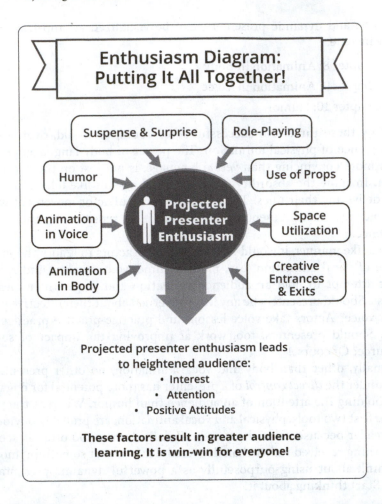

All these tools are useful in that they can contribute to greater *projected* enthusiasm on the part of the presenter.

ENTHUSIASM RATING CHART

How enthusiastic are you as a presenter? A rough indication of your enthusiasm level can be estimated by referring to the "Enthusiasm Rating Chart" (Collins 1981), reproduced in Appendix I. You could simply examine the categories, for example, "vocal delivery" through "overall energy level," and the descriptors that are used to rate oneself as low, medium, or high, in order to get a rough estimate of your overall enthusiasm. Although it is a bit more intimidating, you could ask a colleague to peer-review a presentation using this same chart as a basis for data collection. Repeated measurements, across several presentations, should be taken before any definitive judgment is made.

Is it OK for presenters to incorporate the characteristics typified by the descriptors listed under the "high" column? Is it OK for presenters to move from excited speech to a whisper, to use demonstrative gestures, to change facial expression suddenly, to use unpredictable body movements? Of course!

Like actors, presenters can hone their skills in the use of props, can utilize role-playing, can make better use of subject-matter-related humor (e.g., pun, short story, joke, or riddle), and can create attention-getting suspense and surprise. They also can be creative with their use of space and with their entrances and exits. Not only *can* presenters use all these acting-related tools, they *must* use these tools.

These skills will be addressed, one chapter at a time. Clearly, presenters' *projected* enthusiasm can be enhanced through the judicious use of the skills presented in this book, which until now may have been seen only as relating to the acting world.

These skills, whether used by presenters or actors, are simply a means to an end. They are the tools of one's craft. The more of these acting and performance tools that presenters have at their disposal and the better they can use them, the more effective these presenters will be.

The value of a dynamic presentation often is as important as the delivered content. Otherwise, why would you be delivering your presentation at all? You could simply give copies of your message to interested parties without having to be there to present it.

SUMMARY

Act enthusiastic and you will be enthusiastic.
—Dale Carnegie

For now, concentrate on understanding the acting and performance tools that follow. Most of them you will recognize and, hence, what you read may simply be a bold reminder for you to consciously insert more of each skill into your presentations. For others, the skills might be new, but they are easily mastered. All of them can contribute to your being perceived as a more "enthusiastic" presenter with all the benefits that go with that perception—attention, interest, engagement, more positive attitude, and greater achievement. I believe that you are up to it!

8

Animation in Body: A "Top-Tray" Tool

INTRODUCTION

Actions speak louder than words.
—Anonymous

Actors and presenters, alike, have two primary sets of inherent tools for conveying ideas and information to audiences—their bodies and their voices. Both can be used to provide emphasis, distinguish among ideas, clarify and create connotative meanings, thus complementing the intent of the message. We are about to deal with the first "top-tray" tool in your great presenting toolbox—Animation in Body. It's in the top tray because it needs to be available all the time at a moment's notice.

Our attention to our physical behavior in presenting is especially warranted, since audiences today are more and more attuned from birth to the visual rather than the oral medium. Many presenters have been heard to complain that television and other social media have had such an impact that audiences cannot seem to pay attention to material unless it is presented in a visually stimulating manner. That reality is dealt with in this book as a challenge for presenter action rather than a cause for hand-wringing.

WE ARE DESIGNED TO MOVE

The lens is not quick enough to track the movement of the human body.
—Roger Rees

Humans are designed to move, and we are meant to move. Even my action-figure key chain is designed to move—its legs move, its head twists 360 degrees, and its arms rotate. From the beginning of mankind, well before the development of verbal language, body movement and gestures helped us communicate.

How you move and to the extent that you move while presenting is up to you. Although researchers may disagree, it would be safe to say that from 50 to 80 percent or more of our communication is due to body movement—or lack thereof. When faced with the decision of which message is the truth, body movement wins out over verbalizations. Keep this point in mind.

VALUE OF ANIMATION IN BODY

Believe in your character. Animate with sincerity.
—Glen Keane

Presenters who are at least moderately animated while presenting material will be more successful in getting that material across to an audience. In the specific case of physical animation, I am referring to the use of facial expression, posture, movement, gestures, and more as nonverbal forms of expression that are found in the presenter's enthusiasm toolbox. Although Animation in Voice will be addressed in the next chapter, research shows that nonverbal behavior (e.g., body language) often speaks *louder* than words—sometimes, it seems to scream! A presenter's nonverbal messages, even more so than his or her verbal behaviors of delivery, can convey competence, trustworthiness, believability, and sincerity.

Numerous researchers have investigated the relative value of a presenter's animation in body. In doing so, they have devised various experimental formats, asking presenters to act in a particular way or to imitate certain movements. Other studies have simply analyzed the natural characteristics and unplanned behaviors of successful presenters—just watch them and note what they do. In both cases, the conclusions are similar. A presenter's nonverbal expression is positively linked to his or her effectiveness if that expressiveness is perceived as natural and not distracting.

This perspective echoes the lesson learned by actors that careful, subtle physical expression complements the playwright's words, while excess or unnatural movement "steals the show." The actor also has learned that while some physical expression can be definitively planned, the best is that which seems spontaneously delivered conveying the actor's perception of the feelings and meaning of the words spoken. This is known as "getting into character."

Presenters trained in comfortable, expressive, physical movement can speak with more confidence, thus developing better control of the total communication situation. This would seem to indicate that those speakers who try to be more expressive will develop a certain amount of self-confidence as a fringe benefit.

Like actors, presenters should present with a moderate level of animation as is appropriate to their own enjoyment of the subject matter. Their reward will be enhanced delivery effectiveness due to their own increased confidence and their audience's increased motivation. The all-important "bottom line" is that animated presenters have audiences who learn more!

RAISE YOUR LEFT HAND

> *Words represent your intellect. The sound, gesture and*
> *movement represent your feelings.*
> —Patricia Fripp

"Please raise your left hand and caress your left earlobe with your left index finger and thumb. Continue the caressing for the count of five. Now, relax." Read the next sentence, but *do not* do what is asked of you until I explain further. "Raise your right hand and caress your right ear lobe with your right index finger and thumb." Before you act, you must make a decision. Either choose to follow these instructions or choose not to. It is up to you.

It is *your* choice to act or not act. Obviously, you are perfectly capable of making your body act—you proved that by following the first set of instructions. Animation in body calls upon you to recognize that you, and no one else, oversees your behaviors—your actions. You can emphasize or exaggerate certain actions, or you can understate them or not use them at all.

To highlight the point, you could *choose* to gesture, you could *choose* to sweep your arms, you could *choose* to slam your palms down on the desk, you could *choose* to furrow your brow, or you could *choose* to do none of these at all. You could even *choose* to leap onto a table like Robin Williams did in *Dead Poets Society*, or not. Be careful!

HOW A SIMPLE CHANGE MADE A DIFFERENCE

> *If anyone can make a difference in this life, it's YOU.*
> —Anthony T. Hincks

Following a brief training on how to be more enthusiastic, Williams and Ceci (1997) tested out the impact of using body language when a teacher taught two classes the same verbal content. The same syllabus, audio-visual materials, assignments, and exams were used. In one class, they used their typical body language; in the other class, they used animated body language including emphasizing content through physical gesturing, pointing, varying their voice pitch, and using various facial gestures. In the animated class, they got higher ratings from the audience in *every* single area including, believe it or not, the quality of the required textbook.

Their audience ratings for "How knowledgeable is the presenter?" went from 3.61 to 4.05, a significant difference. "How enthusiastic is the presenter?" went from 2.14 to 4.21, over a two-standard deviation increase. A summary of all the presenter ratings went from 3.08 to 3.92—over a standard deviation increase. The authors conclude by expressing their astonishment that so simple a change (e.g., perceived enthusiasm level) can make such a difference. I share their astonishment.

TED TALKS

TED talks, those invited set of engaging videos that were introduced earlier in this book, are excellent examples of animation in body. A study by Van Edwards (2015) revealed that people decided whether they liked a TED talk based more on the speaker's body language than on his or her actual words. Researchers even compared ratings from audiences who *saw* and *heard* the TED talks with audiences who only viewed them without sound. The ratings were the same. The specific categories of movement that follow capture many of the successful, physically animated and dynamic delivery strategies used by TED talks' speakers.

Ambady and Rosenthal (1993), in a classic study, found that audiences were good at predicting a presenter's overall effectiveness based on first impressions. They showed audiences "thin slices," silent ten-second clips, of a graduate fellow's teaching. The audiences then were asked to rate the presenters on characteristics such as confidence and competence. She then compared these ratings to the ratings earned by presenters whose audience had completed the semester-long course. Her results were the same. The audience had accurately "sized up" faculty in just a few seconds.

This study was replicated with TED talks videos. One group of students saw only seven-second clips of a TED talk before being asked to provide a rating. Another group of participants watched the entire TED talk. The ratings, once again, were the same! The conclusion? You have just seconds to form a positive impression in the minds of your audience. Caldwell (2007), in his book, *Blink: The Power of Thinking without Thinking*, confirms that "just seconds" are needed to form a first impression. Make the most of it.

Humans who had this ability survived; those who did not have this ability did not survive. Sizing up another human being as a potential friend or foe, a dog as docile or rabid, and a speaker as worthy of paying attention to or not, are valuable life skills. If first impressions are lasting impressions, and if you never get a second chance to form a first impression, these first few seconds as a presenter are crucial. Once the audience forms a first impression of you, that audience will look for "evidence" to back up their impressions—and sure as can be, they will find it. The reason? Most people believe that they are "pretty good" judges of character, and thus, the last thing they want to have to do is to admit that they were wrong about their first impressions of someone.

Your first few behaviors, the subject of this chapter, your first few words (the subject of the next chapter), and your ability to provide an engaging "hook" (the subject of the chapter titled "Creative Entrances and Exits"), could make all the difference as to how your audience perceives you. You either will or will not positively engage them. If you do, it is relatively smooth sailing. If you don't, then it will be difficult (but not impossible) to recover.

CATEGORIES OF MOVEMENT

Everybody uses mime and gesture in real life, though we don't realize it. It is very useful as a performance technique.
—Anthony Daniels

Although physical animation most often has the categories of movement that follow (e.g., gestures, smiling, and eye contact) intertwined, for the sake of discussion, I will present them separately. Each of the animation in body categories presented in the following sections is completely under your control. You can choose to use them or not; you can choose to use them a little or not; you can choose to exaggerate them or not. Once again, it is up to you.

Do Nothing, but Do It Well

This first movement category will, at first, seem a bit odd. Do nothing. Even if you try to exhibit no body movement, a really difficult thing to carry off, the lack of movement, itself, projects a message. A lack of movement might suggest a lack of knowledge of how animated movement could be capitalized upon in presenting or reinforcing a point. On the other hand, the lack of movement, but doing it *well*, could project an intended loud and clear message.

Too often doing nothing is accompanied with giving someone the "look." All parents and other "superiors" *think* they know what is meant by giving subordinates the "look." Their "look" is to stare, really stare, at the offender giving him or her a well-practiced evil-eye conveying, "I don't want to see you even breathe heavily, or else!" The evil-eye is normally delivered with teeth clenched and hands sternly on one's hips conveying "I've drawn a line in the sand and don't you even think about crossing it!"

An alternative "look," with one's fists unclenched, breathing under control, and arms hanging limp at one's side, is to portray absolute boredom! Yes, boredom! Think about the chore of doing your dirty laundry if you need some boredom encouragement. This posture, this "look," keeps your blood pressure under control, lets both parties save face, and makes the problem less likely to escalate. The "do nothing" message sent is "I'm not amused. I've seen it all before. I'm willing to patiently wait until you correct your own behavior." Remember, it is very hard to tango with someone who chooses not to tango.

Plan Where You Step

It is unlikely that you will stand perfectly still for your entire presentation. More likely, you will step here and step there. Consider synchronizing the directions of your steps with your delivered message. Step toward your audience to indicate an important point is about to be delivered. Step back from them to indicate that you have concluded an idea and that they can relax for a moment. Lateral movements, left and right, signal that you are leaving one thought (e.g., B. F. Skinner's views) and taking up another (e.g., Carl Rogers's views). Centering yourself in the room signals a new idea or instruction is about to be presented (Princeton Language Institute and Laskowski 2001). Stand with presence; walk with a purpose. This small attention to your movement can contribute significantly to your audience's attention, interest, and understanding.

Gestures

The entire animal kingdom, including man, gestures to communicate. From the silverback gorilla pounding his chest, to the wolf that shows her teeth, to babies who within one year start to make requests by gesturing, each represents a form of communication. "Gesturing can help people form clearer thoughts, speak in tighter sentences and use more declarative sentences" (Gregoire 2016, 1).

Gestures include a nearly limitless range of hand and arm movements. The best gestures to use are those that are natural, purposeful, and non-distracting. Our enthusiasm for the subject matter will typically show itself in gestures that reinforce, emphasize, encourage, and clarify. These might include, but not be limited to, jabbing the air, pointing to objects, contrasting one hand motion with another, or sweeping the air like an orchestra conductor. One award-winning presenter was famous for his repertoire of football referee signals that he used during his presentation.

These gestures, which might seem extreme to some, were well received by the audience. They believed that by his going to such extremes he showed the degree to which he cared about their learning and his willingness to work hard to make it happen.

Fundamentally, gestures, such as sweeping the air with one's hands, are good if they are positively communicative. That means that the gesture should complement the words spoken. The gesture may be a *descriptive* one that clarifies the physical properties of the subject being discussed; it may be an *emphatic* one that indicates the most important aspect of the words spoken; or it may be *signalic*, indicating something the listeners are to do relative to the words spoken.

According to Kolowich (2015), Van Edwards and her team reviewed TED talks since 2010. They found a significant difference in the frequency of use of hand gestures between TED talks' speakers. The most popular TED talks' speakers used an average of 465 hand gestures; whereas, the least popular TED talks' speakers used an average of only 272 hand gestures. When speaker charisma was evaluated, the more hand gestures used the higher the speaker's charisma rating. I am not suggesting that you start running around waving your hands in some sort of frenzy. But the evidence seems clear: proper, coordinated hand gestures are noticed and appreciated by audiences.

Gorman (2010) reports that "authentic" gestures begin split seconds before the words that accompany them. He also points out some fascinating observations, such as a blind person talking to another blind person uses gestures, all of us gesture while on the telephone, and not surprisingly, our gestures become more animated when we are more passionate about a subject. Overall, audiences tend to view more favorably people who use a greater variety of gestures.

Avoid using "finger" or "air" quotations. Here you use two fingers of each hand to draw air quotation marks while uttering a term or phrase that you don't think is appropriate or accurate (*The Telegraph* 2012). Often air quotation marks are used to express distain for both "experts" and "government officials" as in "those so-called 'experts'!" To a listener, the gesture often is seen to connote sarcasm.

Another gesture to avoid is folding your arms across your chest. Some politicians are shown doing this in meetings, with the media, or with domestic and international leaders. This is a closed gesture. It is universally decoded as defensive, resistant, and negative. Finally, avoid what is known as the "fig leaf" position, with your hands crossed over your midsection genitals. The term comes from Adam and Eve's typical stance in Garden of Eden pictures. It suggests vulnerability and shyness.

There has been so much written on the power of gesturing that I recommend you conduct your own Internet search, read what you retrieve, and then put what you think will work for you into action. You will not be disappointed. And, like this book, you should be able to put what you learn into practice immediately. One great source on gesturing is a 2015 article by Van Edwards, "20 Hand Gestures You Should Be Using." Several specific gestures are:

- The easiest and most basic gesture is numerical. Any time a number is said, a corresponding finger(s) is held up for the audience to see.

- A "tiny bit," emphasizing a small point or quantity, uses the index finger and thumb almost closed together. For emphasis, bring the finger and thumb together very slowly stopping just when they are almost going to touch.

- A gesture where two hands come together about the distance apart of a loaf of bread can connote "coming together" or depict the size of something—as in "bigger than a bread box."

- A "this and that" gesture is used to differentiate two things. With your slightly outstretched left hand, palms up, you could say, "On one hand such and such is the best . . ." With your outstretched right hand, palms up, you could go on to say, "But, on the other hand such and such . . ."

- Place your hand on your chin. This suggests that you are pondering something or that you are waiting for a respondent to answer.

- When defining a particularly important term, you might emphasize its preciseness by squinting, raising your eyebrows, pressing your lips together, and announcing it slowly. "One such term might be . . ."

- Bill Clinton avoided pointing or wagging his index finger at an audience because that gesture is often associated with a school teacher chastising a young child. It may be perceived as insulting or condescending to adults. Instead, his version of pointing consisted of closing his fist, placing his thumb on top sticking up just a bit, and using it to point.

- Nodding your head as someone speaks accomplishes several things. It encourages the other person to continue speaking, it reveals that you are in sync with his or her message (you are nodding at appropriate time), and for your benefit it makes you more likeable.

- You could convey that a point is "dear to your heart" by tapping your open palmed right hand on the left portion of your chest. You could simply say the words "This is near and dear to my heart," but the heart tapping drives the point home.

- One rule-of-thumb for gesturing is to keep your gestures within the "box," that area from the top of your chest to the bottom of your waist.

Pretend you are holding a chest x-ray in front of you. Although exaggerated gestures, going beyond the "box," occasionally are acceptable, avoid such grandiose gestures on a regular basis so as to not distract the audience or look out of control.

- Use gestures to purposefully "look confused" with the intention of conveying to the audience that even the master does not know the answer to everything. Solicit their input to help solve the problem or dilemma at hand. To look confused, tilt your head slightly to one side, scratch the back of your head with your outstretched fingers, lean a bit forward (or stare at the ceiling), and maintain that pose for several seconds. If a chair is available, you could sit down on it and try to mimic the "The Thinker" in the gardens of the Rodin Museum, Paris. For a little bit of humor, a topic presented in a later chapter, hold up a picture of "The Thinker" and ask the audience if they can see the similarities!

Facial Expression

Facial expressions are tools for all speakers that exemplify the communication saying, "One cannot *not* communicate." Short of a full head covering, your face gives it all away—your enthusiasm, your boredom, your fear, your devilishness, your wonder, and all the rest of human emotions. Even Fido, your family pet, can "read" your face. When you return home after a trying day, does he bound toward you or slink away?

Our faces always convey some message to our listeners. The catch is that we are not always aware of what that message might be. As presenters, we would do well to sensitize ourselves to our own expressions so that our faces can be assisting our dynamic delivery, not hindering it. For instance, are we smiling and nodding to encourage only certain or almost all audience members to participate? Has a grimace crossed our face before a respondent has finished replying? Do we show an interest in the material by speaking with eyes wide open and animation in our expression?

How do you know for sure what facial expressions you are conveying to your audience? When we say, "He is someone who wears his feelings on his shirt sleeve," we mean that those feelings are visible for all to see. Your face, your whole face, gives it all away. What emotions of yours do you want to project? I hope that "enthusiasm" is one of those feelings.

As a category, facial expression deserves some serious "face time" in front of a mirror. This experience may well be a little new, especially for men, because except for shaving and combing their hair they don't spend a lot of time looking at themselves in a mirror. Practice a myriad of whole-face feelings. Show us (yourself) a poker-face, a scowl, or a dulled expression. Try projecting sadness, amusement, fear, joy, satisfaction, disgust, surprise, calm, pride, amazement, awe, confidence, anticipation, despair, indignation, fascination, puzzlement, intrigue, alarm, and, of course, *enthusiasm*! You *can* project them all. The trick, if it is a trick, is to purposefully convey the specific facial feelings that bolster your message.

Recall my earlier discussion about impressions—first impressions are often lasting impressions, and you never get a second chance to form a first impression. Your face, and the expression your face conveys, often is the first thing others see about you, and, hence, the first thing they use to form their first impressions of you. Before you speak, they see you and they see you most clearly through your face.

Eye Contact

We try to hide our feelings, but we forgot that our eyes speak.
—Anonymous

Eye contact is a sufficiently important feature of facial expression to merit individual attention. Via eye contact, we provide encouragement to our audience, maintain their attention, show interest and concern, signal to them, and portray our own confidence. Audiences tend to be quite sensitive to eye contact. By looking directly at someone whose interest appears to be wavering, we can rekindle his or her attention. We might even use our eyes to convey that we want that individual to respond to a question. In other circumstances, our direct eye contact may be read as a statement of confidence and commitment. By looking directly at the audience, we establish that we feel we have something important to say and trust they will attend to it.

According to Wyeth (2014, 1), "when you fail to make eye contact with your listeners, you look less authoritative, less believable, and less confident." Further, when you look people in the eye, they are "more likely to listen to you and more likely to buy your message." If eye contact is not excessive, "humans tend to rate a person who makes eye contact as more likeable, pleasant, intelligent, credible and dominant" (Akechi et al. 2013, 4).

Braithwaite (2013) suggests that you make some new "friends" by greeting early arrivals and making small talk. When you begin your presentation, these "new friends" can be among the first with whom you engage eye contact. At least at the start of the presentation, in your mind, you are having a one-to-one conversation, not delivering a lecture. Later, move on to establish eye contact with the rest of the audience.

Avoid the "ping pong" back and forth game of eye contact (Dlugan 2013). Instead, break the room into sections and give each one equal time and attention, including those in the back. Make your eye contact in a random pattern. Look at as many individuals as you can right in the eyes for about three to four seconds. Make them feel like you are talking to them.

The purpose of eye contact is to create a give-and-take relationship with your audience (Landrum 2009). Only the audience knows for sure if you are getting across your message. Watch their eyes. Do they convey boredom, excitement, confusion, disbelief, understanding, or empathy? Do their smiles, their nods, their frowns, their wide pupils help confirm their receipt of your intended message?

As depressing as it is, we must acknowledge that audiences may not remember much of what we dispense in a lecture or presentation. Hence, anything that we can do to make our talk more memorable, would be desired. Eye contact makes your words more memorable. If you want people to remember your words, find their gaze and hold it because memory, impression, and eye contact are connected (Harbinger 2015).

It is worth a look at the various and sundry ways that humans can use their eyes to communicate—to send messages. Just what can *your* eyes convey? One of the most exhaustive lists of facial expressions is that prepared by Donovan (2017). She notes that eyes can "flash, sparkle, widen, narrow, dart, twinkle, gleam, burn, glow, bore, gaze, wink, glisten, swell with tears, squeeze tightly closed, display a sarcastic roll, shimmer or beam. Nearby, eye lashes can flutter, eyebrows can waggle, droop or raise, foreheads can crease, furrow or pucker, and mouths can smirk, grin or pout."

The list goes on and on. Think of yourself viewing a dramatic movie, and by simply noting one or more of a character's eye movements or other facial features, you could predict what was going to happen next in the scene. You do not even need to hear the spoken words. Our eyes give us away. Surely, "the eyes are the windows to our soul."

None of these eye contacts, or accompanying facial features, is new to you. You have observed or exhibited each one of them. The important point is how do you purposefully plan to use your eyes, and other facial features, in your enthusiastic presenting?

I stumbled upon the power of eye contact when I read an article claiming that when you approach someone, say a clerk behind the desk at a hotel, you simply establish eye contact for about two seconds. Don't say a word. Let the eye contact connection "sink in" before speaking. I can't tell you why it works, but it does. Receivers, in this case hotel employees, seem to be more cooperative and more willing to respond to your requests.

Different cultures react differently to eye contact and, therefore, you need to be sensitive to this fact. Some cultures might interpret your sustained eye contact as an evidence of trustworthiness. Others may see it as aggressive, confrontational, or disrespectful. Any extended eye contact with an Asian student might embarrass him or her. Middle Eastern cultures, with strict rules regarding eye contact between men and women, present an interesting challenge for female and male presenters trying to engage respondents of the opposite sex.

Then, we have students, themselves, applying eye contact with presenters. They face some of the same cultural-bound eye contact difficulties. For instance, when an audience member does not "look you in the eye," it could be that his or her culture believes that subordinates should not make steady contact with superiors. If cultural differences might be a problem regarding the use of eye contact or, for that matter, any of the other skills presented in this book, it behooves the presenter to research the topic further. Speakers need to respect cultural differences.

Smiling

Sometimes your joy is the source of your smile, but sometimes your smile can be the source of your joy.
—Thich Nhat Hanh

Smiling is one of your greatest assets as a presenter. It is one specific facial expression that contributes significantly to the creation of presenter immediacy and thus to audience attention. The more attentive your audience, the greater chance your presentation will be successful. Smiles tell audience members that we expect them to be interesting and that we are happy to have them in the audience. Smiles tell them that we enjoy the subject matter being discussed. This is not to suggest that we should fake a pleasant expression, but simply encourage presenters to allow their own enjoyment of presenting to be evident. If you want to be considered likable and approachable, put on a smile.

Smile with your mouth, smile with your eyes, smile with your body. Before you even start to present, smile. Don't say anything at first, just smile. Then begin your lecture, conference presentation, or seminar.

If ever there was a beneficial addictive "drug" available to us, it is "smiling." You don't need a prescription for it. You carry it with you at all time. You simply need to turn it on. The act of smiling elicits a chemical reaction from your body—releasing feel-good dopamine, endorphins, and serotonin (Waja 2015). This release brings pleasure—so much so that, like coffee, it (smiling) could become addictive (Wenk 2011). Endorphins act as a natural pain reliever. The serotonin release brought on by your smile serves as an antidepressant filter (Stevenson 2012). And, because smiling often is contagious, once you smile, the audience is likely to smile. Once they smile, you are likely to smile even more. Anyone peeking into your presentation will be wondering what in the world is going on!

Although not necessarily the usual goal sought by a presenter, smiling makes you more attractive. Keep in mind that whether in the court room or the lecture hall, as a pharmaceutical rep or political candidate, people who smile tend to be evaluated more highly. It may not be fair, but it is true. Study after study backs up this claim.

Practice your smiling throughout the day with your significant other, colleagues, friends, Starbucks cashier, and so on. Simply smile while saying "hello." Wait a moment. Look for their response. Watch them begin to "connect" with you. I note that when I smile, perhaps it is a devilish smile, my wife quickly enquires, "What's up?" Sometimes there is nothing "up." Sometimes a cigar is just a cigar—sometimes a smile is just a smile. Sometimes I just "smile" because it feels good.

Did you know, "Smiling makes you look smarter?" If you want people to think you're smarter, smile more. We know that more attractive people are judged smarter. You may not be able to do much about your "attractiveness," but you certainly can do something about your smiling. Remember that the two most cited characteristics of a great presenter are knowledge of content and *projected* enthusiasm. Smiling helps convince an audience that you are smarter—more knowledgeable. Therefore, half the battle is won.

As a caution, don't make your smile too wide. A slight smile suggests that you are more competent, not just intellectually, but emotionally as well (Rivas 2017). Apparently, there is a lot more to our smiling than we first thought.

Do you like company? It doesn't matter whether the tune is belted out by Louis Armstrong, Dean Martin, or Billie Holiday. "When you smilin'... The whole world smiles with you." Start the smiling ball rolling in your presentation venue.

Posture

A good stance and posture reflect a proper state of mind.
—Morihei Ueshiba

Posture is an expressive tool used less frequently than gestures and facial expressions. However, a presenter's enthusiasm can reveal itself in the form of posture changes and overall movement. The best presenters are often described as being unable to contain themselves because they find the material so exciting. Presenters have been known to leap in the air, for instance. This last action is not necessarily recommended for all of us.

But certainly, if we feel so moved by the subject matter itself, or by a respondent's comment, we should allow ourselves to show that in a physical manner.

Posture also should be considered when establishing presenter–audience power relationships. Generally, a person who is standing while others are sitting is an individual with relatively more power. This is true whether in a church, a classroom, or a business meeting. Therefore, if the presenter wants to assert power, it may be wise to stand; whereas, if the presenter wants to establish an equality of power, it may be wise to sit—perhaps suggesting a more relaxed give-and-take session.

A special case of posturing can occur *before* you step on stage. Here, in order to fend off a bout of stage-fright (discussed in a later chapter), you might assume a "power pose"—standing up straight and taking up more space by putting your hands on your hips like Superman. The idea is to bolster your confidence before stepping on stage. Do power poses work? Perhaps. But if they seem to help prepare you for an upcoming presentation, use them. My favorite "power pose" is to picture Alex Karras, who played Mongo in the classic Mel Brooks comedy *Blazing Saddles*. Mongo is shown coming out of a western saloon having trounced a bunch of toughies, beating his chest, declaring, "Me Mongo!" If this reference is a bit dated for some of you, I'm sorry. "Me Mongo" works for me. You may have to get your own version of "Me Mongo."

BEHAVIORS TO AVOID

Normally, psychology tells us to stress what one is supposed to do, not what one is not supposed to do. [Yes, I recognize the double negative in the preceding sentence.] To water ski, bend your knees, keep your arms straight out in front of you, lean a bit forward, and hold on—remembering to "let go" if you are heading head first into the water. Skip all the "don'ts." Normally the same holds true for physical animation. But, while there are no strict rules about what to do in terms of physical movement, there are a few strict rules regarding what *not* to do. Some of our physical behaviors, often committed out of habit, may be interfering with our efforts to create a positive learning environment.

We are trying to attract an audience to our message, not distract them from it. Distracting mannerisms, conscious or not, can interfere with our success as a presenter. According to Smith (2014), some of these distracting mannerisms include wringing your hands, touching your face, keeping your hands in your pockets, jingling your pocket change, twisting your ring, adjusting your hair or clothing, clicking a pen, licking your lips, and pacing back and forth—also known as "Walkie-Talkie." How many of you remember the 1954 Humphrey Bogart film, *Caine Mutiny*, where Captain Queeg (Humphrey Bogart), showing signs of paranoid personality, continually rolls a pair of steel ball-bearings in one shaking hand?

We may inadvertently be sending contradictory messages, that is, our words sending one message and our behaviors conveying an opposite view. For instance, the presenter asks a respondent to speak ("I am interested in your ideas") but then conspicuously checks the time ("Your answer isn't that interesting after all") before the respondent has finished. The respondent receives a mixed message. The presenter's words expressed interest, yet his or her concurrent actions expressed disinterest. Typically, listeners put more faith in a speaker's nonverbal message than the verbal. Consequently, in our time-checking example, the audience will probably have inferred that the presenter's interest in the respondent's response was not sincere. That is an interpretation from which the presenter-audience relationship will be slow to recover. Rule number 1, then, is *Don't use nonverbal behaviors whose meaning conflicts with your verbal choices.*

In the same vein, presenters should not begin to walk while a respondent is talking. In doing so, the presenter would be "walking on the other's line," to use theatrical parlance. As theatergoers, we may have seen a background actor commit such an error, and we called it upstaging. The problem is that the other listeners will be attracted to the person in motion instead of to the person speaking. So, when the presenter upstages the speaker, he or she is essentially stealing the attention that the speaker has earned by participating. That will annoy not just the person who is trying to speak, but others in the room as well. Rule number 2, then, is *Don't upstage your audience respondents.*

Finally, a presenter should avoid any physical actions or behaviors, such as the mannerisms highlighted in the preceding paragraphs, that could be considered distracting. Such behaviors, by their repeated nature, only invite audience mockery. Since the behaviors in this category are frequently subconscious habits, we may be unaware of doing them and of how annoying they have become for the audience. It is in our best interest occasionally to ask a trusted audience member or two if there is anything about our presentation behavior that could be perceived as a nervous habit or distraction in general. Then, of course, work to replace that bad habit with more constructive, purposeful behaviors. Rule number 3, then, is *Do no distracting.*

One of my contributors, Dr. Sivarajah, reports that she routinely performs ultrasound exams in her practice. When she was in the early years of her training, an older tech came up to her and said, "You know you mutter when you are performing the ultrasound exam?" Dr. Sivarajah had no idea. She went on to say, "When you mutter, it sounds like you aren't sure of what you are doing." She hadn't realized that she had developed this distracting habit of "muttering" or discussing the findings and thoughts to herself under her breath. She has been conscious to not do this ever since.

TRUE STORY? MAYBE, MAYBE NOT!

Brunvand (1991) describes a story that has been circling the college circuit for years. It goes as follows:

> A group of psychology students were being taught the operant learning principle of positive reinforcement from a very boring professor. To relieve the tedium, the students concocted a scheme whereby they would all look up and smile whenever the instructor spoke from the left-hand side of the room. The instructor soon began to stand exclusively on the left side of the room while he taught. Pavlov would have been proud.

The bottom line is if you catch yourself presenting from only one side of the room, holding one of your hands stuck into your coat à la Napoleon Bonaparte, or chopping thin air with exaggerated motions to the extent that your watch almost flies off, it could be that your audience is looking for something to relieve their boredom. They may have conditioned you.

SUMMARY

All the recommendations are suggestions for behaviors that *can* be beneficial to you as you aspire to do a more successful job of holding your audience's attention and motivating them. There are no hard-and-fast "rules," and every presenter's individuality will define his or her comfort with physical animation. But none of us should dismiss active gesturing and expressiveness simply because it may make us a little uncomfortable initially. It is too valuable a tool to ignore. As presenters, we are performing artists. As such, it would behoove us to follow the actors' guidelines regarding physical movement. We should allow ourselves to move enough to create character, convey meaning, share enthusiasm, and hold the listeners' attention, but not so much as to become a caricature.

9

Animation in Voice: A "Top-Tray" Tool

INTRODUCTION

It is not enough to know what to say, but it is necessary
to know how to say it.
—Aristotle

We are about to deal with the second "top-tray" tool in your great teaching pedagogical toolbox—Animation in Voice. It's in the top tray because it also needs to be available all the time at a moment's notice. The human voice: it's the instrument we all play (Bariso 2016).

Let's jump right into vocal animation by examining the power of your voice in communicating a message. With the help of Dr. Sivarajah, this example comes from the medical world. I will do this by asking you to read the following sentences, out loud, emphasizing with your *most* emphatic voice, the word that is highlighted each time in **bold** and *italics*.

As an ***intern***, you must be ready to present all pertinent history about our patient.

As an intern, ***you*** must be ready to present all pertinent history about our patient.

As an intern, you ***must be ready*** to present all pertinent history about our patient.

As an intern, you must be ready to ***present*** all pertinent history about our patient.

As an intern, you must be ready to present ***all pertinent*** history about our patient.

As an intern, you must be ready to present all pertinent ***history*** about our patient.

As an intern, you must be ready to present all pertinent history about ***our*** patient.

The same words, but with a different vocal emphasis, can deliver a very different message. Which conveys the most urgency? Which most suggests a superior talking to a subordinate? Which suggests that detail is most crucial? Which suggests that like Joe Friday in the 1960s police series, *Dragnet*, all that is wanted are "Just the facts, Ma'am"? As with animation in body, the focus of the previous chapter, you are in control of your vocal animation. You can purposefully deliver any one of these messages with any emphasis you choose.

GREAT ORATORS

The good teacher is a good talker.
—J. A. Kulik and W. J. McKeachie

Recall Winston Churchill's wartime speech talking about Spitfire pilots, "Never in the field of human conflict was so much owed by so many to so few"; Martin Luther King Jr.'s "I have a dream" civil rights speech; John F. Kennedy's "Ask not what your country can do for you, ask what you can do for your country" speech; and Ronald Reagan's 1987 Berlin Wall speech, "Mr. Gorbachev, tear down this wall." Each of these memorable speeches used the same set of animated vocalizations, pitch, tone, and rate that are available to you as a presenter.

It is true that these speakers probably had good speech writers. But with your extensive subject-matter knowledge, you are, in effect, your own well-informed speech writer. Further, throughout your career you will have multiple opportunities to deliver and, hence, perfect your dynamic presentations. A successful presenter is someone who:

Generates in the audience the desire to learn more; begins a conversation that students are anxious to continue; gives a framework for organizing material; distills complex concepts, making them simple to understand; leaves learners grateful; inspires others to teach; enjoys teaching; mentors other teachers; and believes and makes others believe that medicine (law, politics, business, etc.) is a great and proud profession. (Shields 2010, 3)

The voice is an especially personal element in anyone's expressive repertoire. It reflects our character, background, personality, and moods. Using the voice to create and modify meaning should occur in a completely natural fashion for the speaker, with the expression growing out of—not overlaid on—the presenter's internal understanding and feeling for the ideas expressed. You could hear the sincere, heartfelt feelings conveyed by each of the highlighted orators mentioned. You can hear their leadership, assertiveness, and confidence while they were speaking.

Considerable research has been undertaken to determine whether a presenter's vocal expressiveness influences audience learning. However, one conclusion seems to be firm: a moderately expressive voice correlates with more significant learning.

HURL YOUR WORDS

If the voice is in control, the teacher is in control.
—Anonymous

Practice using emotion—body and voice—in your delivery. Do this with a party-type game that will be fun for everyone. Ham it way, way up; you can always dial it back! Place the following Shakespeare quotations on 3" x 5" cards and distribute them among the game players. Take a moment and learn your assigned lines so that you can maintain eye contact while delivering them. Crank up your emotion. *Hurl* these lines at each other! *Project* these lines. A few of these lines follow.

"Out, dog! Out, cur! Thou drivest me past the bounds of maiden's patience!"
(*A Midsummer Night's Dream*, Act 3, Scene 2)

"Hence, horrible villain! Or I'll spurn thine eyes like balls before me; I'll unhair thy head."

"Thou shalt be whipped with wire and stewed in brine, smarting in lingering pickle."
(*The Tempest*, Act 1, Scene 2)

"Thou art a hodge-pudding, a bag of flax, a puffed man. Thou are old, cold, withered and of intolerable entrails." [This would not be a good yearly review, would it?]
(*The Merry Wives of Windsor*, Act 4, Scene 5)

"Oh thou wicked soul. If I could have my battery on thee, thou sinner, I would touch thy hindquarter with the smarting board of education."
(*The Desperate Instructor*, Act 1, Scene 5)

HOW DO YOU SOUND TO OTHERS?

Be a voice not an echo.
—Albert Einstein

You may recall from the previous chapter on animation in body, I suggested that you use a mirror to practice your gestures. For animation in voice, I recommend that you audio- or video-tape yourself and then listen to it. Do this after you have read this chapter. This can be a humbling experience for some. I know firsthand because it was such a humbling experience for me. You might do it the first time, alone, waiting until later to ask others to listen, too. One of the suggestions under "What Else Can You Do? Lots!" in chapter 17 recommends that you consider seeking feedback from a speech instructor.

It is almost too obvious to say, but animation in body and animation in voice are two critical areas requiring attention by those aspiring to become great teachers and dynamic presenters. There is no substitute for doing these two things well. If audience evaluations regularly cite "boring voice," "her voice puts me to sleep," "heavy accent," "he mumbles," "too soft spoken," "faces the screen while talking," "can't hear her beyond the first two rows," "he speaks in a monotone," then this a wake-up call for action. These are symptoms demanding a proper diagnosis and treatment.

VOCAL FITNESS

When we think of professional voice users, it is natural to consider performing artists such as singers, actors, entertainers, and broadcasters. But, according to Zubrzcki (2015), teachers, too, are high on that list. Whereas many other professional voice users know to take preventative measures to protect their voices, teachers and other presenters have received no warning to do so. Nor have they been trained in how to do so. Presenters simply seem to believe that hoarseness is part of the job—it isn't, or at least it shouldn't be.

When you look at the most common voice disorders, teachers have more of them than any other profession. "Teachers have the highest vocal demands of any profession" (Pitman 2011, 1). The adage "An ounce of prevention is worth a pound of cure" never applied more than it does for teachers to protect their voice—their livelihood. One wonders why such training is not mandatory as part of teacher or presenter training programs. After all, voice-related problems are not *if* they will occur, but more likely, *when* they will occur.

It should seem obvious that if Animation in Voice is a "top-tray" tool in your pedagogy toolbox, then that tool should be kept clean, sharp, and well oiled. A rusty tool, a damaged tool, is of little use to the craftsperson.

Vocal fitness is a prerequisite to effectively using all the other voice-related devices that follow. Actors, appreciative of the voice's potential, work to keep their voices healthy and flexible so that they can be responsive to moderate changes in emotion. Some actors do daily vocal exercises, some take voice lessons, and still others simply treat their voices with care so that the vocal folds will not be strained.

Regular general exercise to maintain an overall level of fitness, well-balanced diets, and avoidance of abusive practices such as smoking are the basics of a sensible approach to maintaining vocal strength and flexibility. Presenters, being equally dependent professionally on their voices, should exercise similar care. Specifically, if voices are to be healthy enough to achieve the projection and expressiveness necessary, presenters should:

- practice deep diaphragmatic breathing
- avoid coffee and other caffeinated drinks
- drink herbal tea or tea with lemon
- drink plenty of water and fruit juices
- whisper more, shout less
- rest the voice when it is not required
- go silent when bothered by a sore throat
- avoid smoking and inhaling others' smoke
- develop and use more nonverbal cues and hand signals to communicate
- design presentations to include, if possible, group work, PowerPoint aides
- get regular ENT exams (ear-nose-throat)

Presenters sometimes must talk for extended periods over the hum of instructional technology, outside traffic, and heating and cooling systems. We sometimes get tense, and we drink still more coffee instead of water. We also commit the sin of pride in thinking that we need to conduct a presentation even though we have a respiratory infection.

The voice is far too delicate an instrument to bear this kind of abuse. It is far too important an instrument to place in such danger. Treat it with respect. What is it about the human voice that makes it such an important tool for both actors and teachers? And what can we learn from actors about the care and use of this tool?

PARALANGUAGE

Paralanguage is a term for the conglomerate of vocal variations that accompany oral verbal expression. Each of us has a certain vocal character that is identifiable as our own. In fact, recent developments in forensic science verify that each human voice is unique, possessing a distinct combination of vocal variations. No one uses only one pitch level, or degree of loudness or rate, of course. We might speak, for instance, an average of 175 words per minute, but that is not a constant speed. We may slow down to 100 words per minute when speaking about something very tragic or somber and speed up to 225 words per minute when sharing exciting news. It is the pattern of variations that is constant for an individual and thus makes that person's voice unique.

Every human being has a range of vocal variations that fit comfortably within their own vocal repertoire. We use those variations consciously and subconsciously to provide shades of meaning to the words we speak. Variation in a presenter's paralanguage can convey the enthusiasm that is positively correlated with higher presenter evaluations, more consistent audience attention, and increased levels of comprehension.

SPONTANEOUS VOICE VARIATIONS

Most vocal variations are initiated subconsciously. Our voices should be responsive to variations in our thoughts and feelings. When conflict is building within the scene of a play, the actor does not need to be reminded to speak more loudly and with greater variations in pitch. That change in voice is going to happen as a direct result of the actor's sensitivity to the developing conflict—he or she will feel angry and tense, and thus the voice will sound angry and tense.

Similarly, as a presenter is delivering material found to be personally fascinating, no thought needs to be given to the idea of speaking with a higher pitch level, a faster rate, and a louder volume. Those vocal variations will likely occur simply because the presenter is so caught up in the material and, having a healthy voice capable of responding to changing emotional states, will experience vocal changes that convey that fascination and enthusiasm.

When telling someone about your latest discovery, thriller book, or vacation, you don't plan to speak faster and louder than usual. It just happens! Each of us probably has that level of enjoyment during moments of our presenting. You catch yourself bubbling with enthusiasm, and you just have to share your excitement—who better than with an audience or colleagues. Our voices will naturally manifest that amazement, surprise, or thrill!

DELIBERATE VOICE VARIATIONS

In addition to spontaneous voice variations, we can make some deliberate decisions in order to provide specific vocal emphasis to our ideas. Again, there is a parallel in acting, for the actor knows ahead of time that, during the performance, a particular inflection is going to be necessary to create a specific meaning at certain key points. Let's look at several vocal characteristics to understand how and why such deliberate variations could be planned for any presentation venue. A special thanks in this section is offered to Cathy Sargent Mester, a valued colleague.

Volume and Projection

Perhaps the most obvious deliberate animated voice characteristic is how loud your voice is, and how well you project it to the far reaches of the audience. Volume changes can be used similarly to convey urgency or commitment about a statement. It is the change in volume that calls attention to the accompanying thought, not the volume level per se. Just being loud is not necessarily more beneficial than being quiet. As a famous commercial line notes, "if you want to get someone's attention, whisper." By purposely changing volume—either by speaking louder or softer—a presenter, like a good actor, focuses the listeners' attention on the point thus spoken.

An adequate volume is a fundamental necessity for both the actor and the presenter, especially since a reasonably strong voice is perceived as conveying confidence, self-assurance, and control. It is a tool particularly beneficial to the beginning teacher or presenter. The general guideline is that, except in cases of confidentiality or emphasis as noted already, a sufficient volume should be maintained so as to make the speaker heard from anywhere in the room.

How loud should your projected voice be? The test is whether everyone in the audience can hear you. My wife directed high school plays throughout her career. To get actors (lecturers or presenters in our case) to speak up, she would move to the rear of the auditorium and repeatedly say, "I can't hear you!" She wore them down; they gave in and spoke louder. It paid off. Come the presentation of the play, no one complained of not hearing the presenters.

Keep in mind that a "strong" volume is characterized by diaphragmatically centered vocal power, not by tensing the throat muscles and screaming. You want a voice that carries well, not that causes an audience to shudder in ear-splitting pain.

Whispering

There is another side to the vocal animation quality of volume. That other side is to whisper. Saying something softly, at barely a whisper, signals intrigue and mystery; it piques interest, commands attention, and arouses curiosity. Leaning forward, giving a furtive glance, looking conspiratorial, or holding your index finger to your mouth (all animation in body movements), help complete the belief that something secret or special is about to unfold. Your audience will be listening and listening extra carefully!

Imagine delivering one of your spirited and enthusiastic presentations and then, at a predetermined time, quickly shifting into a whisper to emphasize a particular point. There is something captivating about being let in on a secret. Whispering a message implies greater importance in what you are saying (Bunny 2017).

You may recall an incredibly successful 1970s–1980s commercial, where a conversation between two men at a business lunch inevitably turned to the stock market. One person said to the other, in a hushed tone, "My broker is E. F. Hutton. And E. F. Hutton says . . ." Immediately, everyone in the restaurant leaned forward to hear the end of the sentence. In fact, much of the viewing world seemed to stop what they were doing in order to pay attention to E. F. Hutton's strategic use of whispers.

Rate

Rate is another animation in voice characteristic that is easily grasped and understood as being important to effective communication. It has arguably the greatest potential as an expressive or enthusiastic tool for the actor, teacher, and presenter. Rate can be varied either by changing the overall speech speed (words per minute), changing the duration of a single syllable or word, or by using pauses of various lengths.

Slower overall rate or duration might be purposefully selected when we need to be perceived as speaking more seriously or emphatically. On the other hand, we may deliberately speed up to convey enthusiasm, panic, or surprise. The actor will have considered the script and plotted specific rate changes to match the intended meaning of the lines. While a presenter may not make such definitive plans, some advance attention to the presentation to determine which points could be emphasized by a simple rate change is appropriate.

Presenter speech rate also has been shown to have an indirect effect on audience learning because of its effect on audience attentiveness. Audiences are likely to be more attentive when a presenter speaks at a moderate and varied pace than at either a noticeably fast or slow, unchanging pace. As with volume, it is the change in rate that catches the listener's attention and provides emphasis.

Tone

My daughter used to say, "Dad, it's not what you say, it is how you say it." She was probably right. An example that all readers will recognize is a parent saying to a child, "Don't use that tone with me!" We all know what the parent is exclaiming. One unknown author describes three tones of voice that presenters use. One, the *disappointed* voice, is where the speaker comes across as disappointed, angry, or upset. Another is the *teacher's* voice, more formal with a clear indication that I'm the teacher and you are the students. Finally, the *people* voice, their adult voice where two equals or nearly equals are talking to each other.

Tone of voice matters. Boyd (2003) says that we tell an audience by our tone of voice whether we are passionate about our topic, whether we have concern for an audience, and whether we are sincere. I offer an example of putting a punch into the tone of your voice when you reach a predetermined "WOW" part of your presentation. You know it's coming. You know from previous presentations that it is considered a "WOW" factor moment for the audience. Let your animation in body, the subject of the last chapter, help you create that "WOW" moment.

Try this simple, yet telling, tone exercise. In Act 1 of the play, *Cyrano de Bergerac*, the big nosed hero, upsets his audience. One especially offended audience member stands up and declares, "Sir, you have a very big nose!" Cyrano is unimpressed with the insult, and he goes on to provide examples of far wittier insults (much to the delight of the audience). Use the suggested tone to deliver your lines! It is good practice (as well as fun) and shows the range of communication possible with your tone of voice.

(1) **Aggressive tone**

"Sir, if I had a nose like that, I would amputate it!"

(2) **Descriptive tone**

"Tis a rock! A peak! A cape! No, it's a peninsula!"

(3) **Gracious tone**

"How kind you are. You love the little birds so much you have given them a perch to roost upon."

(4) **Considerate tone**

"Be careful when you bow your head you might lose your balance and fall over."

(5) **Naïve tone**

"Is that monument open to the public?"

(6) **Military tone**

"The enemy is charging! Aim your cannon!"

(7) **Practical tone**

"A nose like that has one advantage: it keeps your feet dry in the rain."

Pitch

Pitch, the highness or lowness of the voice, has the capacity to reflect a great many emotions and connotations. Rising pitch at the end of a thought group, for instance, typically indicates incredulity or questioning. A lowered pitch, on the other hand, indicates finality or certainty. So, if you were explaining an assignment to an employee and stated the due date in a relatively lower pitch, the employee would likely interpret this as a firm deadline. For example, "Your project is *due by the 24th*" (with the italicized words spoken in a lower pitch).

Pitch changes typically are perceived as signals indicating whose turn it is to speak—the presenter's or the audience's. In addition, pitch changes may be used to encourage audience members to participate. If a presenter asks, "Who can tell us what the Latin term for such and such is?" with a pleasantly varied, higher pitch, it sends a signal that the presenter expects that the audience knows the answer. Such subtle establishment of positive expectations is likely to be rewarded with desired responses.

Quality

Voice quality is achieved as the result of our typical resonance and pattern of vocal-fold movement. Common examples are breathiness, raspiness, stridency, nasality, and mellowness. Again, each one of us has a recognizable personal quality most of the time but may achieve variations in response to changing emotions or the need to convey a specific feeling. We should try to maintain a pleasant quality devoid of any annoying effects such as hypernasality or stridency. After all, audiences may be listening to that voice for long periods of time!

Actors who find that they tend to produce an annoying vocal quality seek professional assistance from speech coaches in order to achieve a pleasant, unstrained voice. Likewise, teachers and presenters should listen to their voices on tape to determine if the quality is pleasant enough for sustained attention.

If the basic quality has no distracting elements, voices should be capable of occasional variations. A teacher of literature, for example, may need to produce a more resonant, almost stentorian, tone when reading from some of Poe's work or a more breathier tone to read from Dickinson. These variations are achieved by modifying the resonating cavities (mouth, nose, and pharynx) or by changing the muscle tension on the vocal folds.

Cadence and Inflection

Cadence refers to the rhythmic inflection or rising and falling of text. Say Poe's opening line, *The Raven*, "Once upon a midnight dreary, while I pondered weak and weary" out loud. Can you hear, perhaps even feel, the rhythm, the lilt? Look back at the opening exercise in this chapter where you were asked to read the same sentence multiple times, each time varying the inflection or cadence.

For a little surprise and humor, both the focus of later chapters, generate different lyrics to Poe's, *The Raven*. "Once upon a time unprepared for an exam, I found myself in an academic jam. Many unread textbooks sat very still while I nodded, nearly napping, suddenly the professor was tapping. Soon on rear he would be slapping."

Pauses

A speech without dashes and dot-dot-dots is an article, not a speech!
—Winston Churchill

You may recall the animation in body suggestion, "Do nothing, but do it well." A similar suggestion applies to voice—"Speak nothing, but do it well." In other words, make effective use of pauses. They can be a powerful communication for emphasizing a point or regaining possibly lost attention from the audience. The pause lets your audience more easily follow your presentation, letting them know when one central idea has finished, and another is about to unfold. Pauses work, not only at the end of a sentence but during sentences.

Actors have long used this technique to build suspense. But, in addition, the pause is a device for punctuating our thoughts by separating items in a list, setting off direct quotes, pointing to key words or phrases, and signaling a change in focus. Consider the spoken pause a parallel to the well positioned written comma in a sentence (Notas 2012). Think of the power of the pauses at each comma in Shakespeare's *Hamlet*, 'To *be*, or not to *be*, that is the question." No one simply reads this line without the dramatic pauses. Strategically placed pauses can sometimes have a more dramatic effect on listeners' attention and comprehension than words themselves.

A gem of a "pauser" was comedian Jack Benny who played the role of a skin-flint (tight with his money) for years both on radio and on television. His classic pause skit where his character feels a gun in his back goes something like this.

Mugger: "Your money or your life!" [Benny just stands there with his arms crossed, hand to his chin, and seems to be lost in thought. The agitated mugger demands, again, "Your money or your life!"]

Benny: "I'm thinking it over!"

DREADED "UMS"

"The most important step toward more fluent speaking is to become aware of your distracting speech habits" (Marshall 2009, 21). It's Sunday and Preacher Scanlon steps before the congregation to make some important announcements. Before he is done, I have counted thirty-two "ahs." I believe it is a new world's record! These "ahs," and its cousins, "ums," "ers," "like," and "you knows" (if I knew, I would not need you to tell me) can be distracting to the speaker's intended message.

These "filler" words clutter your speech and undermine your credibility—they become interrupters that detract from your message (Baral 2016). Your mouth shifts into gear before your brain has fully formed your thought. The goal is not to eliminate all "filler" words, just those that when used too frequently become a distraction. Some claim that "fillers" serve a valuable purpose—give the speaker time to think about what to say next.

Filler words can reveal nervousness, suggest that one does not know the subject matter well, signal that the speaker is uncomfortable with silence, or be used to "hold a place in line" and stall while keeping control of the "talking space" (Shipman 2017). More effective strategies would be to better know your subject matter, become comfortable with pauses (if you are not speaking you can't use filler words), take turns allowing other people to speak, and purposefully deciding to insert filler words in order to emphasize a point—"Our client, 'like,' told me to . . ."

Marshall (2009, 20) ends her article about combating speech disfluencies with a bit of tongue-in-cheek humor. After making her case that fillers are not unique to just U.S. speakers, she reports Swedish filler words such as, "eh, ah, aak, m, mm, hmm, ooh, a, and oh." She concludes by saying, "Hmm, this is starting to sound a bit X-rated!" Now, "like," "you know," her comment is funny.

CREATING CHARACTERS

For a presenter, creative, deliberate vocal changes can also be used to create characters. One may want to read dialogue with a different vocal quality or inflection for each character in the story—a story being one of the most remembered presenter mediums. The differences clarify the plot and character interaction as well as help to hold the audience's interest and attention. This can be done most easily by using different speech rates for the characters, though other vocal variations could be used as well. Br'er Rabbit would probably speak his lines much faster than Br'er Bear, for instance.

In chapter 12, "Role-Playing," you will be reminded of using your voice to convey to an audience the character or characters central to your message. For now, keep in mind that your voice is a primary way to create these roles for your audience.

LARYNGITIS AND SORE THROATS

President Clinton lost his voice at a crucial point in the 1992 presidential campaign. I lost my voice a day before I was scheduled to present at an auditorium full of administrators. Silence is absolutely the best therapy. Even whispering can damage vocal folds. Go completely silent. Have a plan "B" ready. Like insurance, you hope that you will never need it, but it is there just in case.

"Teachers are a particularly high-risk profession, even more so than salespeople" (Vozzella 2010, 1). Over half the population of teachers report voice difficulties—twice the occurrence in the general population.

What can help the problem? Review the suggestions presented earlier in the chapter for avoiding laryngitis in the first place. Drink lots of water—your vocal cords like to stay hydrated, limit caffeinated beverages and alcohol, have some quality throat lozenges available, and so on.

During real or "faked" laryngitis, use your full range of physical motions (review chapter 8, "Animation in Body"), particularly those that communicate a desire for elaboration or that suggest a relationship between two offered points such as nods, shrugs, clapping, snapping, and other hand gestures to assist facilitating or signaling something important (Merys 2014). Note that in a later chapter about feigning suspense and surprise, laryngitis is presented as a purposefully applied presenter skill to get an audience to contribute more.

SUMMARY

Let me share with you a comment from a colleague on the topic of animation in voice. Recalling her own training she stated, "I can't personally think of examples from my own training when instructors purposefully used animation in voice—but I'll keep thinking." This suggests one of two things. Either her memory is faulty or her instructors never, in fact, used animation in voice (from a whisper to a scream) to help emphasize points while teaching. If it is the former, then so be it. If it is the latter, then her instructors may have missed some great dynamic presentation opportunities.

The human voice is an incredible resource of particularly remarkable value to actors, teachers, and presenters. Like any resource, it must be treated with care in order to be appreciated fully.

10

Humor: A "Top-Tray" Tool

INTRODUCTION

Humor helps to convert "Haha" into "Aha!"
—P. J. Herbert

This is the third "top-tray" tool in your presenting toolbox—"Humor." Humor normally is not used as often as the first two "top-tray" tools, "Animation in Body" and "Animation in Voice," but it should be readily available and used far more often than it is. The payoff to both the presenter and the audience is significant.

As the story goes, Joe accompanied his friend to a joke-tellers meeting. At the well-attended gathering, members had such a large repertoire of jokes that they numbered each of them. Then, throughout the meeting, different members simply would stand, call out the number of a joke (e.g., number 42), and everyone in the audience would howl with laughter. Toward the end of the meeting, Joe asked if he could take a turn "telling a joke"—after all, it looked so easy. Joe stood, called out a number, and waited for an audience response. There was none. Joe's friend turned to him and said, "Well, some people can tell a joke, and some people can't."

According to Low (1990), the ability to use humor is a skill that can be acquired. Presenters do not need to create humor, but rather they can use humor created by others. But first, they must learn to appreciate the pedagogical benefits of humor.

Successful joke-teller or not, humor is everywhere. John F. Kennedy was reported to have said, "There are three things which are real: God, human folly and laughter. The first two are beyond our comprehension. So, we must do what we can with the third" (Hunsaker 1988, 285). The powerful assertion that "of the personal dimensions of teaching, humor is the most human of all" (Kottler, Zehm, and Kottler 2005, 19) justifies its instructional use.

Although the following quotation is dated, it is still true. "One of the greatest sins in teaching is to be boring. It's a dull moment when there is no whetstone for the wit. Work mixed with fun goes better" (Baughman 1979, 28). When presenters and audiences laugh together, they stop for a time being separated by expertise, individuality, authority, and age. They become a unit; they enjoy a shared experience. If sense of community can be sustained, a more positive learning environment will have been created. Humor is a powerful tool for improving communication: it is underused in most presentation environments (Borins 2003).

According to Lundberg and Thurstone's (2002) book title *If They're Laughing, They Might Just Be Listening*, humor is clearly connected to sound pedagogy.

IS HUMOR TOO "MICKEY MOUSE"?

Minor surgery is an operation performed on someone else.
—Anonymous

If there is a "Doubting Thomas" among you who thinks that the pedagogical use of humor is too "Mickey Mouse," I say, "Thank you for the compliment!" How is it a compliment? Think about what Walt Disney did with a dream, several theme parks, and a mouse with large ears. He captured and held the attention of the world with his brand of humor—fun! Disney World's attendance at Magic Kingdom, alone, was over 20 million for 2016—a number about the population of New York State.

Disney is not just for children. Disney allows adults to embrace their inner child, and they keep coming back each year. What they experience and what they learn is remembered and, back home, can be recalled in detail. All the characters at Disney act, they perform. They capture the attention of their audience, they engage them, and they inform them. Humor is everywhere. Wanderers through Disney World, laugh, smile, and giggle; they are engaged, attentive, surprised, and amazed. Let's hear it for "Mickey Mouse."

COMPETENT AND CONFIDENT

The art of medicine is in amusing a patient while nature cures the disease.
—Voltaire

Presenters who use, for that matter even attempt to use, humor are seen as brave—plain and simple. More specifically, they are viewed by the audience as being more competent and confident. Sure, there is a risk; life isn't without risk. If you risk embarrassment by using humor, not only are you going to have an audience that learns more, you will be modeling for them that learning is paramount and that you will do what it takes to insure it occurs—even take a chance at humor.

If an audience models the modeler, it implies, "If presenters can teach learners to have a sense of humor about the serious things in life, they are teaching them how to cope in the real world" (Menon et al. 2013, 105). This should serve audiences well throughout their own careers. Dynamic presenters know that to do the exacting work demanded in most professions devoid of humor adds immeasurably to the effort (Aring 1971).

Burns and Woods claim that "a sense of humor . . . and love of your subject will ultimately lead to effective teaching" (1992, 89). I offer two responses. One, we should be aiming for "great" teaching, not simply effective teaching. Two, we don't have time to waste while waiting for effective teaching to *ultimately* happen. We need to speed up the process. The skills in Part II of this book, including this one, use of humor, are designed to speed up the journey toward great teaching.

BENEFITS OF HUMOR

I told my doctor that I broke my leg in two places.
She told me to quit going to those places.
—Henny Youngman

What are the physiological benefits of humor? "The blood flows more freely. The immune response is stimulated, muscles pump, endorphin production is increased and there is some relaxation. All of these, not surprisingly, make us feel better" (Calman 2001, 228). Humor facilitates socialization into the professions because only those with the requisite knowledge or experience are likely to "catch the meaning" of the humor (Ramesh et al. 2011). "Humor can enhance retention, increase learning, improve problem solving, relieve stress, reduce text anxiety, and increase perceptions of presenter credibility" (Poirier and Wilhelm 2014, 2).

Humor can break down barriers to communication between the presenter and the audience. These barriers can obstruct learning. When presenters project a sense of humor and are not afraid of using it, audiences relax and listen better (Menon et al. 2013). It can link presenters and audiences together through shared enjoyment.

Victor Borge, a famous comedian of late, believed that laughter is the shortest distance between two people. Non-hostile humor, directly related to a presenter's message, can also help make taboo subjects, such as politics, law, religion, terminal illness, death, and sex, more approachable. It is a powerful way to reinforce learning.

Ron Berk wrote in his book *Humor is an Instructional Defibrillator* (2007) that there are two reasons for presenters using humor. Even his book title has us laughing. Reason one: humor can improve the connection between the presenter and the audience. Reason two: humor can bring dead or dying, boring course content and, hence, almost expired audience members back to life.

On one hand, for both actors and presenters, humor should be the easiest skill area to address. Probably more has been written about humor than on any of the other acting or presenting skills highlighted in this book. Endless examples of humor exist in medicine, economics, business, politics, and law. No subject area is immune.

On the other hand, humor often is seen as the most threatening of the skill areas. For presenters, humor must serve a subject-related purpose, not simply entertain. Further, humor that "bombs" for an actor one night with one audience can be forgotten—a new audience will be in the theater tomorrow. For a presenter, humor that "bombs" may carry over to the next class or presentation.

Because the use of humor can be a bit scary, it might be wise to announce to your audience, "I'm not a natural at humor, but from what I've read its use should help me present and you to learn. Bear with me. I'm going to give it the old college try." Chances are that the audience will cut you some slack. You could always have a Plan B available such as "Yep! My wife (or husband) was right when she rolled her eyes and said, 'You are going to do *that*?'"

According to Glasser, fun (i.e., humor) is one of five basic needs that motivate human beings. Fun is no less important than the other human needs of survival, love and belonging, power, and freedom. Fun is nature's reward for learning. "Students feel pain when a need is frustrated and pleasure when it is satisfied" (Glasser 1998, 26). Presenters are in a key position to help an audience experience the pleasure of having needs satisfied—including the need for fun.

Despite the anxiety that beginning users of humor might experience, it is worth the effort. "Humor, like sin, sun, and self-righteousness, exists virtually everywhere people congregate" (Herbert 1991, 2). Humor holds great potential for positively impacting an audience no matter the venue. Who can argue with the fact that learning is most effective when it's fun?

HUMOR: ITS IMPACT ON AUDIENCES

One of the most important qualities of a good teacher is humor.
—Gilbert Highet

Having a sense of humor is a positive trait often listed by an audience when they are asked to rate effective presenters. The humor to which I refer here is non-hostile humor directly related to the presenter's message—not just some funny joke. Humor is a recommended presenting strategy for facilitating learning (Torok, McMorris, and Lin 2004). If we allow such humor to be a vital part of our presentations, we will add a strategy to our repertoire that is sure to stimulate audience attention and interest.

Humor can take many forms including that of playful exaggeration or an intentional expansion of emotional responses reinforced by gesture, posture, tone of voice, and role-playing. According to Starratt (2012), using humor is a form of acting that falls in between playing a role with sincerity and playing an imposter or fraud. It recognizes that a presentation cannot tolerate relentless melodrama, but neither can it endure uninterrupted frivolity. This type of presenting includes, among other exaggerated responses, mock indignation ("How dare you, sir!"), mock surprise ("I never would have suspected!"), a playful moralizing ("That's what happens to little boys who disobey their mothers.") and stock rationalizations ("The devil made me do it!").

Humor invites an audience to take risks because it softens the blow of failure. In *Dead Poets Society* (1989), Mr. Keating, played by Robin Williams, often used humor to inspire his students to participate. One notable moment occurs when a student incorrectly answers a query about a certain poet. Williams makes the sound of a buzzer with his voice, giving the impression that the student is on a game show. The buzzing sound is followed with the line, "Incorrect (Charlie), but thank you for trying." This creates immediate laughter from the other students, as well as from Charlie. The students were discovering for the first time that participating in class, even if the incorrect answer is given, can be exciting, fun, and safe.

Humor can help promote a point of view. Nightly monologues from comedians often combine domestic and international political events with humor to make pungent points. We laugh, but we also learn. Humor also can help presenters assess whether an audience grasps the concept that is the subject matter—if they laugh or smile, and do so at the right time, they probably have an understanding of the concept behind the humor. What a "cool" way to tell if an audience has grasped the material—they laugh!

We must remember, though, that humor is a tool that should never be used to lower the self-esteem of someone. One must be careful to note the difference between genuine humor, which allows us all to see our more vulnerable human side, and derision, that which creates laughter at the expense of another person.

CATEGORIES OF HUMOR

The job of the teacher is to get students laughing, and when their mouths are open, to give them something on which to chew.
—E. M. Lundberg and C. M. Thurston

It soon becomes apparent when using humor that there are various categories of it. See Wandersee's classic article titled "Humor as a Teaching Strategy" (1982), for a description of such categories. All have potential for livening up a presentation and engaging an audience. When used for pedagogical purposes, humor falls into the following categories:

- Joke (a relatively short prose build-up followed by a surprising punch line)

  Did you hear the one about the young man who was hired by a supermarket? He arrived the first day and the manager greeted him, gave him a broom, and said, "Your first job will be to sweep off the sidewalk in front of the store." The young man replied indignantly, "But, I'm a college graduate!" The manager responded, "I apologize. Here, let me show you how to do it!"

- Riddle (a puzzling question containing a problem to be solved)

  I am personally the number 79. They once tried to make me from 29. What am I? (McKay 2000). The answer is gold. Gold occupies the number 79 on the Periodic Chart and once upon a time, efforts were undertaken to make gold from copper, number 29 on the Periodic Chart.

- Pun (a play on words that has different possible meanings, or sounds the same but has different meanings)

  Here is one for your nieces and nephews. What is black and white and "read" all over? A newspaper! Someone hearing this may well assume that the word "read" is actually "red." Then the answer might be "an embarrassed zebra!"

- Oxymoron (combination of seemingly exact opposite words)

  Business ethics, military intelligence, genuine imitation, resident alien, working vacation, peace force, vegetarian meatloaf, pretty ugly, act naturally, jumbo shrimp are all examples.

- Rule of Three or Comic Triple (a first item is related to a second item, thus establishing a pattern; third item, both unexpected and unrelated, disrupts the pattern)

  "Suppose you were an idiot. And suppose you were a member of Congress. But I repeat myself" (Mark Twain) or "Be sincere, be brief, be seated" (F. D. Roosevelt).

- Funny Story (a series of connecting events or the activities of a single incident as a tale)

  "A funny thing happened on the way to the Forum." We all have these kinds of stories, don't we? Audiences love stories.

- Parody (a feeble, transparent, ridiculous imitation in voice or body)

  Saturday Night Live is probably the king of parody on television. Think of the many U.S. presidents, as well as others, who *SNL* has mimicked.

- Humorous Comment (brief humorous statement that does not fit in any other category)

  Shakespeare's *Romeo and Juliet* was "a tragedy that could have been averted if Verona had a decent postal system" (Boerman-Cornwell 1999, 69). We suppose that a good Internet texting service would have averted the disaster, too. No one told Shakespeare.

- Murphy's Law (if it can go wrong, it will—and at the worst possible time)

  Everyone has his or her own example.

- Anecdote (humorous connected events described by the speaker)

  My young daughter told me she was playing "doctor" with her friend, Sammy. I was concerned until she explained what she meant. She proudly exclaimed that she had kept him waiting more than an hour for his doctor's appointment. Come on now, that was funny.

- Limerick (light or humorous verse form)

  There once was a principal named Harry, a wooden paddle he would
     carry.
  Through the halls he would swing it, up and down he would bring it,
     and not a lingering student would tarry!

- Deadpan (emotionless immobile face)

  You might remember Ben Stein who capitalized on a delivery of a deadpan look as the Economics teacher in *Ferris Bueller's Day Off*.

- Knock-Knock (call and answer form of a joke)

  Knock-knock. Who's there? You finish it . . .

- Irony (incongruity between actual results and expected results)

  It is ironic that presenters receive little "coaching" on how to present, yet are called upon to regularly do so.

- Doodles (simple drawings that can be interpreted to mean several things)

  A viewer, in sort of a version of a Rorschach test, is asked, "What does that look like to you?"

- Humorous Titles (makes one wonder how some experiments or articles got funded or published in the first place)

  "Statistical analysis reveals drug wars increase homicide rates" or "Nifty ways to leave your lover: The tactics people use to entice and disguise the process of human mate poaching."

- Slapstick (exaggerated, unexpected movements and gestures)

  Think of the Three Stooges or Chevy Chase and Steve Martin for more contemporary images, but tone it down a bit!

What is in common about all these categories? No matter the category, humor allows the recipient to experience and appreciate, once they "get it," a certain incongruity, absurdity, and ludicrousness about life (Sultanoff 2002).

You may have noted that I have left sarcasm out as a category of humor. Although sarcasm can be funny, it also can be dangerous. *Webster's Seventh New Collegiate Dictionary* defines sarcasm as "to tear flesh, bite the lips in rage, sneer; a cutting, hostile, or contemptuous remark; the use of caustic or ironic language" (1972, 764). More current definitions say that it means the opposite of what it appears to say and usually is intended to mock, make fun of, or insult someone. Avoid sarcasm at all cost.

By the way, if students don't bust out laughing at your attempts of humor, keep at it. You will get better.

SELF-DEPRECATING HUMOR

Reagan and Lincoln (among others) all used it and used it effectively. Here are a few of their self-deprecating quotations. Reagan: "There are advantages to being elected President. The day after I was elected, I had my high school grades classified as top secret" and "To show you how youthful I am, I intend to campaign in all 13 states." Lincoln: "Honestly, if I were two-faced, would I be showing you this one?" (Famous Lincoln-Douglas debate).

Clearly, these individuals used self-deprecation differently than, say Rodney Dangerfield ("I get no respect!"). Properly used self-deprecation humanizes presenters and creates and strengthens connections with an audience. It keeps the presenter from seeming too snooty or self-important (Coenen 2011). It is hard to "talk down to someone" while being self-deprecating. Further, it signals to the audience that if you can mock yourself, you must be confident in your own abilities.

Although not the specific focus of this book, for those of you unmarried and looking for a mate, Greengross and Miller (2008, 403) report, "Many studies have found that a sense of humor is attractive to women, but we've found that self-deprecating humor (by high-status presenters—that's you) is the most attractive of all!"

Being "up in years," I find it easier and easier to use self-deprecating humor. Gray hair (white my wife tells me), thinning hair, morning aches and pains, failing eye sight and hearing, all make self-deprecation not only easy, but seemingly natural. My attitude these days is like the insurance company commercial that says, "We've seen it all." Nothing any longer embarrasses me. Yet, when I first started teaching science, even discussing the reproductive system of flowers with "sexy" words such as stamens and pistols caused my face to turn red.

LETTERMAN'S *TOP TEN REASONS*

Let your audience help you deliver humor. Try David Letterman's approach. It never gets old. Share with them an example, such as where a nurse announces his or her *Top Ten Reasons* why it is "cool" to be a nurse. Some of these reasons include (*250 Funny Reasons* 2015):

#10 "drugs, I know them all"
#9   "fingers get to go places you never thought possible"
#8   "celebrate major holidays with friends—at work"
#7   "wear sexy white uniforms"
#6   "acronyms (COPD, PPN, DNR, SGOT) become your new best friends"
#5   "know it is a full moon without even looking at the sky"
#4   "favorite TV program is the BBC *Call the Midwife*"
#3   "basted a Thanksgiving turkey with a Tommy syringe"
#2   "consider a tongue depressor as an eating utensil"
#1   "courteous infallible doctors who leave clear orders in perfectly legible handwriting"

Ask the audience to help compose their own list of *Top Ten Reasons*. For medicine, it might be reasons for going to med school, itself, or for becoming an anesthesiologist, a radiologist, a cardiologist, or a gynecologist (this last specialty ought to generate some interesting responses).

For a law audience, they could create reasons that prompted them to be a defense versus prosecuting attorney, or what have they learned from watching *Matlock, Boston Legal, Law & Order*, or, of course, *Perry Mason*. I always wondered in the case of Attorney Matlock, did he only have one suit—a seersucker one at that?

Save a copy of these lists for future presentations. Many will be creative and funny. They will always be informative.

BRAINSTORM HUMOROUS SENTENCE ENDINGS

Humor is also a way of saying something serious.
—T. S. Eliot

Ask an audience to brainstorm humorous endings to sentences such as, "You know that you are a bit anxious about your upcoming speech when you . . . ," "You know you have chosen to be a politician because you . . . ," or "You know that you are not cut out to be a lawyer when you . . ." Save these, too, for your future use.

You could have your audience answer any one of life's time-honored questions. For instance, "Why did the chicken cross the road?" Unscientific, yet just as plausible as any other answers, might be:

- "It had a dream" (Martin Luther King Jr.)
- "Because it's there" (George Mallory)
- "The news of it crossing has been greatly exaggerated" (Mark Twain)
- "Define 'road'" (Bill Clinton)
- "That's the way it is" (Walter Cronkite)

Your audience would, of course, use their own subject-matter situations and would be called upon to explain why each answer is plausible. Anyone participating in this humorous exercise is unlikely to forget it.

HUMOR IN PATIENTS' HOSPITAL CHARTS

The best doctor in the world is the veterinarian. He can't ask his patients what is the matter—he's just got to know.
—Will Rogers

I thank Dr. Sivarajah for contributions to this humor source. Humor is all around us. It even is found at the foot of a patient's bed or in the rack at a Nurse's Station. I am talking about what doctors write on a patient's chart. It could be your chart! Be sure that you are not in a library where "Quiet" is enforced because you will find some of these comments hysterical.

- "The patient had no previous history of suicides."
- "The patient refused an autopsy."
- "She is numb from her toes on down."
- "The patient is tearful and crying constantly. She appears to be depressed."
- "Patient has two teenage children, but no other abnormalities."
- "Between you and me, we ought to be able to get this lady pregnant."

Here are a few humorous one-liners from the world of politics. Think of the possibilities for discussion.

- "An honest man in politics shines more there than he would elsewhere" (Mark Twain)
- "Politics is still a land of promise, especially during a political campaign" (Alfred E. Newman)
- "The trouble with practical jokers is that they often get elected" (Will Rogers)
- "I am extraordinarily patient, provided I get my own way in the end" (Margaret Thatcher)
- "There is no trick to being a humorist when you have the whole government working for you" (Will Rogers)

Lawyers, speaking in court, have their own humorous offerings.

- "How far apart were the vehicles at the time of collision?"
- "And when you returned, were you no longer gone?"
- "You were there until you left, is that true?"
- "Did you say "order in court? OK, I'll have a ham sandwich with fries."

WHAT YOU SAY MAY NOT BE WHAT THEY HEAR

Cure sometimes, treat often, comfort always.
—Hippocrates

These "laymen" definitions for legitimate medical terms are priceless. Behind the humor, keep in mind that patients or their families might not really "hear" exactly what you said, especially in a moment of crisis. The same use of highfalutin (at least to the listener) language, as shown in the list that follows, could be delivered by any presenter in any field.

What you said	*What they heard*
• Pelvis	cousin of Elvis
• Dilate	die later than expected
• Urine	opposite of "you're out"
• Seizure	Roman emperor
• Nitrate	lower than day rate
• Herpes	what women do in the Ladies Room
• Morbid	a higher offer

CARTOONS: A SAFE FIRST STEP INTO HUMOR

Blessed is he who learns to laugh at himself, for he will
never cease to be amused.
—John Bowell

One safe way to begin using humor is to incorporate into your presentations cartoons that carry a message related to the subject being presented. Cartoons are normally a drawing accompanied by a caption that together are humorous. "They [cartoons] are particularly useful if a presenter knows he or she is not good at telling jokes or making quips" (Norris 2012, 33).

A cartoon can be useful in helping an audience to remember a concept or for reducing anxiety about difficult content. Today, with the use of the Internet, thousands of subject-related cartoons can be quickly and easily obtained. Your biggest problem will not be locating great cartoons but deciding which to use. An audience's recognition of the point of the cartoon involves a flash of insight that shows a familiar situation in a new light, not unlike the insight that accompanies scientific discoveries. This leads to learning.

I use a punishment-oriented cartoon depicting a father porcupine who is just about to use his hand to paddle his son. The father says to his son, "This will hurt me more than it will hurt you." The cartoon highlights both the possible physical and emotional pain that administrators of punishment can experience, let alone the receivers of such corporal punishment.

Another cartoon I use shows Jean Piaget, famous child psychologist, sitting in an easy chair (with his telltale beret) smoking his pipe surrounded by his young children. His wife stands in the doorway with her coat on ready to go shopping. She instructs Jean Piaget to "Watch the kids, while I'm gone." The key word is "watch." Do you get why this cartoon is so funny? It is funny because if his wife had not told him to carefully watch his children, it is unlikely that he would have ever developed his four stages of cognitive development—sensorimotor, preoperational, concrete operational, and formal operational. Piaget constructed these stages by "watching" his own children (and then, later, other children). Although parents since the beginning of time have watched their children, apparently, they never made the connections that Piaget did.

Could these same messages or discussion starters have been delivered without the cartoons? Sure. But, like a picture, a cartoon is worth a thousand words. Further, cartoons add some welcome variety to a presentation. Cartoons are especially valuable because they help maintain interest, create a visual example of the topic at hand, and add some levity to the presentation. Consider starting a collection of subject-related cartoons for possible inclusion in future presentations.

Sources include professional journals within a specific subject area, as well as journals relating to the teaching profession in general. Some wonderful cartoons are included each month in the sophisticated *New Yorker* and the witty *Atlantic Monthly*. At the same time, though, one should not overlook sources such as *TIME* and other magazines. Another great source would be cartoons from the editorial pages and the comic strips in newspapers. For a one-time use, you might consider either showing them directly or, by respecting copyright laws, displaying them via media projections (e.g., PowerPoint). Fair use by educators makes even more of these cartoon resources available.

A hysterical cartoon viewed recently was that of a lawyer in a courtroom wildly gyrating in front of the judge. The judge is shown saying, "Your *motion* is still denied!" Another cartoon shows a prosecuting attorney standing in front of the witness box, holding a baseball bat, and asking, "Permission, Your Honor, to treat the witness as hostile."

A telling political cartoon, showing Justice Ginsberg holding up her fingers, announces three words that might scare conservatives. "Five more years!'" A business-related cartoon shows a cat, presumably the company CEO, sitting behind his or her big desk listening to an employee representative who is saying, "They find you to be aloof, haughty and distant." Any reader who has a feline knows the truth of this statement.

You may want to create your own cartoons. If you do not have the talent to do so, you could solicit audience members who do possess such talent and who, in fact, would be flattered to assist. On several occasions, I have worked with commercial art students from local vocational-technical schools who have created original cartoons depicting my subject matter. On more than one occasion, the cartoons have not only been used in lectures, workshop presentations, and conference deliveries but also as pictorials to accompany journal articles and books published both nationally and internationally. Appropriate releases were secured.

USING HUMOR: A GAGGLE OF IDEAS

One doesn't have a sense of humor. It has you.
—Larry Gelbart

Although not intended to be a definitive list of suggestions, the following do represent a variety of ways in which presenters can incorporate humor. Like all the acting or presenting skills highlighted in this book, the humor should have an academic purpose.

All humor has structure. In order to create humor or to understand it, one must have a degree of mastery of the concepts within it (i.e., joke, riddle, pun) and recognize the logical sequence of any process or steps suggested.

*   Use humorous cartoons to introduce or support lessons. Encourage the audience to locate and then bring in their own subject-related cartoons, puns, and so on.
*   Share a humorous event from your life in the form of "A funny thing happened to me on the way to the Forum." Solicit such events from your audience.
*   When citing a string of examples of a concept, end with a humorous or unexpected event. When teaching the concept of "positive reinforcement," one could offer examples such as receiving scratch-and-sniff stickers, consumables (e.g., candy), or a shiny red Maserati!
*   Use mnemonics and acronyms. Humor is an excellent mnemonic device. As a memory aid, humor can help audiences to visualize and remember a concept, principle, or operation. All of us remember, "Every Good Boy Does Fine?" (white piano keys), "My Very Extravagant Mother Just Sent Us Ninety Parakeets" (Mars, Venus, Earth, Mars, Jupiter, Saturn, Uranus, Neptune, Pluto), and ROY G. BIV (rainbow colors—red, orange, yellow, green, blue, indigo, violet). Your mnemonics can be words or visualizations, even music. Seek mnemonics that are unusual. The mind forgets the ordinary. That's a major reason for you incorporating humor, the unusual, unexpected, and surprising (e.g., a skill soon to be introduced) into your presentations in the first place.
*   Include appropriate humor on tests. In a multiple-choice question, limit your humor items to the body of the question, not one of the "a" through "e" choices. Occasionally, toss in Elvis, Kermit the Frog, or perhaps even a *Mr. Rogers'* character. Test takers enjoy characters from their childhood. It seems to relax them.
*   Make your syllabus, program, or handout a bit funny. Place toward the top, "My mother believes that I am a great presenter. Let's not disappoint her." Ham it up.

- Look for the humorous side of situations that naturally occur. Something that falls to the floor during your presentation could elicit a "Newton was right. Gravity does exist" comment.

- Combine humor with other acting or presenting skills (e.g., use of props) such as donning a pair of "Wellies" (Wellington boots) while telling an audience that "We are going to do some 'deep' thinking today."

- Comment upon one's own hand-drawn chalkboard sketches with the statement, "It is pretty obvious why I didn't major in art."

- When stumbling over one's words in a presentation (especially likely to happen early on a Monday morning), comment, "Gosh, I forgot to put in my upper plate of dentures this morning." You might keep a plastic set of "uppers or lowers" in your pocket for just such an occasion.

- Propose humorous decoding challenges. Create your own subject-related examples. Humorous or not, decoding information is part and parcel of what professionals do no matter their specialty. Try this one. What is the only word in the English language that has three double letters in a row? Hint: You are currently reading a "book."

- Bring in an unusual prop. Give it a funny name. "Include" it in your presentation. When the audience groans, take that as a sign that they are paying attention!

- Share humorous journal titles from your discipline found via a quick Internet search. Here are a few examples: "Finding Comedy in Chaos," *Journal of Nursing Jocularity*; "The Jurisprudence of Yogi Berra," *Emory Law Journal*; "The Anatomy of Coping: Medicine's Funny Bone," *Med World News*; and "Wills: Witty, Witless, and Wicked," *Wayne Law Review*.

Spooner (2014) reminds us that a generation or more might exist between a presenter and the audience. He cites an example of where he delivered a joke about Winnie Cooper, a much-loved character in the television sitcom *The Wonder Years*, that did not get the intended effect. Only then did he realize that *The Wonder Years* was last broadcast in 1993! Keep in mind that the more we age, the greater that "humor" gap might become. Believe me, I know!

POSSIBLE UNEXPECTED BENEFITS OF HUMOR

A sense of humor is part of the art of leadership, of getting along with people, of getting things done.
—Dwight D. Eisenhower

A newspaper article by Oldenburg (2005), titled *Laugh Yourself Skinny*, may have some application to today's audiences. With obesity a serious problem in our country, perhaps humor, and the laughter that results from it, can serve two purposes. One, it can enhance learning and heighten presenter and audience satisfaction. Two, it can help people lose weight—and, it is claimed, bring about lower stress levels and strengthen cardiovascular muscles.

Colmenares (2005, 1) has found "ten to 15 minutes of laughter could increase energy expenditure by 10 to 40 calories per day, which could translate into about four pounds a year." So, can we eat calorie-laden foods with impunity? Unfortunately, the answer is "no." "You'd have to laugh for 15 minutes just to burn off two Hershey's Kisses" (Colmenares 2005, 1).

Although physiology experts may say that laughing is not the most effective way to shed extra weight, it just may be an idea that is worth a laugh or two (Ross 2005). What do you have to *lose*? Get it? What do you have to *lose*? Just to prove that laughing can help you reduce weight, weigh yourself with a very, very accurate scale. Now, read the hypothetical dissertation title that follows. Get ready to laugh.

> "Spikes vs. Platforms: The Relative Effectiveness of
> Two Height Enhancement Techniques in the Reduction of the
> Napoleonic Complex"

If this hypothetical dissertation title (Kher, Molstad, and Donahue 1999) didn't get you laughing, try the *Family Circus* (Keane 2005) cartoon where, just prior to the Christmas holiday, an elementary teacher asks, "Who can tell me what a subordinate clause is?" A student responds by saying, "One of Santa's helpers!" Surely this one got you laughing.

Now, after you have laughed, weigh yourself again on that same very, very accurate scale and see if you have dropped a micro-ounce or two. Even if you did not "laugh yourself silly," the exercise of walking to and from the scale, twice, should result in burned calories. In either case, you come out a winner.

SUMMARY

A merry heart doeth good like a medicine.
—Proverbs 17

Humor can be a powerful instructional resource that helps presenters in several ways including: attracting attention, improving communication, soothing difficult moments, delivering "delicate" topics, and reinforcing desired behaviors. Humor can help presenters positively affect changes in an audience's knowledge, attitudes, skills, and aspirations.

Spooner (2014) points out that although humor seems to be a universal phenomenon, cultural differences do exist. What is humorous in one culture may be taboo, not understood, or unappreciated in another. In addition to possible different cultural reactions, even some audience members within the dominant cultural may never have experienced a presenter who used humor. How are they to react? It might take some accommodation on the part of both the presenter and the audience.

Properly used, humor clearly sends the message that you are confident, competent, comfortable, and in control. The fear of feeling foolish when attempting humor should be, in part, offset by the aphorism, "Education should teach us to play the wise fool rather than the solemn ass" (Herbert 1991, 17). Presenting is serious business, but there is a big difference between being serious (e.g., no humor) and being solemn (Deiter 2000).

While not all presenters can or should act like a Robin Williams, the thoughtful, spontaneous, or planned use of instructional humor can bring the wonder of wackiness, wit, and wisdom into the presentation. Clearly, humor, and its connection to *projected* presenter enthusiasm, is a skill that should be developed by all presenters.

One writer summarizes the value of presenter humor in the title of her book (Spangler 2000), *She Who Laughs, Lasts.* If you want to "last," then laugh; if you want to "last" longer, laugh more often!

At the start of a presentation announce, with a bit of exaggerated fanfare, "Dear attendees. I know when you're texting in class. Seriously, no one continually looks down at their crotch and just smiles."

11

Suspense, Surprise, and Storytelling

INTRODUCTION

It is by surprises that experience teaches all she designs to teach us.
—Collected Papers of Charles Sanders Pierce, Vol. 5

Let's immediately create some surprise and suspense. "Why does ice float?" It shouldn't! Really, it shouldn't! Are you a bit *surprised* by this claim? Probably. You will have to wait until chapter 13, "Use of Props," to read why ice should not float. This is a bit of *suspense*, holding off the *surprise* explanation until later.

What common complaint do many audiences have about presentations today? "They are boring." When asked "What is boring?" they respond, "The presenters!" Keep in mind the quotation from earlier in this book, "Audiences don't dislike lectures and presentations, they dislike bad or boring ones."

Variety, as we all know, is the spice of life. The introduction of suspense, surprise, and storytelling, as the fluid to transport the first two into a presentation, can help resolve this common complaint. Suspense and surprise are two of a presenter's most potent weapons to engage, enthuse, and educate an audience. Let's use them; let's purposefully use them.

If you are a presenter who likes to do things differently and occasionally pull rabbits out of a hat, then surprises (and suspense) are your bread and butter. At the end of the day, learning has got to stand out and it must be sticky. If surprises can give your presentations the Velcro® quality, then it is worth every ounce of your effort (Dabell 2017). It must be "sticky" in several ways. It's sticky because if you incorporate more suspense and surprise, you probably will end up presenting a little differently than you have to date. It's sticky because you really don't know ahead of time whether these new approaches will work. But the best way that it is sticky is that by incorporating more suspense and surprise into your presentations, more of what you present will "stick"!

According to Ramsell, in a seemingly dated, but still pertinent, claim, "when we are reacting physically and emotionally to surprise, boredom cannot be part of that response" (1978, 22). Most, if not all, people love suspense and surprise. They also simply love storytelling. All human beings come into this world with what is known as epistemic curiosity—curiosity about knowledge. Their daily dose of suspense and surprise spurs them on in their life's quest to learn. On a more primitive level, being curious as to why a simple plant rubbed on a cut stopped infection, wondering what lies beyond the next mountain or sea, or the concern (e.g., suspense) about what lies around the next bend in the road, all helped mankind survive, and in fact, thrive.

Humans have never lost their awe of suspense and surprise. They are time-tested pedagogical strategies for dynamically engaging an audience. Both presenters and audiences have something to gain through the attention-grabbing and holding power of suspense and surprise.

The degree of suspense and surprise attained is often more dependent on the acting or presentation skills of the presenter than on the physical event itself (Estes 2005). You might note that I "teased you" in the Preface but delayed until chapter 4 actually introducing the word "enthusiasm" as the most often cited characteristic of a great presenter.

This was an effort to introduce some suspense and surprise early in the book. Enthusiasm, when finally unveiled in chapter 4, became the catalyst for you to want to learn and master the acting and performance skills presented in Part II.

CREATING SUSPENSE AND SURPRISE

Surprise is the greatest gift which life can grant us.
—Boris Pasternak

Although both elements, suspense and surprise, are included in this same chapter, there are differences between the two. Suspense is something that is developed over a period of time as the story, demonstration, or event unfolds. Intrigue, especially dramatic intrigue—whether on stage, in film, or in the classroom or lab—helps develop this suspense.

Creating intrigue, and hence suspense, is possible in physics (Why does the earth stay in an orbit around the sun?), in mathematics (What is the probability of at least two people in the same room of thirty having the same birthday?), or in chemistry (What is "heavy" about heavy water?). Suspense is equally possible, and useful, in history (Why did Napoleon hold his hand inside his coat?), in law (Gee, the jury has been out a long time . . .), in politics (Nail biting voter results to follow . . .), and in business (What will be the features on the new iPhone?).

Surprise is said to depend upon unexpected events or special effects. It is a feeling one gets *after* something unexpected has happened. Surprise takes place when people encounter something that violates the expectations they hold for existing beliefs. An expectation, first established, is challenged by a contradictory, unexpected event. Cognitive dissonance, the theory that people experience tension when a belief is challenged by an inconsistent behavior, is created.

With a little imagination, no subject matter is alien to suspense—even an unexpected package arriving on your front porch. It is bigger than a breadbox. You wonder what it is. You pick it up and, seeking a clue, test its heft, its weight. It is not all that heavy. You then listen while you give it a little shake. One more clue to the mystery. What could it be? You give in and try to read the sender's address. It is too blurry to decipher. Finally, you do what you could have done from the start and that is you get a knife, cut the sealing tape and open it. What you have done is to impose the elements of suspense and surprise on yourself.

Should an event, effect or outcome be totally unexpected? We are much more likely to perceive surprise if we have reason to expect it. This sense of a suspense leading up to the surprise creates a shared experience helping to bond the audience and the actor—the audience and the presenter. Taken together, suspense *and* surprise, not simply suspense *or* surprise, are powerful delivery tools.

The unexpected interjection of suspense and surprise helps presenters to be more spontaneous because they both generate tension. This tension prompts us to attempt to resolve the dissonance, to explore further for answers, to ask "Why?" questions, and to search for cause-and-effect explanations. We are, in fact, motivated! Order is sought for unexplained events. It's the chase, not necessarily the achievement, of order that is so stimulating. Achievement, itself, might just be a welcomed, appreciated, and, yes, "surprising" outcome.

Surprise calls us up short—didn't expect it, it happened, it is over, it can be dealt with. Suspense, on the other hand, can keep us on the "hook" for an extended time (Napoli 2018). Surprise seems to come out of nowhere; it blindsided us. With suspense we know something is coming, but we just don't know how, when, where, or why.

Suspense and surprise create an emotional impact upon audiences' senses. In fact, the emotions associated with learning, itself, are surprise, awe, interest, and confusion (Holmes 2016). The more we involve our audiences' senses, the more we sharpen their ability to learn. While you are at it, involve your own senses by venturing into the unknown—be surprised *with* your audience! Capture once again some of those feelings that you found so surprising earlier in your career.

IGNORANCE 101!

> *Genuine ignorance is profitable because it leads to humility,*
> *curiosity and open-mindedness.*
> —John Dewey

Professor of Physiology, Robert Root-Bernstein's quotation that follows justifies the value of ignorance in any and all disciplines. Does this surprise you?

> Ignorance is excitement, the perpetual challenge to grow. Ignorance is everything yet to be: places you've yet to go; people you've yet to meet; facts you've yet to learn; things you've yet to discover. Ignorance is viewing the world through the eyes of a child for whom all is fresh, new and unexpected. Ignorance is the possibility of surprise. (Root-Bernstein, cited in Witte 2017, 6)

Too often presenters present as if the world were predictable. We present a world of facts as if we know all there is to know. The black-and-white world of clearly right and wrong answers is a fallacy. Poetry and literature are not predictable. Psychology and sociology are not predictable. Mathematics and chemistry are not predictable. Outcomes in law and politics are not predictable. Ask any scholar in his or her field. They will tell you this is so. In every field, much remains unknown and, thus, unpredictable.

Audiences need to grow comfortable, not just with the idea that failure is a part of learning, but with the idea that confusion is, too (Holmes 2016). I don't know whether it is part of some grand plan or not, but the world, not just our presenting arenas, would be boring if total predictability prevailed.

Dr. Marlys Witte, a Professor of Surgery at the University of Arizona, College of Medicine, recognized the dearth of medical knowledge and authored a course titled, "Introduction to Medical and Other Ignorance," known simply as *Ignorance 101*. Surely this could have been done for law, politics, business, or any other field, too. Dr. Witte has presented a 2013

TED talk on the topic, as well as delivered a seven-week summer workshop titled "Summer Institute on Medical Ignorance (SIMI)." This unique program champions ignorance (Witte 2017).

As part of the course, the audience must demonstrate their ignorance of a medical topic by writing a term paper setting out everything *unknown* about it. In effect, audiences are setting themselves up for experiencing their own suspense and surprise as they try to fill in some of the knowledge gaps they have identified. Ignorance can be bliss, or so says Gelatt (2015). It is a catalyst for inquiry that produces learners driven by curiosity who are delighted, if not surprised, to learn that science is an endless frontier.

Perhaps audiences would be better served if they were taught that the world is full of the unexpected. Not only would presenters' use of the unexpected, then, be a sound pedagogical tool, but its use would reflect the reality of the world. Without the feelings of uncertainty and insecurity that accompany suspense and surprise, learners would quickly fall into a state of complacency and overconfidence where unthinking approaches to problem-solving are mechanically applied. No one, then, would consider "thinking outside of the box."

STORYTELLING

Eureka!
—Archimedes

Observe the delight in a child's eyes when a parent says "Would you like me to read you a bed time story?" Consider that all a lawyer has to do is approach a jury, pause for a moment, and then say, "Let me tell you a story . . ." Jury members all lean forward a bit in anticipation. Lawyers simply must be good, no, make that great, storytellers—presenters! The jury wants to hear the story. They want the lawyer to weave all the seemingly endless divergent facts and hypotheses together.

Storytelling is included in this chapter because most stories are built around suspense and surprise. Suspense and surprise can be found in children's stories such as *Goldilocks and the Three Bears*, "Someone has been eating my porridge," growled Papa Bear, or in *Cinderella* (will the slipper fit?).

Think back on your own life. The odds are that your memorable moments mostly have to do with stories, not theories or definitions or dates, but an unfolding narrative, complete with suspense, drama, humor, or perhaps a personal anecdote (Green 2004). Stories can spark audience interest, aid the flow of presentations, make material memorable, help overcome a listener's anxiety or resistance, and build presenter–audience rapport (Green 2007). Urban (2008) claims that audiences may tune out a presentation (not yours, of course), but they'll always listen to a good story. All good presenters are good storytellers. No matter the age, no matter the subject matter, people love good stories and good storytellers.

Partially for your entertainment, but primarily to show how a story can capture our attention, I offer several surprise and suspense stories. I'll bet that you will remember them and probably tell them to others.

FIRST STORY: JUST FOR THE SUSPENSE AND SURPRISE OF IT!

Then there is the classic campfire story of the young couple parked on lovers' lane. Steamed windows accompany some adolescent necking. The music on the radio is interrupted by an announcement, "An escaped murderer, nicknamed the 'hook' due to his having one artificial arm, is rumored to have been seen in the area. Beware." The frightened young couple quickly put the car in gear and speed away. Upon arriving at the young lady's home, the boy gets out and walks around the car planning gallantly to open the door for his girlfriend—only to find a bloody "hook" hanging on the passenger-side door handle! Do you have goose bumps?

SECOND STORY: TURTLES—NO LEARNING, NO FUN!

According to William Glasser, MD in Psychiatry, sea turtles have no fun in their lives. They don't smile. Why? Think back on a National Geographic story about female sea turtles coming ashore on a warm sandy beach to lay their eggs. They lumber up the beach beyond the high tide line and laboriously scoop out a depression in which to deposit their eggs. Once the eggs are laid more laborious effort goes into covering them. Then what happens? The mother sea turtle waves "bye, bye" (not really) and returns to the ocean. The sea turtle eggs are on their own. About sixty days later they all hatch and make a beeline in mass to the sea hoping to avoid any predators. Still no smiling on their part. Why? Because sea turtles do not have to learn anything, and "fun" is nature's reward for learning. Sea turtles, unlike let's say lion cubs, have no mother and certainly no father around to teach them anything. The parents are long gone. Sea turtles are born knowing all they need to know. How boring. Hence, no learning, no fun, no smiling. Remind your audience that they are not sea turtles, they can have fun learning.

THIRD STORY: KENNEDY'S INFANT SON, PATRICK

A very personal story hits close to home for Dr. Sivarajah. She reports that President Kennedy's wife, Jacqueline, gave birth to their son, Patrick, five and a half weeks prematurely. The newborn lived thirty-nine hours. He died a victim of hyaline membrane disease, a deficiency in a substance that lines the air sacs called surfactant. Today, surfactant can be administered to premature infants allowing babies much more premature than Patrick to survive. Dr. Sivarajah's own son was born thirteen weeks premature. Without such medical advancements, her son (now a normal preteen) also likely would not have survived.

These examples have in common the fact that people will continue to pay close attention to interesting stories as they unfold. As presenters, we just need to create or relate those stories, or at least events or situations, that capitalize upon an audience's love of suspense and surprise. Tell just enough of the story to whet their appetite. Once the audience is "hooked," we can begin to reel them in via our talk or presentation. Save the surprising end for the end because what would be the purpose of being told a story to which you already know the ending? Few people jump to the final pages of a really good book, find out the surprising ending, and *then* start to read the story from the beginning! It just isn't human nature to do so.

Effective storytellers have long known the power and persuasion of using suspense and surprise. Storytellers are part and parcel of human existence. Whether gathered around a primitive campfire or a formal dining-room table, storytelling was, and in many societies continues to be, an important medium for the transfer of knowledge and skills. Then and now, storytellers present.

Whether in film or on stage, a story is told. The audience, often purposefully deceived by the movie's or play's plot, waits with anticipation to find out "whodunit." These are called "cliff hangers." Suspense and surprise are used to grab, as well as hold, the attention of the audience. Did the butler really do it? Will the damsel in distress be saved? Will the Road Runner ever be caught by Wile E. Coyote?

Presenters can infuse their presentations with suspense and surprise. They can create a sense of dramatic tension and excitement that comes from expecting something important or unusual. Presentations can be delivered as if a story were being told. The excitement of discovering an unfolding plot, using only "clues" that have been dropped along the way, can heighten an audience's suspense. Presenters can *act* (e.g., use their animation in body and voice) as if they, too, are just now discovering the plot. They can share in an audience's suspense and drama.

Note the parallel between storytelling and most presenters' fields. In a good Agatha Christie thriller (e.g., *Murder on the Orient Express*), clues are revealed one at a time until it is determined who whodunit! In medicine, doctors examine their "clues" in the form of symptom after symptom in hopes of making a proper diagnosis. In law, a collection of clues can, with a good story to connect them, sway a jury. In business, one must decipher today's clues in order to plan effectively for tomorrow. Every profession seeks its own sort of clues.

What is not so parallel between presenter storytelling and these professions is that our minds, seeking closure, may latch onto answers too quickly and might miss beautiful and important moments along the way (Holmes 2016). We, as presenters, *want* audiences to experience those beautiful and important moments. Often as presenters we can purposefully hold off exposing a surprising ending if we choose. But doctors, lawyers, and business persons want to reach the end of their story as soon as possible.

Superb lecturers and dynamic presenters share many qualities with storytellers. They, too, save the conclusions or most crucial points until the end, having teased the audience and whet their appetite along the way with preliminary clues, findings, or interpretations. Presenters can learn to be better storytellers if they relax their inhibitions and react to the natural suspense inherent in most content.

RELATIONSHIP TO OTHER PERFORMANCE SKILLS

Mystery is at the heart of creativity. That, and surprise.
—Julia Cameron

Almost anything presenters do that is seen by an audience to be out of the ordinary will be viewed with curiosity. Therefore, each of the acting or presenting skills highlighted in this book are all part of a presenter's repertoire of behaviors and have the potential for creating suspense and surprise.

Unexpected animation in voice—perhaps a shout (surprise), perhaps a whisper (suspense)—can do the trick. Animation in body, possibly conveyed through sudden demonstrative body movements, can create both surprise and suspense. Greeting an audience after having unexpectedly moved their desks into a new seating pattern might do it. They wonder, "Gee, what's up?" A presenter, himself or herself, playing a role, complete with supportive props (e.g., costumes), can be surprising and heighten suspense. Content-related humor, delivered at just the right moment, can be surprising. Presenters should keep their eyes open for opportunities to evoke suspense and surprise when using these acting and performance skills.

SURPRISE! DON'T TALK

When I was born, I was so surprised I didn't talk for a year and a half.
—Gracie Allen

Although this idea could have simply been listed with the many suspense and surprise ideas that follow, I felt it was interesting enough to be addressed separately. A presenter feigned laryngitis on the day that a wrap-up discussion was scheduled for an earlier off-site visit. He kept to his silence script by making sure that no one overheard him speak before class.

In an uncharacteristic fashion, the presenter kept quiet; the discussion, then, was *dominated* by the audience. Apparently, all the presenter could do was scribble boldly on the chalkboard, "Tell us more." "Why is that?" "What about such and such?" Further limited "communication" consisted of, at appropriate moments and timed well, tapping on the board, snapping fingers, clucking his tongue, clapping his hands, using "thumbs-up" (or down), or vigorously nodding his head. But nothing empowers an audience as immediately and profoundly as does removing the presenter's voice from the room (Finckel 2014). Our not talking might, at times, be the best way to engage an audience.

Imagine the audience's surprise when, while leaving the venue at the end of the exciting presentation, one dominated by audience input, the presenter said, in a clear voice, "I will see each of you on Wednesday."

Believe it or not, there is a wikiHow website titled "How to Fake Losing Your Voice: 9 Steps (with Pictures)"—"hold your neck and go Aa-ahh-aahh," "throw in some whispering," "write little notes to communicate," "be seen taking throat lozenges." Try to keep a straight face!

USING SUSPENSE AND SURPRISE

There is no way that I could create sample surprise and suspense eye-openers and attention-grabbers for every field reflecting each reader's content specialty. The next best thing is to offer examples of surprise and suspense activities that *all* readers could identify with and, with a bit of tweaking, could customize each to their own specialty.

- Do not always announce to an audience what activities will take place during the presentation. Let each activity, revealed one at a time like the layers of an onion, help create suspense and surprise. If you are up to it, a different "hook" could be used each time a topic transition is made in your presentation (see the chapter titled "Creative Entrances and Exits").

- Use "what-if" exercises. A what-if exercise asks the audience to extrapolate information, to go beyond what is known for sure and venture into the suspense of the unknown. It is a tool for audiences to create their own suspense and surprise. What if free access to lawyer representation was rescinded? What if ice did not float? What if people were regularly to live to over one-hundred years old? Every discipline has a past, present, and unknown future. Each is ripe for surprising what-if exercises.

- Turn to the chapter titled "Use of Props," where John Lennon's *Imagine* is played, first with the original lyrics, and then with substituted lyrics from other content areas. Everyone pays attention when this song (e.g., tune) is played. The lyrics tell a story.

- Use self-disparaging comments in moderation. Before doing so, one should have a healthy rapport with the audience. Mild presenter self-disparaging comments are unexpected in an audience's experience. They find it surprising to hear presenters "pick" on themselves for a change. Skillful presenters are confident enough to exploit their own fallibility.

- Role-playing by making *intended* mistakes. An audience is delighted and surprised when a normally accurate presenter makes a mistake. An intended mistake is neither deceptive nor dishonest in spirit when the purpose is altruistic. Aware of this, enterprising practitioners occasionally engage in a bit of "planned error." The presenter could accompany this error with an exaggerated display of consternation or despair. The more the presenter "hams it up," the more surprising it is. The audience, then, can be asked to help correct the error—a useful, but surprising effective, pedagogical tool.

- Pretend (e.g., act) that you are "giving in" (once again, acting a part) to a view that you don't really, in your heart, support. For instance, I contrast the views of behaviorism versus humanism—B. F. Skinner versus Carl R. Rogers. While identifying and discussing characteristics for both philosophies, it becomes clear to the audience that, personally, I supports the often less popular humanist position that shuns the providing of punishment and rewards. As my presentation continues and the audience makes their compelling arguments in favor of behaviorism, I finally appear to "give in" and say—with all the sincerity possible—"I give up, it's too hard trying to defend humanism. I think that just maybe you are right, behaviorism is the preferred position."

Students are so surprised at my apparent change of heart—perhaps they just feel sorry for me—that they immediately set about trying to convince me that humanism is the better view!

- One presenter starts class by asking, "What are the three most important words in real estate?" If you have not heard this question before, you might be surprised to find out that the answer is the same word, three times—*location, location, location!* This same presenter sometimes places the word *location* on three separate 3" × 5" cards and then, just before his presentation, "hides" them somewhere in the room. When she asks the audience "what are the three most important words in real estate?" she walks around the room and "pretends" to find the cards, one at a time, that she has hidden. To add some additional drama, the professor looks surprised, really surprised, each time she finds and reads aloud one of the cards. Are there "three words" (more or less) in your field that you could substitute in this exercise?

- Another presenter has a partial outfit for the Lone Ranger—just a white hat and mask. While wearing the hat and mask, the presenter plays the theme song from *The Lone Ranger* radio and television program. The students are surprised to find out that the theme song for a classic children's cowboy program is the *William Tell Overture*! It is claimed that only a true intellectual can listen to the *William Tell Overture* and not think of the Lone Ranger.

- Consider a science teacher demonstrating the impact of an active volcano. Even though the audience was told it was going to "explode," even though they knew it was going to "explode," and even though they knew *why* it was going to "explode," the suspense is still there until it does "explode." What concepts or procedures in your field would be this engaging or explosive?

- Bait students. Ask students to do something that, although it appears possible, can't be done. For instance, use paper bull's-eye targets to present the concepts of "Validity" and "Reliability." Tell the audience that you are testing a rifle scope's validity and reliability. Pretend that you have five shots to fire at each of four bull's-eye targets. Show the students what a "Reliable" and "Valid" pattern of shots would look like—all five shots closely (reliably) grouped in the bull's eye (validity). Ask them to create shot patterns for the three remaining combinations—"Not Reliable" and "Not Valid," "Not Valid and Reliable," and "Valid and Not Reliable." Looks easy, but it is *impossible* to do! There is no way to have a pattern of shots that are "Valid" and "Not Reliable." Why? By definition, all things that are "Valid" are "Reliable!" Surprising? Yes! Remembered? Yes!

- Still another version of baiting is telling enough of a story, or revealing enough of an event, to pique the audience's curiosity. "Once baited, the audience wants to find out who wins, who loses, whether the villain receives his just deserts" (Rubin 1985, 113). One presenter taught the Roadblocks to Communication from Thomas Gordon's, *Leader Effectiveness Training: L.E.T.* (2001). When introduced to these twelve road blocks, the audience realizes that they unknowingly use them all the time. Just when they are begging to know what alternative behaviors they could use, the presenter announces, "Sorry, but we are out of time. We will have to wait until tomorrow to hear Gordon's alternatives." Healthy suspense is created. This is precisely the format of every good television program or movie for which each show is one episode in a series. The audience is sure to tune in tomorrow!

- Make a seemingly outrageous statement and then go on to "back it up." For instance, I announce with authority and some arrogance, "The best thing about praise is that it beats getting hit in the eye with a stick!" I let that message sink in for a minute or so. I go on to tell them, "By the end of class I will convince 85% to 90% of you to either stop using praise *or* to significantly reduce your use of this behaviorist, controlling, manipulative, authoritarian tool." Finally, I say, "After my pitch against praise, I will offer a recommended alternative." I have their attention. No one believes that I can do what I claim. Many students have their arms crossed with a projected attitude of "I dare you to convince me!" Well, fifty minutes later, a poll of the audience reveals that they are, in fact, convinced. Talk about surprise! Suspense and surprise were so thick that as the saying goes, "You could cut it with a knife!" My audience at this point is literally "begging" to be told the recommended alternative. The suspense was killing them!

- Change the rules occasionally. One presenter I heard about has a team-building exercise variation on the popular game of musical chairs. Instead of pitting players against each other so that one player *must* lose each round, she designs the game so that the players act cooperatively with everyone a winner. How does she do this? In her version of the game when the music stops, and a chair is taken away, if a player can't find an empty chair, he or she simply sits on another person's lap who is on a chair. The only "rule" is that all participants must have their feet off the floor. At some point, keeping safety in mind, they figure out that building "bridges" between chairs with audience legs can keep the game going longer. Laughter is heard. Cooperative, team-building and problem-solving dominates the win-win game. Search the Internet using "musical chairs," specifically, "Happy New Year, Charlie Brown—Musical Chairs—YouTube." Note, the classic musical chairs game is a win-lose game designed, no matter how many players and chairs, to purposefully have loser after loser, and at the end, just one winner. Isn't shooting for more and more winners and not more and more losers a more laudable goal?

- Provide the audience with the opportunity for meaningful guessing—call it forming hypotheses if you like—before solving or presenting solutions The anticipation associated with guessing "who done it," "how high (or low) can Apple stock go," or "when will we have a female president" heightens the suspense.

- Buy a child's musical jack-in-the-box and "equip" it with the ability to grasp a $3'' \times 5''$ card holding a message. When it comes time to deliver a particularly important point, enlist the help of your "assistant," Jack, to help answer an earlier posed question. Crank the crank and watch the audience stare at the box in anticipation of Jack popping out with the message. It never fails to surprise them.

- An instructor presents the concept in engineering that a thin-walled vessel usually fails along its longitudinal axis due to "hoop stress" as illustrated for all of us when we overcook a hot dog and it "splits." If this has not caught your attention, yet, it will. While explaining the concept of hoop stress, the presenter "happens" to notice an "old" hot dog in the trash (one he secretly and carefully placed there before class). All of this, of course, is purely theatrical on his part. With some green food coloring previously applied to simulate mold, the audience is surprised (e.g., shocked) when he plucks it from the trash and takes a bite. At that point he leaves the classroom (no, not ill from the hot dog), only to return with a tray of hot dogs (and buns), each of which is microwaved, and each of which demonstrates the hoop stress split (Estes 2005). Lunch was served! The presentation and the learning were memorable.

- Start the class off with a surprising—even shocking—behavior or event. I know of one presenter who, about to lecture on the subject of discrimination, walks toward the door as if someone has hailed him from the hall, and screams in a booming voice at that person, "What do you mean I am prejudiced? Some of my best friends are black!" After an uncomfortable pause, he screams, "What do you mean I am prejudiced? Some of my best friends are Jews." Surprising behavior for Professor X? Yes. At this point, a fidgeting audience begins to suspect something is up. The presenter asks the audience what goes through their mind when they hear such statements. The universal response is that the screamer must, in fact, *be* prejudiced. Otherwise, why would he protest so much? The presentation continues. Everyone is paying very close attention.

- Bring in a child's battery powered fireplace or campfire. Set it on the desk, turn it on, turn down (off) the lights, and announce "Gather round, I have a story to tell!" For small audiences they could actually "gather round." For larger audiences tell them to "gather round in spirit." You also could simply turn to the Internet and do a search for sites such as "Burning Fireplace with Crackling Fire Sounds" or "Virtual Camp fire with Crackling Fire Sounds." Some of these "burn" for over an hour!

- Use an accomplice. In an administration of justice course, one presenter had a primed student burst into the classroom, "throw" a bucket of water on him (just cut up paper from a paper shredder) and then quickly exit—not the usual classroom experience. The audience was then asked to describe the perpetrator. Few could do so accurately. The presentation on the reliability and validity of eyewitness testimony followed.

- Display a prop and let the audience wonder about its use. Let it just sit there in full view of everyone. Or, who would not experience a feeling of suspense if a presenter walked into class, placed a paper bag (obviously full of something) in a prominent place, and then proceeded to "ignore" it? It would have our curiosity piqued. Suspense, and possibly, later, surprise, is created. Audiences would be paying attention. Paying attention is a prerequisite to learning.

- I teach the difference between praise and encouragement—the former evaluates, the latter, supports. They are not synonyms. For those who cannot give up their addiction to sending praise, I at least ask them to avoid sending *inflated* praise as in "That was *incredibly* good." To drive home the point, I write the word "praise" on a deflated balloon with a marker and then inflate it so that the word "praise" is *incredibly* enlarged. You know what happens next—I jab the balloon and it breaks! Surprise! No more praise inflation!

- Play music from *Jaws*. It doesn't get much more suspenseful than this. Enough said!

SUMMARY

> *This suspense is terrible. I hope it will last.*
> —Oscar Wilde

Oscar Wilde's quotation captures a happening that we have all experienced. You've been there, haven't you! You may be embarrassed to admit it, but you want that tingle that accompanies suspense (and, later surprise) to continue! So does an audience.

People seem to really enjoy being placed in suspense. This fact is evident from the earliest measures psychologists made of kindergarten children where they expressed a clear preference for stories based upon a suspense theme (Jose and Brewer 1990). Whether it is Hitchcock's classic *Rear Window* or Spielberg's thriller *Raiders of the Lost Ark*, theater and film directors exploit this fact. Although presenters cannot be expected, especially daily, to present such attractive themes of good and evil forces, presenters can capitalize on those opportunities that do exist.

I need only to remind the readers of the interest, no, the passionate interest, that children, as well as adults, show in reading *Harry Potter* books. The books are thick, there are lots and lots of words, and pictures are kept to a minimum, yet readers cannot put them down. What is the attraction—suspense and surprise! Reflect upon your feelings when a favorite author of yours announces that he has decided to stop writing his incredibly exciting mystery novels. Where, now, will you get your suspense and surprise "fix"?

12

Role-Playing

INTRODUCTION

To be confident, act confident.
—J. Eison

I am talking about having *you*, the presenter, play a role. We know that the medical field hires actors to role-play patients who pretend to exhibit symptoms associated with different diseases in order to hone med students' diagnosing skills. We know that lawyers conduct "mock" trials and politicians use "focus groups" in preparation for the real thing. The rationale by which we decide to use this audience-based role-playing to intensify the learning experience also applies to the use of a *presenter* role-playing.

The intention here is to have you engage in role-playing—for you to be the actor, you to convincingly assume a role, and you to use that role-playing to present memorable "performances." I guarantee such behavior will be attention-getting and, like the message, it will be remembered!

DR. EAKIN: GREAT SCIENTISTS SPEAK

Can you or your colleagues identify with the following? As a presenter, are you concerned that your audience may become progressively more

111

inattentive and absent? No doubt the answer is "yes." These are almost the exact words, back in 1970, that Dr. Richard M. Eakin from Berkeley wrote regarding his Zoology 10 class. What should he do?

It hit him! He would use himself as a human prop. He would engage in role-playing, something that he had never done before. Dr. Eakin decided to dress up, with some help from a make-up coach, as some of the great biologists and present their discoveries and thoughts in their own words in order to help alleviate audiences' apparent boredom. He would, in costume, address the audience in the most engaging form of communication of all—the first person. The goal was to convince the audience that they were listening to the actual, live scientist or researcher. It worked!

Enrollment and attendance dramatically (note the pun—dramatically) increased with even colleagues attending his presentations. He claimed that he did the acting simply to make the course content more graphic and memorable. It certainly worked. Back then it probably took a great deal of courage to step outside of the delivery norm for presenters. Today, with predecessors such as Dr. Eakin having blazed the role-playing trail for us, and with research in role-play delivery methods before us (e.g., this book for one), it should be easier, but probably still a bit scary.

As his first character Dr. Eagan appeared before his audience as William Harvey to describe how, reportedly with a cow's heart in his hand and food coloring as blood, the heart circulated blood through the body. He received a standing ovation, and the rest was *history*—or perhaps more correctly, was a view of the *future*—the use of presenter role-playing.

For the next seventeen years, he offered Zoology 10 with six "dress up" lectures—William Harvey (Circulation of the Blood), William Beaumont (Alexis' Stomach), Gregor Mendel (Genetic Inheritance), Hans Spemann (Embryonic Development), Louis Pasteur (Pasteurization), and Charles Darwin (Evolution). Different beards, different make-up, shaved head, or today a skull cap, for Mendel and Darwin completed the transformation.

Eakin's role-playing has spurred others to action. Dr. Urbanowicz, Professor of Anthropology, does much the same Darwin role-playing today for his audience. He says:

> I believe the theatrical device works well because the theater-like classroom creates an ephemeral sense of intimacy for both the presenter and the audience. Although a theatrical performance lasts only for an afternoon or evening and ends, the classroom theater can create a sense of intimacy that may last for weeks or years, creating a positive atmosphere throughout the rest of a term. (Urbanowicz 2003)

Imagine the impact upon your audience if you dressed up like William Jennings Bryan or Clarence Darrow from the 1925 *Scopes Monkey Trial* and delivered your legal (and moral) positions. Imagine role-playing Winston Churchill (classic hat and a cigar) and, pretending over the telephone, to literally "beg" FDR to send more war supplies. You would have the audience eating out of your hands!

PLAYING A ROLE

Role-playing means temporarily transforming oneself into a different person by means of modifications of expression and appearance, and often by the use of props and language. To play a role successfully, one must *become* someone else and do so convincingly, at least for the moment. Obviously, it is a process that is totally synonymous with the profession of acting. In addition, it can be a very valuable tool for a presenter.

Many actors report that they can feel a transformation of self, occurring each time they don their makeup or costume and walk on stage. The transformation is not just into the character being portrayed but, more fundamentally, into the role of "actor." By *acting* like the person you want to be, your self-confidence will likely improve, thus allowing you to *be* that person—at least for your presentation. That hypothesis is confirmed in the experiences of many successful presenters who note that they are less shy and more dynamic when putting on their "presenter role" (Hanning 1984).

As with role-play, in general, playing the presenter role may require some, often modest, costuming in order to be most successful—to make us *feel* more like that person we are attempting to represent. A case in point was the experience of a member of the clergy queried about why she chose to wear the heavy ministerial robes on the hottest Sundays of the year. Her reply was that by wearing the "costume" of the clergy, she felt more confident in the role of pastor and thus was more likely to be received attentively and respectfully by persons unaccustomed to a woman minister. Her experience, consistent with all that we know about self-confidence and communication, testifies to the value of a little costuming for role-playing to create a persona.

While some degree of a professional "costume" may be helpful in creating the role of presenter, it is not a prerequisite. The most important precondition for successful role creation is simply to have identified and adequately researched the characteristics of the person you aspire to embody. Then, using some combination of expression, posture, appearance, props, and language, go on to act (e.g., present) that role. In doing so, remember that the goal of this presenter role-playing is to gain and hold the attention of an audience in order to get across your message.

CREATING A CHARACTER

We can play an innumerable assortment of character roles in order to enliven our presentations. Let your imagination run wild. Because role-playing is such a vivid and enriching instructional tool, however, it merits the effort. Many institutions invite reenactors to visit their classes, portraying everyone from George Washington's soldiers to operators of the Underground Railroad. These are semi-professional actors whose work has been proven to capture and hold an audience's attention, making the actions and issues of that era come alive.

"Come alive" are the key words associated with role-playing—you come alive and the audience comes alive. If these "invited actors" can do it, you can do it, too. As a presenter you can get the same results with a little bit of effort and creativity and, dare I say it, some guts. Don't be afraid to do things that others may consider "different" when your instinct tells you that "different" may be better.

As a presenter, Neil Bates uses not only the incredibly moving photograph (e.g., a prop) of Dorothea Lange's *Migrant Mother*, but himself, to teach and transport his audience back to the Depression era of America (Drury 2013). He attempts to become the photograph. He comes into class wearing a tattered 1920s dress and hat, holding a baby (toy), and sits down on a tire next to a battered suitcase, saying nothing. The scene he has created says a lot. With his hairy legs on display he sits just beneath a sign hung on the wall saying, "Any questions or comments?" And, questions the audience does have! "What happened?" "What are you going to do?" "How do you get food?' "Where do you shower and go to the bathroom?" "Can't you just get a job?" "Don't you have family or friends who can help you?"

The key components to successful role-playing are (1) research the character; (2) have the audience write down "interview" questions; (3) create some atmosphere (e.g., a simple back drop, lighting); (4) choose a prop (when holding it you *are* the role-playing character; when you put it down, you may be addressed as the presenter; and (5) get on with it (Drury 2013).

Put on your own "creativity hat." Note, by doing so, you are getting into the role-play mood. Use this "hat" (code word for creativity) to help you generate ideas of how role-playing a character could facilitate your presentations and, for both you and your audience, interject a bit of fun into the learning experience.

DEAD POETS SOCIETY

The writing and the delivery skills of Robin Williams make the movie *Dead Poets Society* one not to be missed. In fact, it should not only be seen once but several times in order to pick up on pedagogical didactics. You will see my entire book in the movie from animation in body, animation in voice, humor, and role-playing, to use of props, space utilization, suspense, surprise and storytelling, and creative entrances and exits. Without these presentation skills, Mr. Keating (Robin Williams) probably would not have stood out as a presenter so capable of engaging his audience.

I know it was only a movie, only entertainment, or was it? Several quotations from the movie reveal Keating's powerful messages to his audience, but they also can be messages to us, as presenters. "Carpe diem. Seize the day!" In every scene that could be characterized as "presenting," Keating is not standing or acting in the way that traditional presenters most often do. He got close to his audience, he had them huddled around him, he stood on a desk, he towered above them, they towered above him, they romped across the school grounds, he sat among the students as an equal. He had the courage to do this.

As I ask you to incorporate many of the acting and performance skills presented in this book into your presentations, two thoughts come to mind. One, just when you think you know something (e.g., how to present), you might want to look at it in a different way. Even though it may seem silly . . . give it a try. Two, as you read this book, don't just consider what I think, consider what you think. I hope that you think the ideas in this book are worth trying.

MEETING OF MINDS

One of the more memorable examples of educational role-playing occurred in a classic television show some years ago called "Meeting of Minds." The program, produced and moderated by Steve Allen, the Father of All Talk-Show Hosts, consisted of "live" conversations that he had with great intellectuals of the past discussing contemporary issues. Allen interviewed people, from Aristotle to Theodore Roosevelt, from Thomas Aquinas to Thomas Paine, and from Voltaire to Susan B. Anthony. The important point here is *why* Allen chose the role-playing vehicle for this program. His goal was an educational one: he wanted the contemporary public to appreciate the sage insights from the past and be stimulated to discuss the issues themselves. One could have attempted to accomplish that goal via a more conventional presentation. But, in Allen's view, that approach would not have held viewers' attention; something more dramatic was needed.

Role-playing enlivens material. By portraying a character pertinent to the specific subject matter, the presenter, communicating in the first person, can make abstract concepts more concrete, hold the audience's attention, clarify depths of meaning, and stimulate audience reflection on the material covered. Numerous presenters who have tried playing a role confirm the success of the tool in motivating their audience and provoking them to a more thorough understanding of the material.

Not only is role-playing a motivating device for the audience, it is also a freeing device. By pretending to be someone else for a while, the presenter creates a situation in which the audience seems to feel freer to challenge and question ideas presented. The "whys" and the "how comes" burst forth. After all, that person up front is not an evaluating superior, but rather Jonas Salk explaining how he created a polio vaccine, or Dr. Charles R. Drew, a black American surgeon who during World War II improved techniques for blood plasma storage and without which many of our grandfathers would not have survived their wounds. Come to think of it; if they had not survived, you and I might not be here! Ponder that thought!

"While I (pretend I am Dr. Drew speaking) have your attention, did you know that white soldiers died in World War II, partially as a result of the U.S. Army and Navy telling the Red Cross that they would only accept blood from white donors even though blood was desperately needed? Did you know that the American Medical Association spoke out against the ban? Did you know that I resigned, in protest, from my position as the director of blood banks for the entire Red Cross?" This paragraph about Dr. Drew could also fit my book under suspense, surprise, and storytelling, as well as a great attention-grabbing entrance hook!

Give role-playing a try. After all, if it does not work as planned, you can always claim "It wasn't my fault, it was the fault of the character I was role-playing." Only kidding!

Before going on to describe the specific elements involved in doing role-play, it should be emphasized that this is a tool that can accomplish those pedagogical goals only if used in moderation. If the audience becomes too accustomed to the presenter being someone else, the role-play may lose the element of surprise and may diminish its interest value. To work, role-play should essentially be a tool kept in the "bottom of the tool box" to be used somewhat for special emphasis and impact.

THE ROLE-PLAY PROCESS

Everyone who has performed a role-play characterization agrees on one key point: it *must* be well prepared. While we may use audience members to role-play on a somewhat spontaneous basis, presenter role-play will be only as valuable as the advance planning that has gone into it. That is where the process of role-playing begins.

First, the presenter must begin by carefully choosing and researching an appropriate character to portray. It could be an obvious choice—the central figure in the material being studied, or it could be something more creative. The character simply must be one that you, the presenter, is comfortable with. Research about the character should focus on biographical data as well as information about the times and setting in which this character lived. Enough information must be gathered to allow you to develop a sense, not just of the person's actions, ideas, and achievements but also of his or her feelings, values, and attitudes.

Second, in doing such research, the presenter now is ready to address the process of character creation—deciding about costuming and props. By studying the character thoroughly, you will develop a sense of how this person would have dressed, stood, moved, and behaved. It is a matter of personal choice whether to *imitate* the character (full costume, props, and staging) or *suggest* the character (minimal costume and props, no staging). Some props will generally make the role-player feel the part more fully and will assist in creating a more credible representation for the audience.

Third, the dialogue must be constructed. In choosing what words to say, decisions should once again grow out of the research done on the character. If possible, using the person's exact words would be most appropriate. That makes the characterization valid and conveys more clearly that the speaker is *not* Presenter X, but a completely different character. When verbatim texts of the person's speech cannot be found or are not suitable, a script should be prepared using a manner of speech that seems consistent with that person's character and intellect. The more comfortable you feel with the character, the more you may want to build into the script some openings for spontaneous dialogue with the audience. Be prepared to remain in character, no matter how the audience responds.

Fourth, and final step, once the materials for the role-play are assembled and rehearsed, is the actual performance. There is no one right way to initiate the role-play in class. In some cases, it may be fitting to prepare the audience in advance for the arrival of this character, having them do some research and prepare questions. In other cases, the presenter may simply appear in character unheralded and begin to speak. Both approaches have advantages and disadvantages.

No matter how the role-play is initiated, it is critical that it be brought effectively to a close. There should be an opportunity for "debriefing" either at the end of the period or on the succeeding day to monitor the impressions the audience had about the "guest." This is necessary because role-playing can be such a dramatic device that it is possible some people in the audience may have gotten caught up in one of the characterization's special elements and missed the overall point.

The presenter's creation of a character is a process moving from selection, research, planning, costuming, scripting, and rehearsing to presentation and review. If that sounds like the same process that an actor goes through in creating a character, it is not coincidental!

SKINNER VERSUS ROGERS

I use what is called a "two-hat" (not actually two hats) role-play technique when staging a hypothetical debate between B. F. Skinner, a behaviorist, and Carl R. Rogers, a humanist, and the opposing philosophies they represent. These views have important ramifications for any and all professionals who must make philosophically based decisions.

The gist of this technique is a staged debate between real or hypothetical persons representing opposing viewpoints. The presenter plays both characters and distinguishes the speakers simply by putting on a hat, or holding up a picture, depicting each character. The costuming is minimal.

To get ready for his role-play, first, the presenter captures a picture of both Skinner and Rogers off the Internet and enlarges each one to approximately 8½″ × 11″. Second, he visits a discount store and purchases several "fans" that folks use to keep cool in a warm church when there is no air-conditioning. These cardboard fans have a wooden handle that looks like a very large tongue depressor. Third, he tapes Skinner's picture to one of the fans and Rogers' picture to the other fan. In minutes, the role-play is ready.

The two-hat role-play technique comes from holding one of the two pictures up next to your face and delivering that person's portion of the dialogue. The other fan remains at your side. When it is time for the opposing speaker to deliver his dialogue, up comes his picture and down to the side goes the other picture. To emphasize the contrasting views of the two debating "participants," their dialogues are delivered from different sides of the room (or desk)—normally to the right for Skinner and to the left for Rogers. Repositioning yourself before delivering each participant's dialogue reinforces their philosophical differences. At the end, be sure to "thank" your debating participants.

It takes just minutes—copy image, tape it or staple it (not counting writing the script that will be delivered)—to prepare the props for your role-play. Nothing fancy. But it works!

THE ACTUAL DEBATE

Address your audience, tell them that two guests, B. F. Skinner and Carl R. Rogers, have agreed to join us for a brief debate. The audience was informed ahead of time and, therefore, has already researched a good bit about both guests, as well as prepared interview questions. These two guests are familiar enough to most all professionals and, hence, their use for this example. No matter your subject matter, if you used a role-playing exercise like this, you would invite your own, more relevant to your subject matter, guests to speak.

> **Narrator (you):** Welcome to the both of you. We know that the two of you hold very different views, one a behaviorist and the other a humanist. We look forward to your debate. By the toss of a coin, Dr. Carl Rogers, please go first.

> **CR:** Behaviorism does seem to have a lot of followers from parents, to teachers, to bosses. What do you think makes it so attractive?

> **BFS:** It is about having control. A behaviorist's real power to control lies in his ability to supply consequences, thereby controlling someone's future behavior. If you do something we like, we supply one consequence. If you do something we do not approve of, we supply a different consequence.

> **CR:** Let me clarify something. You say behaviorism is about control, but you hinted at the fact that someone must do something, first, before you can supply your chosen consequence. So, behaviorism is designed to impact future behaviors, not current behaviors.

> **BFS:** That is absolutely correct.

> **CR:** But, where is the "control" you are talking about if as a behaviorist you have to wait for the other person to voluntarily exhibit a behavior that you either want to encourage or extinguish? What if he chooses not to exhibit that behavior? It would be his choice, wouldn't it?

> **BFS:** Of course, we can only supply consequences *after* the subject acts. That is why it is called Operant Conditioning. The subject first has to "act" or "operate" on his environment. Then we can supply the appropriate consequence.

> **CR:** It sounds to me as if the subject is the one who has the most control (to act or not act), not you. Let me ask this question. "Are most behaviorists in relatively good physical shape?"

> **BFS:** I don't understand the point you are trying to make.

> **CR:** Well, if behaviorists must not only wait until a subject chooses to act, they have to be there, say next to each of thirty students in a classroom, to "catch" the subject's behavior. What if they miss seeing or hearing the behavior? This must be exhausting.

> **BFS:** Scoff all you want but supplying consequences *does* impact a subject's future behavior. It has been proven over and over.

> **CR:** I have another question. "Do you like to be manipulated?" But before you answer, let me turn to the audience and ask them the same

question, "Unless you have gone to a chiropractor, how many of you like to be manipulated?" "I see that almost no one raised their hand."

BFS: No, I do not like to be manipulated.

CR: Well if you don't like to be manipulated, then what makes you think that it is OK to manipulate others with your supplied consequences?

BFS: The difference is that when we supply consequences, say to a child, student, or employee, we are doing it for their own good.

CR: Oh, Oh! The hair on the back of my neck just stood up at the words that you claim to know what is best for me. Do you really? Let me ask this question, "Do you have your life completely in order?" If not, I would ask behaviorists to make sure that their own life is completely in order before telling me how to live mine.

BFS: You make us sound callous and uncaring. That's far from the truth. The truth is simple, if someone does something good, he or she should be rewarded.

CR: Does this also mean if someone does something bad, he or she should be punished?

BFS: Behaviorists would say, yes, with the punishment fitting the crime.

CR: Let's say you punish a child for doing something wrong and he or she continues that behavior. Is it likely that you would increase the intensity of that punishment? Do we swat the child even harder? Where does it stop?

The exciting dialogue between B. F. Skinner and Carl R. Rogers continues. Time is saved at the end of the allotted time for the audience to ask questions of either "guest" speaker.

STORYTELLING: HERE IT IS AGAIN

A much simpler and briefer technique than the formal role-playing I have described, storytelling is still a form of role-play in that the speaker takes on a different persona, the role of narrator. The art of the storyteller is a time-honored tradition in many cultures and has carried over very effectively to many venues. No matter the age of the audience, no matter the audience, there is still a noticeably captivating effect when one says, "Once upon a time" or something equivalent.

Whether the story told is truth or fiction, it is told best if told simply. The presenter should play the part of narrator as well as any and all other characters in the story using slight modifications of posture or expression to suggest the identity of the character speaking. As with the more extensive role-plays, storytelling may incorporate a few simple props. Hint! Practice storytelling at home with your children or grandchildren. They will love it.

MIME

A particularly unique role-playing creation available for the presenter is that of a mime. By removing dialogue from the role portrayal, a presenter is challenged to convey a message or concept to an audience with facial expression and movement alone. Mime's lack of words challenges audiences to think more analytically and sparks their creativity.

Mime is a more challenging form of acting or presenting than that used in the other examples I have described here. It might be considered as an "advanced" level of role-play suited to presenters who have already developed some comfort with the basic form of character portrayal.

SUMMARY

Presenter role-playing is the pedagogical tool probably most resembling the tools of the actor. It may be a most difficult role for many presenters. If a presenter's self-confidence is still "under construction," the one role-play that is ideal is the role of presenter itself. We benefit by acting in the way that we think confident, successful presenters act. We then can grow into the role, *becoming* confident master presenters ourselves. Once that self-esteem begins to develop, we may want to try the creation of character roles to further enhance our delivery. All role-playing should be planned, rehearsed, and presented in a well-organized manner. By doing so, you will have added another dynamic presentation tool to your repertoire.

13

Use of Props

INTRODUCTION

Give me a lever long enough and a prop strong enough,
I can single-handedly move the world.
—Archimedes

A recognized prop worldwide is Shakespeare's graveyard scene where Hamlet, brooding over the finality of death, holds up the grotesque skull of his favorite court jester saying, "Alas, poor Yorick! I knew him . . ." (*Hamlet*, Act 5, Scene 8). The words remain the same; the delivery varies by actor—Laurence Olivier, Richard Burton, and even, Mel Gibson.

I know that if readers listed all the props that they have used over their years of presenting, the list would fill this book many times over. The prop examples that I offer may not necessarily come from your specific field. It would be impossible for me to offer examples of your sort of props without ignoring the props of others. Someone would feel "left out." Instead, I have offered some unusual ideas for props along with some guidelines for using any and all of props.

Imagine the myriad of props in medicine. Probably, over the course of your life, you have seen many of them as patients. You also see the realism they add to the endless, and endlessly popular, television hospital programs. Although there are fewer props used in lawyer programs, the statement, "I would like to offer 'Exhibit A into evidence'" suggests that it will.

be an important prop to be referred to later in the trial. Politicians decrying the size of the federal budget and wanting to make a visual point, show a stack of 74,000 pages (e.g., a prop) just for the federal tax code. Advertisers make sure that yearly auto shows (props, in themselves) are shown adorned with beautiful women (e.g., more props).

PICTURE PROPS

> *I love to come in and play with a wig or glasses or clothes.*
> *I love using props.*
> —Dan Aykroyd

A picture, as we are all told, is worth a thousand words—both in creating emotion and delivering information. For the actor, props help set the stage, conveying information that is crucial to the film or play's message. It is no different for a presenter.

Earlier I offered a description (mental picture) of Hamlet holding his jester's skull. Assume for a moment that a presenter giving a medical presentation holds up a picture of a skull, bone, or other body part as part of her presentation. There is no reason why Hamlet's famous lines could not accompany its display. The audience would find Hamlet's accompanying words curious but engaging. Of course, holding up the "real thing," an actual skull, would be preferred.

To emphasize the power of a visual prop, recall the emotion-evoking picture titled *Migrant Mother* introduced in chapter 12 "Role-Playing." The destitute mother is shown, with her two children turned away in despair, clearly having lost all hope, having nowhere to turn for relief. Before showing the picture to an audience, stare at it for a minute. Look at the detail. Look into her lifeless eyes. Look at their ragged clothes. Think, "There, but for the grace of God, go I!" Now, show the picture to your audience. Let them, too, look at it—really look at it before you continue.

So, what is the point of showing the picture? There could be many "points." You could tell the audience the points or they could offer theirs. There are those who have good health care, poor health care, and *no* health care. There are those diagnosed with a terminal disease who wonder, "Why me?" There are those who just learned their life-long partner of fifty years has died—"What am I going to do?" There are those who know they must commit their aging parent to a nursing home but are overwhelmed with guilt, let alone having no idea how the costs will be paid. Showing an audience the *Migrant Mother* picture (as a chapter 15 "Creative Entrances and Exits" "hook") as part of your presentation can help them, in the best sense possible, get in the proper mood, empathize with the woman, her children, and her circumstances, as opposed to seeing her as just another "case," "customer," or "voter."

Start identifying and collecting physical as well as picture props that you feel could enhance your presentations. Be on the lookout for some particularly powerful ones! Ask your audience for some help in this task.

SOUND PROPS

Consider purchasing a child's sound bites machine. These inexpensive, usually less than $15.00, versions of a tape recorder have a pre-recorded selection of sound effects on them available at just the push of a button. Among the sound effects are Applause, Soap Opera Drama (dum, dum, dum, daaa), Charge (as in taking San Juan Hill), Whistle, Drum Roll, Uh Oh! and more. When triggered at the right moment, for example, applause after making a significant point, an Uh Oh! after making an intentional (or unintentional) error, a Drum Roll just before an important utterance, a Charge!!!! sounded where you think it might best fit, these unexpected sounds can augment your delivery. Attention is refocused, laughs occur, tension is reduced—all taking but a push of a button. Practice inserting these suspenseful and surprising sounds into "discussions" with your grandchildren, nieces, and nephews.

Another handy device is a miniature digital tape recorder that allows you to store, in folders, previously inserted dialogue, sounds, or music. Up comes a recording of the give-and-take that you and a colleague recently had regarding a controversial government decision. Up comes thirty seconds of an exhilarating theme song from a movie (discussed further in chapter 15 "Creative Entrances and Exits"). Up comes last night's evening news announcement from the Surgeon General regarding e-cigarettes.

MUSIC, MOVIES, AND TELEVISION PROPS

There simply is not enough space to fully address the value of turning to music, movies, and television (all of which involve presentation skills), let alone literature and art, to help in delivering dynamic presentations. Here are just a few resources to whet your appetite.

- Use of fine art to enhance visual diagnostic skills. *JAMA.*
- From ABBA to Zeppelin: Using music to teach economics. *Journal of Economic Education.*
- Teaching medical students psychiatry through contemporary music. *Medical Education.*

- Teaching molecular biology with watercolors. *Smithsonian.com.*

- Visual thinking strategies: A new role for art in medical education. *Family Medicine.*

- What great leaders and music have in common. *TEDtalks.*

- Teaching physics with music. *The Physics Teacher.*

- Using "The Merchant of Venice" in teaching monetary economics. *Journal of Economic Education.*

- Show a portion of films (or TV programs) such as Rodney Danger- field's 1986 comedy *Back to School*, where as a nontraditional student with building experience, he incurs the wrath of the dean of the busi- ness school for suggesting that "bribery," in fact, was part of most large city building projects.

- Use Seinfeld's episode, "The Sponge," where Elaine buys an entire case of these birth control devices and begins to hoard her ever dwindling scarce supply. She must decide whether her boyfriends are "sponge- worthy!" Review the many economics principles displayed in *Seinfeld* by turning to yadayadayadaecon.com.

ALEX TREBEK'S *JEOPARDY!*

> *Please form your answer in the form of a question.*
> —Alex Trebek

For almost forty years, viewers have tuned in to try to beat contestants to the punch in answering questions. No doubt Alex Trebek, as a low-key yet engaging presenter, has had a lot to do with the show's success. Lectur- ers and presenters can create their own version of *Jeopardy* (or similar games) as a prop to engage, inform, and motivate an audience. Their ver- sions can be low tech with categories and clues written on 5" × 8" note- cards, or high-tech electronic versions such as "Internal Medicine Jeopardy Game," "Accounting Jeopardy Game," or "Legal Ethics Jeopardy." Present- ers can provide simple "answer buzzers" that actively engage audience members with the "game-show" host.

Whether played as individual contestants or as teams, these games are interactive, fast-moving, and fun! When played at the very start of a ses- sion, it is guaranteed to get the audience there on time ready to "partici- pate." Here is a sample *Jeopardy* clue from me. "Humor, suspense and surprise, animation in body and voice, role-playing, props, and creative entrances and exits." Answer: "What are presenter skills that *project* enthusiasm?"

Trebek is quoted to have said, "My job is to provide the atmosphere and assistance to the contestants to get them to perform at their very best." Isn't this exactly what great presenters do?

"IMAGINE": A JOHN LENNON PROP

The more I see the less I know for sure.
—John Lennon

I credit Dr. Sivarajah for the following, creative and engaging, John Lennon example of how to present valuable information and make it have a lasting impact on an audience.

If there ever was a song that hits right to the heart of most folks, it is John Lennon's "Imagine." You may start humming it right now if you wish. I will wait. The original lyrics are thought-provoking. But what I am going to describe here is something that could have easily been inserted in the chapters on humor, suspense and surprise, role-playing, or creative entrances and exits.

Here are the steps for using "Imagine" as a prop.

Step 1

Locate via YouTube or some other outlet, John Lennon's song, "Imagine." The tune is about three minutes long and shows John and Yoko Ono walking toward a mansion and then entering a bright white room with only a piano where John sits and starts to play and sing. Yoko Ono proceeds to open the drapes and lets light stream in.

Step 2

Write original lyrics for the tune using terminology related to your specific subject matter. Give yourself some lead time to do this. Dr. Sivarajah generated the following original lyrics for the field of Oncology. Original lyrics, of course, could come from any and all fields—including yours!

Step 3

Just before the clock indicates that your presentation is to begin, don't say a word, just start to play the original "Imagine." All heads will turn, everyone will be listening. Depending upon the available time, you could play the entire song or just part of it. The tune now will be cemented in their consciousness.

Step 4

Stop the music. Tell the students—as seriously as you can muster—that you lead two lives, one as a presenter, and two, as a frustrated wannabe "America's Got Talent" singer. "Ham" it up a bit! Tell them that you have written your own "Imagine" lyrics. "Sing," and I *generously* use this term, your substituted Oncology "Imagine" lyrics.

Imagine there is a heaven
It's somewhere in the sky
No pain and suffering
Cancer has gone bye, bye
Imagine all the people still living today

Imagine there's no one denied treatment
No one bankrupted with money due
Everyone has access to healthcare
Rich people, poor people, me and you
Imagine all of us living life without pain

You may say it's just a pipe dream
Now our curing of cancer has begun
Join with our oncology practice
We will treat people one by one

Imagine no chemo or radiation needed
I wonder if you can
No loss of hair by children
No nausea, vomiting or diarrhea by man
Imagine the people experiencing cancer cures

You may say I'm just dreaming
But we can and will reach our goal
I hope one day you'll join us
Then cancer will no longer take its toll!

As a presenter, the question you may now have is "What should I do with this?' "What is the point?" Only you can answer these questions. You wrote the lyrics, you sang your lyrics, you decided what substitute lyrics to insert, you put the words together to express a message. What was that message? Is it just a dream where no chemo will be required? Is it possible for all people ("rich and poor people, too") to have access to early screening? Will cancer finally be beaten? Or, was Lennon correct when he sings that he's just a dreamer?

Imagine (get the pun?) all the other lyrics that you, or if asked, your audience could write for your specific field. Imagine all the other tunes that could be the base for your creative terminology lyrics. You don't have to imagine it—just do it. Music and creative lyrics can deliver a powerful, sure to be remembered, message. Your presentation will be remembered.

"THE RAVEN": EDGAR ALLAN POE PROP

> *All we see or seem is but a dream within a dream.*
> —Edgar Allan Poe

Here is one more prop from Dr. Sivarajah that substitutes medical terminology for the original words. In this case, Edgar Allan Poe's "The Raven" is used. You can read the original and then with some dramatic fanfare proceed to read your version of "The Raven." Feel free, of course, to choose terminology that best fits the focus of your presentation. The point is that the delivery of the two poems, the original and the altered version, takes only a minute or two, but would be an eye-catching, actually an ear-catching, hook (relates to chapter 15 "Creative Entrances and Exits") to start a presentation.

Edgar Allan Poe, "The Raven"
Once upon a midnight dreary, while I pondered, weak and weary,
Over many a quaint and curious volume of forgotten lore—
While I nodded, nearly napping, suddenly there came a tapping,
As of some one gently rapping, rapping at my chamber door.
"Tis some visitor," I muttered, "tapping at my chamber door—
Only this and nothing more."

Dr. Sivarajah reports that this new version of Poe's poem could be used in a medical school cardiology block or to teach med students or residents rotating through a clinical cardiology rotation. It could be used to reinforce the timing of certain abnormal heart rhythms and sounds.

Edgar Allan Poe, "The Raven" (altered lyrics)
Once upon a midnight dreary, I, a resident pondered a patient, weak and weary,
Over many up-to-date articles and volumes of textbooks I searched
While I nodded, nearly napping, I could hear my patient's heartbeat tapping.

An arrhythmia of rapping unfamiliar to me—so for the differential I
     researched.
Tis irregularly irregular, I realized, now knowing I would not be
     besmirched.
"You have atrial fibrillation," I explained to patient at the side of his bed
     I was perched.

SPANDEX REVEALS ALL

Be original; don't be scared of being bold!
—Ed Sheeran

A presenter in the Netherlands recently raised more than a few eyebrows by stripping off her clothes, layer after layer, from the outside in,
showing her body's entrails, eventually getting to her skeleton. She began
by taking off her normal street clothes. No doubt she had everyone's attention. Beneath her outside clothes, she had on a top-to-bottom full-suit of
spandex illustrated with accurate muscles and organs. Underneath that
suit, she had on another spandex suit showing all the bones in her body.
Certainly, this was a memorable prop for her audience. See for yourself
by doing an Internet search using, Netherlands Biology Teacher and
Spandex.

I am not recommending that all readers run to their spandex store, but
you must give this presenter credit. She played the cards given to her, both
in courage and physique. She grabbed her audience's attention big time.
Short of seeing a human's organs, muscles, and skeleton in textbook pictures or in slides, her delivery method was creative. It certainly was memorable. And, it was easy—such spandex suits are readily available for sale on
the Internet.

Another university presenter who teaches computer courses wears a
Spider-man spandex outfit while presenting. Why? Just because it works!
Still one more presenter occasionally teaches his math class in a Darth
Vader outfit with accompanying *Star Wars* music. Why? Once again, just
because it works!

You would not have to wear a full body suit. You could, as in Superman's
case, simply wear a long-sleeve light blue jersey, with a bold red "S" pinned
on it, underneath your dress shirt or blazer. At the proper time, displaying
some sort of urgency, remove your "Clark Kent" black-rimmed glasses and
your dress shirt. "Voila"—it's Superman. To this day I could never figure
out why Lois Lane never caught on! You also could do something similar
with Batman, but this time including a flashlight projecting an image of

the "bat signal," the kind that was shown over Gotham City when Batman was needed.

Finally, you don't have to do any of these things—spandex or otherwise. That is part of the fun of it all. It is entirely up to you.

PRESENTER PROPS

I trained as a theater actor and you had a bare stage and you had to pretend, one prop and you are in the middle of 8th Ave. and traffic is just going by.
—Benicio Del Toro

While the actors' props are essentially limited to artifacts and costumes in the theater, the options are considerably more extensive for presenter venues.

Dabell (2017, 3) recommends: "All presenters need a bag of tricks, a suitcase of curios and a pile of props to supplement their lessons. Unusual artifacts and objects can flabbergast, entertain and educate and we should utilize them to power home a point, illustrate an idea or make a concept stick."

Whatever the form, presenter props, like those in the theater, help set the stage. They provide context and character. For the audience, props may clarify information, capture and hold their attention, and make the presentation more memorable. Using props can render a special benefit to a presenter. Using a prop gives anxious presenters something to do with their hands. By keeping physically busy, the presenter is less likely to be perceived as nervous. In this circumstance, the props also serve the function of "notes," reminding the presenter of the sequence of points to be made in the presentation.

Many props can be considered universal in that, with a little imagination, the same prop can serve very different purposes in a variety of situations. Take, for example, an apple. In an art class the apple may be used as a still-life prop to be painted. In a chemistry class the apple (in both its peeled and unpeeled state) may be used to test the reaction of oxygen. The significance of taking a bite out of the forbidden apple may be explored in a religion class. The historical accuracy of Newton's having been hit on the head with a falling apple could be investigated. As shown in the film *Stand and Deliver*, Jamie Escalante, the Los Angeles calculus teacher, used an apple to teach fractions. In medicine, the truth of "An apple a day keeps the doctor away" could be explored. Each of these lessons could have been taught by the presenter's use of words alone. But a simple apple prop makes those words much more captivating and memorable! One other use for the apple is that after class it could be eaten!

What about using a piece of taffy as a prop? A colleague takes several pieces of salt-water taffy with him when he presents his spiel. After covering a particularly challenging concept, he stops talking and slowly chews the taffy—"digests" it—a function that he would like his audience to emulate mentally regarding the subject matter just presented. Corny? Of course. The time used to chew the taffy provides the pedagogically sound equivalent of "wait time." After the "food-for-thought" has been chewed and digested, he entertains questions or comments.

A physics professor, Jonathan Hall, demonstrates the concepts of force and pressure. Like an Indian guru, he lies on a bed of nails while an eager audience member proceeds to nail two pieces of wood together that are placed on his chest. Hall dramatically makes his point about how force can be dispersed.

Even an everywhere-present, taken-for-granted book can be an effective prop. There is something captivating about a presenter reading a quotation directly from a book rather than from her notes. The words may be the same, but the dramatic impact is different. Reading from a book adds a dimension of reality and importance. A prop does not have to communicate anything directly; it is not even critical that the audience can see it closely. Props, books, or otherwise are used to add credibility and enhance interest.

PUPPETS AS PROPS

The public has been infatuated with *Mister Rogers' Neighborhood* and his puppets, King Friday XIII, Daniel Striped Tiger, and Lady Elaine Fairchilde for over fifty years. Joining the puppet obsession, Jeff Dunham, an American ventriloquist, is among the most popular stand-up comedians in the United States today. Dunham uses his hand puppets, such as the grouchy old man Walter, to have biting conversations regarding current events—politics, medicine, law, race, religion, and the economy. You just never know what is coming next out of Walter's mouth! Even Dunham often seems surprised. The audience is engaged, informed, and at the end, wants still more.

This brings to mind a joke (e.g., humor). Kermit the frog, in some stomach discomfort, is shown across the desk from his doctor who is holding up Kermit's full body x-ray. The physician, with some degree of pride in his diagnosis says, "Here, I think that I have found the source of your internal discomfort." The x-ray reveals an entire hand and upper part of a human being's arm stuck inside Kermit's body! Go ahead, laugh.

I have a small collection of approximately four-inch-tall "finger puppets." They include, among others, Carl Jung, Albert Einstein, and Isaac Newton. I also have several "hand decorated" padded or rubberized oven mitts character puppets. I have a pair of Sigmund Freud slippers that I wear when discussing Freud's work, and a hand puppet "dummy" raccoon that when I told my wife I was going to use it in class, she remarked, "Good idea, but which one of you is going to play the role of the dummy?" *Ha Ha*!

The puppet "guests" that you present can be an assistant, colleague, antagonist, doubting-Thomas, or anything you want them to be, and you don't even have to buy them lunch! Corny? Perhaps. But they engage, engage, engage an audience.

SELECTED MEDICAL PROPS

Dr. Sivarajah contributes here by offering simple, down-to-earth, props that can be used to help deliver a dynamic and memorable presentation. This shows how easily simple props can be used that are sure to highlight a lesson. Feel free to create your own set of props.

- Picture of a normal lung and one from a smoker on a pulmonary talk.
- Use life size pictures, or the real items, of food arranged by increasing sizes. Poppy seed—lentil—blueberry—grape—kidney bean—olive—fig—lime—lemon—apple—avocado—turnip—bell pepper—mango—cauliflower—coconut—cantaloupe—watermelon. Unveil them one at a time. This would be used to review sizes of a fetus at different gestational ages.
- Pictures of Muhammad Ali, Michael J. Fox, and Jesse Jackson, people with Parkinson's disease, in a talk about neurodegenerative disorders.
- Caput Medusa is a sign of portal hypertension in a patient with liver failure. It's when there are vessels in the region of the belly button that look like the hair of Medusa. You could put up a picture of the Greek goddess Medusa at the start of a liver failure talk. You could even play a clip from Clash of the Titans with the Medusa scene. This definitely would be attention-getting.
- A cardiologist teaching about cardiac sounds could place a pretend (imaginary props) stethoscope on an imaginary patient and then use his other hand to demonstrate the heart sounds moving his palm up and down to the sounds of "lub-dub, lub-dub."
- An internal medicine doctor as a prop, himself, might describe the appearance of a Parkinson's patient when he walked. He could get up in front of the room and recreate the shuffling gait associated with

Parkinson's disease as he would slowly walk from one side of the room to the other.

- The small intestine is twenty-two feet long. Imagine the impact of giving an anatomy lecture and showing something that is as long—like twenty-two notebooks or a two and a half story high building. You could use a Twenty-five-foot tape measure, easily available at a home improvement store. Ask them to "picture" their lunch time Philadelphia cheese steak making its way through the intestine.

USING THE AUDIENCE AS PROPS

Admit it, most people love to be "on stage." This may well be their "fifteen minutes of fame." In the following exercise, both the presenter and the audience can safely "ham" it up!

Why Does Ice Float: It Shouldn't?

"Why does ice float?" Silly question? Not really. Until one realizes that water is the only liquid whose solid form is not heavier than its liquid form, the audience takes the floating ability of ice for granted. If ice did not float, our world would be significantly changed, perhaps even unable to sustain life as we know it. For instance, the Great Lakes would freeze solid and during the summer melt an insignificant amount of water—not enough to sustain a fishing industry, allow giant lake freighters to move raw materials, or provide fresh drinking water for citizens.

In order to demonstrate the phenomenon, nine participants (e.g., human props) are asked to come to the front of the room, stand together in three rows of three, and play (e.g., act) the role of water molecules. At the start of the exercise, the "molecules" are told to moderately vibrate (e.g., more acting) just as molecules do. There is laughter in the room (e.g., humor). Now, the presenter pretends (e.g., acts) to raise the room thermostat (e.g., imaginary prop) and asks them to demonstrate (e.g., role-play) what would happen. The "molecules," now warmer, become more agitated (e.g., act) and vibrate more violently thus needing more space (e.g. space utilization) in which to do so. As a result, the molecules move a bit farther apart from each other. They become less crowded, less dense. More audience laughter.

The presenter now pretends (e.g., acts) to lower the room thermostat (e.g., prop) and asks them to demonstrate what would happen.

Being colder, the molecules vibrate less violently and naturally move (e.g., act) closer together because that is what molecules do when they get cold. Now that they have moved closer together—still vibrating, but not as much as before—they are denser (e.g., heavier). In real life, let's say in a swimming pool, the now heavier molecules would sink to the bottom just like cold water does in a pool. If we kept lowering the temperature of our water molecules, they would get colder and colder, more and more dense, get heavier and heavier, vibrate less and less aggressively, and be even more likely to sink to the bottom. At some point our water molecules turn to ice and, somehow, *MAGICALLY* become less dense than the surrounding water and thus bob to the surface! Uh, Oh!

It's not magic at all. The presenter explains (e.g., surprise) that between four and zero degrees centigrade water molecules move farther apart, not closer together. Strange, but true. The result makes the frozen form (ice) lighter, thus causing it to float. The role-playing water molecule participants are thanked, the point of the presentation is discussed, and a memorable fun-packed learning experience comes to an end.

Everyone had fun; everyone learned!

PROP BOX

Acting is all about big hair and funny props. . . . All the great actors knew it. Olivier knew it. Brando knew it.
—Harold Ramis

A prop box is a "hope chest" of items that the presenter thinks may be useful for some future presentation. What does one use for a prop? The answer is "anything and everything." Where does one get his or her props? The answer is "anywhere and everywhere." Ask colleagues what props they have successfully used and add those to your box. Ask your audience for suggestions of what to include.

If you have decided to use props, costumes, special lighting, or any other kind of "staging," help can be sought in locating suitable free materials. Custodial staff, for instance, may be a good source of knowledge about what materials are lying around that could be used. Naturally, the theater department at your institution or nearby in your town would be another good resource.

If presenters must go shopping, they should start with yard sales. One professor's two-hat technique depends upon the hats salvaged from yard sales and thrift stores. Either he has purchased them himself, or others, knowing of his presentation style, pick up some unique hat or other item of clothing for him that they happen to run across.

Other things can go into your props box, too. Included may be a collection of humorous cartoons (see chapter 10 "Humor"), striking anecdotes, great opening lines (see chapter 15 "Creative Entrances and Exits"), and more. Journaling of personal stories, yours, and those told to you, is an effective and easy way to build such a resource. Every event that happens to you or that you read about that leads you to say "that's really interesting" ought to be recorded. You never know when one of those stories will be just what you need!

GUIDELINES FOR USING PROPS

Before anything else, preparation is the key to success.
—Alexander Graham Bell

Whatever the nature or purpose of a prop, they all come with risks. Murphy's Law is certainly applicable when it comes to props. Nearly every presenter has stories of props that flopped because a light bulb was burned out, the supplies didn't arrive in time, it rained on the poster, or the dog ate it! Like any good actor who double-checks all the props before the curtain goes up, a presenter should rehearse with the prop to make sure it is working. This would be the equivalent of a pilot doing a "walk around" of his plane before taking off.

The best prop is one that is large (yet transportable), clear and visible to the audience all at the same time. Are all the necessary pieces there? Do you have the proper equipment for displaying the prop—an easel, a projection screen, a display table? Do a "dry run" of all experiments to make sure that the procedure will result in the desired conclusion—every time! But, being realistic, be prepared for the experiment *not* to work. Here is where you whip out the adage, "Every experiment, even a failed one, teaches you something!"

Generally speaking, props should be displayed, not passed around the room. Passing just increases the odds of Murphy's Law kicking in! If every audience member must hold and pass on the prop, it is going to get dropped somewhere along the line. In addition, passing an object is a distraction to the entire audience who are watching it go around the room instead of focusing on what the presenter is saying about it. Also, it is quite likely that the object will still be in someone's hands after the presenter is already done explaining it, diminishing its usefulness as a clarifier.

Keep props simple enough to be clear. Remember that any visual aid or prop should be exactly that—an aid, not the complete source of information. This means displaying just the main gear in a linkage assembly, not the entire contraption!

Display the prop only when you are speaking about what it depicts. Until that moment and after than moment, it is a distraction; keep it out of sight. The only exception to this rule is when you want to use the presence of the prop, or the bag or box that it is concealed in, to heighten the audience's suspense about the topic for which it will later be used.

Finally, there is one more risk in using a prop. It does draw attention—both the audience's and the presenter's. It is very tempting to continually look at the prop while speaking about it, even if that means looking down or back and, thus, away from the audience. Practice with your prop so that you know exactly where the various parts are that you will be pointing to, and then you should not need to take much more than a quick glance when presenting with it.

TECHNOLOGY PROPS INVADE

You know, he's so capable—just the way he deals with props is amazing.
—Meg Ryan

Being up-in-age, I occasionally have difficulty streaming a favorite Netflix program. I am not proud of it. The age of technology has arrived and brought changes everywhere. Now that's an understatement! We have all had to learn digital technology for simple things like using the telephone or watching television and are observers of the technology used for much more complicated operations in manufacturing, global communications, medicine, and transportation.

Those transformations have certainly not been lost in the worlds of the theater and education. Technology has created a vast new world of "props" available to the performer and the presenter, alike. As with the traditional props, there are many similarities between the two worlds. In movies, they may be called "special effects" and include everything from the creation of believable flying creatures to enhanced views of microscopic realities. In live theater, technology has created new prop possibilities via projected images, creative sounds production and sophisticated artifacts.

The presentation medium, too, has seen an absolute explosion of possibilities as technology has given the presenter new tools for clarifying and enhancing his or her delivery. With more options, of course, come more, or at least different, challenges.

Just as with any prop, the technology we use in our presentations is meant to serve the purposes of clarifying information, capturing and holding student attention, and making ideas memorable. It is critical to keep those purposes in mind as we consider the options newly available to us, lest we fall for the notion of using the technology simply because we can.

POWERPOINT

Most of the presentation skills, by design, presented in this book are pedagogically sound, rather low-tech (e.g., animation in body, humor, suspense and surprise). Learn them and they can be used to deliver more dynamic presentations in any venue. Having said that, one must mention a particular instructional technology.

No discussion of instructional technology could be complete without a reference to PowerPoint. A search of articles about the rationale for using PowerPoint yields many reasons like its "ease," "availability," "colorfulness," and "compatibility." The same might be said of crayons! That doesn't justify using crayons all the time any more than it justifies using PowerPoint slides in every presentation. The actor does not use fireworks in the theater, even though he could. Instead, he or she chooses the most appropriate technology for the setting and for the goals in that setting. That is the lesson for us as presenters.

One caution about the use of PowerPoint revolves around the fact that the "slides" are just so much fun to prepare—different colors, different fonts, animation, and so on. PowerPoint slides are an opportunity for adults to recapture some of that creative childhood fun. It is easy for presenters to spend too much time "formatting" the slides to the possible detriment of strengthening the message of what the slides are to help convey.

The saying "it was cast in stone" can apply to PowerPoint presentations that, by design, have been prepared well before a presentation and are supposed to be presented one way—slide after prepared slide. The slides and the presentation sequence virtually are set in stone.

In the area of technology props, perhaps more than any other lessons we take from the theater, careful selection of one's tools is vital to the enthusiastic presenter's success. The best presenters are not the ones who incorporate *all* the latest "bells and whistles," but rather the ones who choose the best bell or whistle for the task.

Finally, if you choose to use PowerPoint, research both its benefits and drawbacks, an undertaking that could easily fill an entire book.

NOTES AS PROPS

One of your most used, but sometimes too often relied upon, props are your notes. If we continue to see the parallel between acting and presenting, we must point out that actors and actresses generally learn their lines needing only an occasional prompt. The best speakers, the best presenters, are those who can speak without notes. Shoot for a goal of not looking at your notes more than 20 percent of the time (Goulden 1991). Of course, there are ways such as displaying PowerPoint slides, poster boards, and so on, that could "stretch" this 20 percent goal.

SUMMARY

Do you remember "show and tell" days of kindergarten years? The prop, the "show," was used to promote the real reason for the exercise, the "tell." And it worked! Do you recall *The Bob Newhart Show* where Newhart's wife, an elementary teacher played by Suzanne Pleshette, asked Bob (a psychologist), neighbor Howard (an airline pilot), and friend Jerry (a dentist) to speak at her school's "show and tell." When the time came, Howard brought along a rather large model of a commercial airplane that wowed the kids. Jerry brought along a large toothbrush and giant set of dentures. Bob, as a psychologist, brought along . . . ! Whoops, he had nothing physical to bring along as a prop to show. Luckily, the majority of fields are ripe with applicable props. Props can be a key ingredient in helping to set the stage and convey the intended message. Props—tongue-in-cheek—can really "prop" up a lesson!

14

Space Utilization

INTRODUCTION

People like to be close enough to obtain warmth and comradeship,
but far enough away to avoid pricking one another.
—Robert Sommer

Once upon a time, at the small Montgomery Bell Academy, boys entering their American literature class found the door closed and no sign of their teacher. When they knocked, however, they heard Mr. Pickering's voice inviting them in. Imagine their surprise when entering the room to not find him anywhere in sight. The meaningfulness of this classroom episode lies in the fact that the next sound the boys heard was Mr. Pickering enthusiastically reading Thoreau from under his desk! Their teacher's choice to read to them from such an unexpected spot made the students curious and attentive (Pickering 2004).

For those of you who may not know, Pickering's maverick pedagogy influenced one of his students, Tommy Schulman, who later wrote the screenplay for *Dead Poets Society*. We have Robin Williams, as Mr. Keating, to thank for bringing Mr. Pickering's antics to the big screen. This example provides us with a reason to think about how we use the space of our presentation venues. Are we doing so in a way that contributes specifically to the success of learning?

Another reason to give this issue some attention is that many times a presenter, particularly newer presenters, may feel uncomfortable in front of an audience. By using the space of the room in a manner that *looks* comfortable, presenters can convey to an audience that the presenter *is* comfortable in that room.

When asked by an aspiring actor, "What is the success to becoming a great actor," Spencer Tracy is reported to have said, "Learn your lines and don't bump into the furniture." When I, previously a physics teacher, would bump into something in my classroom causing it (or me) to be jostled, I would say, "Note, I have just demonstrated the physics exclusion principle which states that two things cannot occupy the same place at the same time." Through this statement, I demonstrated a bit of physics and used a bit of humor.

I now turn to the consideration of constructive, purposeful use of space that can contribute to presenter confidence and to greater audience learning. Imaginative use of space is, therefore, a means, not an end in itself, to achieving positive learning outcomes.

LECTERN LINGERING

This will be short and to the point—*move out from behind the lectern!* Use the lectern as a point of departure, not a barrier to hide behind. Medley (2017) cautions speakers to not hide behind the lectern claiming that you must be visible to the audience. Be brave and step out to the side. Don't stand in place and lean heavily on the lectern. Once out, don't rock back and forth, shifting your weight from one leg to the other, like a chained elephant in a zoo. Getting out from behind the lectern helps connect you with your audience and turbocharges your performance.

Standing behind a lectern encourages hand "death grips" and discourages natural hand gestures (the focus of an earlier chapter). It encourages reading from your notes or outline, which is often boring for your audience. The physical barrier, the lectern, also acts as a psychological barrier between you and your audience. Just seeing a lectern can cause audiences to roll their eyes believing that an old-fashioned, one-way communication presentation is about to unfold.

Have you noticed the warnings posted on the rear of trailer trucks that say, "If you can't see me in my rearview mirror, then I can't see you"? Lecterns partially, or totally at times, block the audience from seeing you and, hence, if they can't see you, they are less inclined to listen to you. It's sort of like getting the "cheap seats" at a play that block your view by a thick pillar. You are less likely to pay attention to the delivered message. And, if the audience can't see your hands, they may well not trust you. Mankind learned this "let me see your hands" survival message eons ago.

Venture from behind the lectern to deliver material that you know well and, thus, have little need to refer to notes or other resources resting on the lectern. Although there may well be a need to use the lectern, it should be by design, not by default or habit.

PROXEMICS

The study of the communicative effect of the physical space between interacting people is known as proxemics. We learn that you consciously or subconsciously choose a spot in relationship to others depending on their interpersonal relationship, the context of the communication, and your particular goals—even something as simple as where you prefer to sit at a restaurant.

Our interpersonal locations are interpreted as sending messages—of coldness, interest, intimacy and so on—whether we consciously intend them to or not. It is on the basis of these principles of proxemics, then, that the actor or director plans the placement of actors for each scene. In real interactions with others, of course, we do not *plan* each and every placement of ourselves, but the proxemic message is still present.

SPACE AND ITS LIMITATIONS

As oral communicators, both actors and presenters can benefit from being observant of the effect of space on the impact of their communication. Since nonverbal elements are part of the message communicated, actors and presenters must, for instance, consider how well the listeners can see and hear them when they speak. The physical nature of the venues within which we all must work will vary in terms of such things as acoustics and sight lines, and those elements will, in turn, impact the listeners' ability to attend to our messages.

Classrooms or other presentation venues should have no bad seats. If you can't properly arrange the seats (discussed later), rearrange yourself. Poorly designed learning environments can distort the information presented and hinder an audience's ability to see, hear, and participate. This hampers their ability to learn.

No matter the room we happen to present in, its space provides both opportunities and challenges. Some presentations are held in rooms where the acoustics are awful. The audience may hear an echo in some rooms, and in others the presenter may be inaudible to all students beyond the fifth row of seats. In order to move students closer to the presenter, some presenters rope off the rear rows of seats.

The issue of sight lines should also occur to presenters, just as it does to actors and directors. The question in this instance is: From what point can I be seen by listeners seated at various points around the room? Being seen by the listeners is, after all, a prerequisite to being heeded.

BLOCKING

As a cast prepares for a performance, each piece of dialogue is thus blocked—determining the precise placement of each character within the stage space. Through rehearsing, the placement of the actors becomes firm and is ultimately perceived by the audience as integrated totally into the scene's creation. You can do that same kind of purposeful planning of movement and placement within your presentation space.

Movement around the presentation venue will be most effective if planned. Some portions of a presentation, for instance, are going to demand that the presenter be near the chalkboard, while other portions allow more options in using the available space. Technology, with wireless controls for audio-visual presentations, also increases space utilization options.

Whatever the case, whether a presenter has many or few constraints on how the classroom space can be used, the goals of selecting the best use of space are the same for the presenter as they are for the actor. A presenter should place himself or herself in such a way as to maintain the audience's attention and to provide emphasis for the most important ideas of the presentation.

A presenter's awareness of the proxemic effect of free use of space necessitates occasionally breaking away from the lectern and chalkboard. Pedagogically, such movement is beneficial in that it allows the presenter to be more physically expressive, to establish meaningful proximity with the audience, and to create a more confident, professional image.

The lectern, discussed earlier, is especially problematic. Since most of us want our audience to perceive us as *not* wanting to be distant, we need to get out from behind the desk or lectern. But, some consoles in technology classrooms are particularly challenging. Those that provide built-in units for all the computers and projectors that might be used can create a "Great Wall" of technology between the presenter and the audience. Stepping out from behind that wall may be no easy feat. We can conceive of several ways to break away from the chalkboard or lectern during the lecturing mode, however.

The break from the chalkboard can be accomplished when using a lecture format, for example, by planning and preparing transparencies, flip charts or PowerPoint slides of the desired notes. A front row student could be drafted to "turn the pages" as required, while the presenter is free to place himself or herself within the room where it makes the most sense for both holding the audiences' attention and emphasizing the key points of the material.

Another possibility would be to use poster boards placed strategically around the room in place of the chalkboard. The posters could be prepared in advance but revealed at the most appropriate moment or left with some blank spaces to be filled in as the presenter moves about the room. Unveiling poster by poster carries with it a bit of surprise and suspense.

VENUE SEATING

The classroom seating arrangement—a factor that both influences audience attentiveness and constrains the presenter's use of space—deserves special attention. Presenters have long realized that audience members sitting in certain areas of the room tend to be more attentive and responsive than others. While this is due in part to the tendency of more communicative students to select seats within the presenter's direct line of sight, the seats learners *happen* to choose can be a factor that can impact their pattern of responsiveness. If we want to encourage an audience to be more responsive, we can either move ourselves so that we will come within their direct line of sight or move the students, or both. If the mountain (the entire class) cannot come to you, then you must go to the mountain!

As we think about the possibilities of moving the presenter, the image of Professor Keating (*Dead Poets Society*) again comes to mind. Keating evidently was aware of the need to place himself in the most attention-getting position in the room, despite the constraints of the prep school's classroom. So, we saw Keating in one memorable scene standing on the desk to deliver his presentation and, in another instance, kneeling down between rows of students so that they could huddle around him as he revealed an important insight about the lesson. While these situations may seem extreme, they illustrate the range of options available that a presenter may want to consider ahead of time in order to increase student attentiveness and learning.

Moving the audience, on the other hand, is a somewhat more complicated undertaking, not as open to extremes. With a reasonable number of students in a fair-sized classroom, for instance, the desks can be arranged in a circle in order to promote better communication. Even the most inflexible of arrangements—chairs and desks bolted to the floor—can still allow some rearrangement, however. We should not be too quick to concede defeat.

One presenter dealing with this most inflexible of seating arrangements developed a rotating seating chart. She had observed that certain seats in the room were "dead spots" because the audience members seated there had a poor view of the demonstration table at the front of the room. Certain other seats, however, were known to encourage the holders to be more attentive and responsive due to their bird's-eye view. The presenter adjusted to this constraint by numbering the seats and establishing a regular rotation so that each student would move up one number each week of the course. Thus, everyone had a turn at the "good seats."

Except for lab rooms with demonstration tables needing certain gas and water hookups, most rooms have a "front" only because that is where someone has arbitrarily placed the presenter's desk, wastebasket, or flag. In other words, the "front" can be moved just by moving those accoutrements. By occasionally doing so, we change the audiences' visual focus and thus renew their attention.

To a certain extent then, presenters, like actors, can block their positions within the confines of the "scenery" (e.g., chalkboard, projectors, desks, walls) in order to enhance audience attention, clarify focus, and establish intergroup relationships. Such blocking is done by carefully considering the nature and substance of the material to be presented and both the limitations and creative possibilities afforded by the available classroom space.

WHERE AUDIENCES CHOOSE TO SIT

You may want to share what research has to say about where someone chooses to sit in a classroom, lecture hall, or meeting room and what that seat position says, loud and clear, to a presenter. "First impressions are lasting impressions." Proximity to the presenter does have an impact on these first impressions.

All things being equal (of course, they never are), presenters size up audience members by whatever information they can quickly garner. One of the first bits of "evidence" as audiences enter the room is where they choose to sit. Good students tend to sit up front and toward the middle. These students will find it easier to develop a better relationship with the presenter, will receive more eye contact from him or her, are less likely to have their minds wander, will be less likely to use social media devices, will pay closer attention to what is being presented, and will more often be called upon to participate. All of this leads to greater learning on their part and more positive impressions being formed in the presenter's mind. It is a circle. One influences the other and so forth.

It may not be perfectly clear which came first—sitting up front contributing to the audience member learning more, or because the student learned more, he or she felt more engaged in the class and, therefore, chose to sit up front. There may be no direct cause-and-effect relationship between seat choice and student learning (I wish that it were that simple), but there may well be a link between the positive learning outcomes precipitated by the likelihood of greater eye contact, heightened attention being paid, and greater engagement opportunities for front seat occupiers. Seat choice may not guarantee greater student learning but, just like in Las Vegas, it might just give some students a bit of needed "edge."

SPONTANEOUS USE OF SPACE

Just as good actors can improvise on occasion, so good presenters can also make spontaneous decisions about where to place themselves, their audience, or their materials within the presentation space. Such decisions grow out of the presenter's continual sensitivity to the audience—their moods, levels of comprehension, and interests.

The point is that in order to use space most productively as a presentation tool, one must be comfortable enough in the space to move about it spontaneously as dictated by the material and audience responses. The presenter must be able and willing on a moment's notice to pick the spot that will enhance the relationship between him or her and the audience, and that will be most conducive to learning.

One could, for example, lean on the window sill, sit in a student desk, stand in the doorway, or walk slowly among the student desks. Each of these actions represents a break from the typical or expected presenter behavior of standing by the desk or lectern—a break that could change the audience's perception of the presenter's meaning or attitude.

For instance, in conducting a discussion, a presenter may convey an attitude of respecting and encouraging respondent opinion by sitting in a spare student desk instead of standing at the front of the room. Standing at the front, after all, reinforces the perception of the presenter as the person in charge. Thus, if the presenter notes that the audience seems reluctant to share ideas, it may be that a change in space relationship is needed. By moving to sit at eye level with the audience, or to crouch (needs strong knees to get back up again), a different power relationship is indicated.

Spontaneity, though, can lead to some hair-raising experiences—literally. While speaking before an audience in Darwin, Australia, I decided to emphasize a point by leaping onto one of the classroom tables. I thought, if Robin Williams can do it in *Dead Poets Society*, certainly I could do it in Darwin. There was "good" news and "bad" news. The "good" news was that the table held my two-hundred pounds. The almost "bad" news was that I had neglected to consider my six-foot two-inch height and the classroom's slowly turning ceiling fans! My head just missed those swirling blades. It was almost an event everyone, *except* perhaps me, would have remembered for a lifetime. The moral of the story is that creative use of classroom space is a pedagogical tool, and, like any tool, one needs to be careful in it use!

SUMMARY

Those in the theater apply the principles of proxemics to determine the best placement for each of the characters within a scene. This is done to help the audience better understand the playwright's intended point. The blocking of positions is planned and practiced well in advance of a performance, with some allowance for improvisational movement under certain circumstances.

Similarly, effective presenters should consider, prior to their presentations, the best placement of the people involved in the class to enhance the likelihood of meaningful learning. This planning may result in the preparation of certain teaching aids, in the rearrangement of furniture or seat assignments, or in rehearsed movements within the classroom space available. The presenter is always prepared to modify such plans and spontaneously make decisions about his or her placement in the room.

Just as an actor learns a part gradually, so a presenter should attempt to learn new approaches to using his space gradually. Jumping up onto a table like Robin Williams is not recommended as one of your first new approaches to space utilization. If it is, make sure that you have ceiling clearance and that your insurance is paid up!

15

Creative Entrances and Exits

INTRODUCTION

Well begun is half done.
—Anonymous

A verbal entrance can be as simple as having a catchy title. Think of a fictitious book or article title that you have thought about writing. Use your imagination. I, as a gutsy young professor, wrote a manuscript titled "Praise. It Beats Getting Hit in the Eye with a Stick. Maybe!" This rather outrageous sounding title grabbed the reviewers' attention. The paper was accepted and delivered at a professional conference and, with an editor-suggested modest change in title, published in a national journal. A physical entrance, too, can be just as engaging. Think *Seinfeld*'s Cosmo Kramer's spirited attention-grabbing entrances into Jerry's apartment. His entrances had pizzazz. Kramer may well be the king of memorable entrances and, as a point of trivia, he *entered* Seinfeld's apartment almost three hundred separate times!

As a contrast, think Fred Rogers, from *Mister Rogers' Neighborhood*, comforting, low-key and soothing entrance into his "home," five days a week, week in and week out. Drastically different entrances, but the effect was the same. We were hooked—Kramer for a couple of moments, Mister Rogers for a good half an hour. More on Mister Rogers, later.

One's entrance, let alone one's exit, can make a huge pedagogical difference. My job was to get you to read these first couple sentences of this chapter hoping to propel your eyes and your interest to the rest of the sentences in this chapter. Did it work?

ENTRANCES AND EXITS

As everyone knows from having taken a speech class, the opening and closing of any message are critical to its overall impact. You have sixty seconds, or less, to grab the attention and interest of your audience. The good news is that listeners are at the peak of their attentiveness at the opening and closing of an oral message.

Every message ought to begin in a way that captures the listener's interest and attention and ought to end in a way that makes the message memorable. We see the incorporation of these principles in advertising, public speaking, political speeches, lawyer summaries, newscaster deliveries, and, of course, in theater and films. When presenting, most often you are your own "opening" and "closing" act.

The earlier chapters on animation of body, animation in voice, humor, suspense and surprise, role-playing, use of props, and space utilization come into play here.

USING "HOOKS"

Hook, line, and sinker! This age-old combination works. But we are not talking about fishing. "The hook" is a strategy to get an audience engaged by introducing what's interesting about it in a brief, up-front manner. We will then "reel" them in to our intended message. Newscasters use several "hooks" at the start of their show (tease you with what you have to look forward to) and offer additional "hooks" just before going to commercial in order to keep you glued to their station. As presenters, you need to make the most of this precious time.

There are a variety of rhetorical "hooks" (or *WOWS*) that we can use to engage an audience. Among these are a story, question, quotation, visual, statistic, startling statement, personal anecdote, humor, expert opinion, sound effect, physical object, or testimonial.

If you don't hook them, like trout fishing, your story may be nothing more than, "You should have seen the one that got away." Too many audience members are "getting away" mentally. We need to grab them, we need to hook them. We need to "reel" them in. But, telling 'em what you are going to tell 'em might just deny you of a good "hook." Genard (2016) recommends simply starting off with one of your rhetorical "hooks," avoiding the temptation to provide an introduction. When you say too much about what you are going to talk about, you tend to lose people's attention. Just deliver the story or the quotation. Introducing it tends to water down its potency.

You can make or break your presentation, talk, or speech in the first sixty seconds—even less time if you are visible to audience members ahead of time. Remember, first impressions are lasting impressions. Even before you speak, the audience will be "sizing" you up using whatever stimuli is available to them, from your scuffed shoes to your tousled hair. When you begin your presentation, your opening seconds are where you can put into practice all that you learned in earlier chapters—importance of eye contact, a smile, body language, animation in voice, and more. It is now or never!

Dynamic presentations need a "Wow" factor—something that makes the audience pay attention and think, "Wow, I didn't know that!" Great presenters should shoot for more than one "Wow." As the presenter you know what is coming next, what "Wow" is just around the corner, and thus it helps energize you and maintain your enthusiasm (Boyd 2010).

USING LAW QUOTATIONS AS "HOOKS"

Imagine the spirited discussions in law, or any other discipline, that could emerge by a presenter providing audiences with a famous content-related quotation or two. Here are just a few. These quotations can act as an audience "hook."

- "If the law is against you, bang on the facts. If the facts are against you, bang on the law. If both are against you, bang on the table." (*Drop Dead Deva*, TV series, season 2, episode 8)
- "If there were no bad people there would be no good lawyers." (Charles Dickens)
- "Justice denied anywhere diminishes justice everywhere." (Martin Luther King Jr.)
- "Justice delayed is justice denied." (William E. Gladstone)
- "If you laid all of our laws end to end, there would be no end." (Mark Twain)
- "If we desire respect for the law, we must first make the law respectable." (Louis D. Brandeis, Justice)

ETHICS OF PLAYING MUSICAL CHAIRS

We wrestle by weight classes to help insure fairness to the competition. But in musical chairs, we play by survival-of-the-fittest! Wishing to demonstrate the ethics, or lack thereof, of playing a game such as musical chairs, as a "hook" a presenter planned to select a mismatch of fifteen players by gender, size, and perceived agility (i.e., human props) from the audience and actually play the game. Her institution stepped in, though, and said "Don't do it, our insurance would not cover any injuries likely to occur in such a spirited activity."

Not dissuaded, the presenter turned to "Plan B" and enlisted her audience to help write poems that captured the often unfairness of pitting those less able against those more able. This, too, was a "hook." Here is one of those poems.

Musical Chairs Poem
There's a children's game with music and motion that starts out with
    great promise.
But soon children realize the game is rigged so it is seen as a bit
    dishonest.
Big kids and small kids, those coordinated, those not,
Are pitted against each other, success for some a very long shot.
Where do all the children go when they cannot grab a chair?
They find themselves labeled as "out," and are told to stand over
    there!
As the pile of "losers" grows and grows, their fun begins to diminish.
At least in a game like kickball kids are all involved from
    start-to-finish.
More and more children are sidelined, realizing they should have
    fought harder at all cost.
The message they've learned is that their happiness derives from
    others' loss.
With every passing moment fewer and fewer kids will be having fun.
Their positive self-image, cooperation and confidence undone.
But if this is what really happens, why do kids continue to play?
Could it be that as children they simply do what adults say?
The final chair grabber is the one who clearly beat them all,
But maybe winning by beating weaker friends is not winning at all.

                                                  Anonymous

It turned out that this substitute activity about the ethics of pitting the weak against the strong caught fire, and audience members ended up writing their own poems centered around still other concepts and ideas. Later, they were collected, printed, bound, and shared!

PHYSICAL ENTRANCES

Many actors and actresses have created memorable, almost signature, entrances. As a presenter, keep in mind Gorman's (2012, 2) advice when making your entrance:

Stay relaxed, walk out on stage with good posture, head held high, and a steady, smooth gait. When you arrive at center stage, stop, smile, raise your eyebrows and slightly widen your eyes while you look around the room. A relaxed, open-face and body tells the audience that you are confident and comfortable with the information you're about to deliver. Since audience members will be reacting to any display of tension, your state of comfort also will relax and reassure them.

Recall Johnny Carson on *The Tonight Show*. For more years than most viewers can remember, Johnny Carson's late-night entrance would be announced by Ed McMahan saying, "Here's Johnny!" Sometimes Johnny would "fight" with the curtain while trying to emerge from backstage. Was this unplanned or was it really sort of a comedic entrance, setting the audience up for his humorous monologue that followed?

VERBAL ENTRANCES

The following scenarios demonstrate two attempts at providing a "hook"—one a bit bland, one a "grabber." In each scenario we have the "Professor" and the "Students." The topic is B. F. Skinner's behaviorism with which most readers have some background. Recall that behaviorists have at their disposal only four consequences that they can supply to someone in order to increase or decrease that someone's behavior in the future. It is too late for the past.

Here are two examples of how a class might start—two different verbal entrance "hooks."

Verbal Entrance 1
Professor: This morning we are going to compare and contrast Skinner's four consequences.

Apparently "this," and this alone, is the Professor's chosen "hook." Did it work? Did he grab their attention? Did he grab *your* attention? As the Professor starts to lecture, he senses several faint tweeting phone taps. His extra sensitive ears tell him that the tweets are messages to roommates to get themselves out of bed, skip breakfast, and run over to the lecture hall in their PJs in order to hear the Professor's, about to commence, stimulating four consequences lecture. Even you don't believe this, do you? There may be lots of tweets, but I would bet they are not about the upcoming presentation. This lecture may be heading downhill, and it has just begun. Few, if any audience members, have been "hooked."

Verbal Entrance 2
Professor: We are going to have an oral brief quiz. You may win a trip to the closed and rusted PA steel mill depicted in Tom Cruise's, 1989, "Born on the Fourth of July" movie. Are you game?

The "prize" is so outrageous that students know that it isn't for real. They realize that this is one of the professor's "hooks." It worked. They are curious. They are paying attention. After all, who would not want to win such a prize? Now that they are hooked, the surprising (another acting skill) dialogue continues.

Professor: Question #1, what is it called when one *supplies* a reward to a someone?

Student: [*said with assurance, Joe responds*] That's called "positive reinforcement."

Professor: Correct! Right on target. You are well on your way to winning. [*Laughter is heard.*]

Professor: Question #2, what is it called when one *removes* a reward from a someone?

Student: [*after a bit of awkward silence, Sue tentatively responds*] Punishment.

Professor: OK. How many of you agree with Sue that *removing* a reward from someone is correctly called punishment? [*Most of the audience raise their hands in agreement.*]

Professor: Excellent! [*hamming it up a bit*]. Excellent try! Unfortunately, that answer is incorrect. Sorry. [*The audience is more than a bit surprised, some actually shocked. A soft murmur, with some indignation, begins to spread.*]

Student: But, but, but! Why is it wrong?

Professor: It is incorrect because the definition of negative reinforcement is *removing* an aversive stimulus (e.g., pain or discomfort), not *removing* a reward.

Professor: Removing a reward is called "time-out." Think taking away a misbehaving child's TV privileges (or your new Porsche) for a certain amount of time. No pain has been *supplied*, only something found rewarding by the person has been removed.

Student: What, then, is punishment?

Professor: Punishment is the *supplying* of an aversive stimulus. Here one administers, or causes to happen, pain or discomfort.

Professor: [*To be sure that the audience grasps these operant conditioning terms, the presenter asks*] Do you look forward to receiving positive reinforcement?

Students: [*Now informed, almost in unison, the audience responds by correctly saying*] Yes!

Professor: Do you look forward to receiving negative reinforcement? [*For those who understand the correct definition of negative reinforcement, there is no surprise. They answer "yes." For those who remain confused about the definition, they find the "yes" answer still a bit surprising.*] (Tauber 1988)

Chances are that jumping right into the lecture, without telling 'em what you are going to tell 'em, and having students take this "quiz" as a hook and be promised an outrageous and humorous prize of traveling to a rusted steel mill, will have grabbed their attention, engaged them, and, thus, have them more effectively learn.

MUSICAL ENTRANCES

I don't suggest that you hire a band or orchestra to accompany your entrances and exits, although if you can pull it off, go for it. I am talking about using music to enhance your opening, closing, and the stuff in between. That music can come from the Internet or from a little digital pocket recorder that you would bring along to the presentation.

For instance, according to Dr. Sivarajah, let's say that you are talking about cancer treatment. It has the *good* (may well kill the targeted cancerous cells before they spread), the *bad* (possible damage to heart, kidney, bladder, or lung cells), and sometimes the *ugly* (hair loss, nausea, vomiting, or diarrhea). For Parenting 101, we have the *good* (positive parenting, logical consequences, firm limits or encouragement), the *bad* (yelling, frustration, shame and blame, too much praise, and child entitlement), and the *ugly* (corporal punishment, physical and verbal abuse).

These topics could be accompanied by a brief, but ear-catching entrance "hook." You could play thirty seconds of the theme song from Clint Eastwood's (the "Go ahead. Make my day" guy!) movie *The Good, the Bad, and the Ugly.* Play it loud. You will have their attention—attention directly related to the day's topic. Then, you can point out the connection between the day's presentation and Eastwood's movie title.

Do you want to go for a "full musical gusto?" Tell the students that the topic today is so important that it just must be delivered with fanfare! Play sixty seconds of the main theme from *Star Wars*, play sixty seconds of *The Phantom of the Opera*, or play thirty seconds of *Eye of the Tiger* by Survivor (instrumental). This will get their blood flowing! Make sure, though, that your exciting presentation lives up to the tease of the exciting music. Want the entrance to be a bit lighter? I often lighten the mood of my day's presentation by playing thirty seconds of James Harriot's *All Creatures Great and Small* theme, or the opening theme song from *The Andy Griffith Show* starring Andy Griffith, Ronnie Howard, and bumbling Barney Fife, played by Don Knotts.

Your music selections are endless. Use your creativity to select snippets of selections that can enhance your dynamic delivery, and through the selection of song lyrics, your content. Occasionally I try to squeeze in Susan Boyle's, "I Dreamed a Dream" performance, one where the judges were brought to tears and to their feet! Thirty seconds of music "has

charms to soothe the savage beast." Could your audience use some soothing? Could you?

Other ways to use music in a presentation is to select offerings with a
message related to the topic of the day. Take, for instance, coping with cancer. Guitarist Tom Searle wrote a song about skin cancer when he had surgery to address the melanoma on his leg. Initially, upon learning the
doctor's diagnosis, he said that as in *Harry Potter* you are not supposed to
mention the name Voldemort. He felt that way about the big "C"
word—*cancer*! Nick Jonas, from the Jonas Brothers, wrote the song, "A Little Bit Longer," to help him deal with his Type 1 diabetes. Elton John wrote
a moving song about AIDS. Dolly Parton wrote the song, "Chemo Hero,"
complete with animations, on behalf of her young niece who had con-
tracted leukemia.

In 2007, Mary Chapin Carpenter was diagnosed with pulmonary
embolism—blood clots in her lungs. Her "Holding Up the Sky" song lyrics
speak to her feeling completely helpless. Surely, many patients feel this
way, too. Sheryl Crow sings the song "Make it Go Away (Radiation Song)"
about undergoing treatment for breast cancer. Could listening to this song
help care givers step into her shoes for just a bit? The seemingly prehistoric
1959 Coasters song "Poison Ivy," first thought to be about the itchy plant
irritation that could be cleared with lots of calamine lotion, was really
a metaphor for a sexually transmitted disease—the clap. Thanks to
Dr. Sivarajah for her contributions to these examples.

The potential for incorporating music and accompanying lyrics reflecting your specialty into any presentation is limitless. These all can contribute to exciting entrances, memorable exits, and surprising revelations.
The question, then, is not "Why would I want to introduce music and
its accompanying lyrics into my presenting?" The real question is
"Why not?"

Enlist your audience to help locate content-related musical examples
and then contribute them to your ever-growing "Props Box."

MISTER ROGERS' NEIGHBORHOOD

Let's again refer to Fred Rogers, from *Mister Rogers' Neighborhood*, and
his low-key and soothing invitation to us to enter his "home." His program,
as of 2018, just passed the fifty-year mark and, although Mister Rogers is
no longer alive, Fred's program lives on.

Mister Rogers was enthusiastic in his own way; you could tell he had a
passion for what he was doing and for the information that he was delivering. There was a sparkle in his eyes. He really wanted us to be his special
guest. It was clear, too, that he was a caring person and someone who knew

how to listen. I have just described characteristics of a great presenter. Entrances do make a difference, whether on television, screen, stage, or in boardrooms and classrooms. Fred's daily *Mister Rogers' Neighborhood* entrance "hooked" all of us.

The commonly held view, as you have been repeatedly told, is that audiences today have an attention span of just fifteen minutes. Yet, children remained "glued" to Mister Rogers' half-hour educational television programs. I believe that quality programming and good delivery, like good lecturing, speaking, or presenting, are perfectly capable of engaging any audience for more than fifteen minutes!

WHAT'S IN A NAME OR TITLE?

"What's in a name?" The answer is often "everything!" Because names or titles are often the first thing we know about someone or something, they demand our attention. They are something directly under our control. Why not take advantage of it even if the advantage is slight? If you were a player in a Las Vegas casino, you would more likely be a winner if you had even a "slight advantage" over that of the house.

Would you go to a movie titled, *Gone with the Breeze, The Maltese Palmetto Bug*, or *Snow White and Just One Dwarf*? Probably not. Just like in a classroom, movie actors must *get* the audience's attention before they can *hold* their attention for the hour or more movie or play. A catchy, surprising, snappy, sexy, emotions-tugging title can help with the "get" part.

Actors and actresses have long known the value of "what's in a name." Would you put down good money to view a film starring Oscar and Emmy winning Ilyena Lydia Vasilievna Mironov? I bet not. This actually is the given name of actress Dame Helen Mirren! A good name, a strong name, or a powerful name can make the difference between recognition, fame, and fortune or obscurity and poverty. What happens if you are not born with an engaging name? No problem, change it. Here are some actors' and actresses' stage names and their given names.

- Michael Caine   Maurice Micklewhite
- Hulk Hogan   Terry Jean Bollette
- Kirk Douglas   Issur Danielovitch Demsky
- Dame Helen Mirren   Ilyena Lydia Vasilievna Mironov
- Cary Grant   Archibald Alexander Leach
- Lady Gaga   Stefani Joanne Angelina Germanotta
- Elton John   Reginald Kenneth Dwight

I am not suggesting that you change your name in order to better engage audiences. This example is simply to show the power behind "what's in a name or title." You don't need to change your name, but you might decide to liven up the title of your lecture, submitted manuscript, conference presentation, or paper now that you see the power (or lack of) it can project.

In addition to the serious side of "what's in a name," a good deal of humor can be found in titles for conference presentations, scholarly papers, and less formal lectures. It could be used as attention-getting verbal props, as entrance "hooks," or simply as content-related humor. As stressed in the chapter on humor, students "catching" the nuance of these creative titles indicates that they grasp the concepts behind the title.

For contrast purposes, Dr. Sivarajah starts us off with a selection of accurate, but a bit on the bland side, presentation titles. An examination of several 2018 medical conferences, Gynecology, Clinical Neurology, and Body Imaging revealed these less-than-exciting program titles. Among those included were:

- Osteoporosis for the Gynecologist
- Contraception 2018: What Do I Need to Know?
- Adnexal Masses: The Guidelines Have Changed
- SERMs and SPRMs: What's Now? What's Next?
- Update on Management of Spine Diseases
- CT Angiography: What's New
- Pediatric Female Pelvis

There is every reason to believe that each of these conference sessions would be informative and, no doubt, worth attending. The point, though, is that you first need to "get them through the door." Your session, paper, or presentation title is the equivalent of your theater marquee. It is advertisement to potential customers—attendees or readers.

Here are just a few, may I say, more creative titles. You might shoot for presentation titles that are a little more engaging than those already mentioned and maybe a little less cutesy than those that follow. You decide. It is your presentation, conference session, or professional paper.

- Chickens Prefer Beautiful Humans
- Ovulatory Cycle Effects on Tip Earnings by Lap Dancers: Economic Evidence for Human Estrus?
- From Urethra with Shove: Bladder Foreign Bodies, A Case Report and Review
- 5 TIWIKLY Things I Wish I Knew Last Year

- A Comparison of Jump Performances of the Dog Flea and the Cat Flea
- Sword Swallowing and Its Side Effects
- Pressures Produced When Penguins Pooh—Calculations on Avian Defecation
- Cure for a Headache [Note, the presenter wore a full woodpecker head-dress (prop) while accepting his 2006 Nobel Prize in Ornithology.]

Which one of the titles was made up by me? None!

Surely playwrights and movie producers spend time, effort, and money trying to come up with play and movie titles that they believe will capture an audience's attention. Presenters should do the same thing. Consider the title of George Plitnik's three-credit university honors seminar. This Professor of Physics labels his course, "The Science of Harry Potter." He could have named it "Physics 101." Which course title do you believe will best capture his audience's initial attention? Plitnik's demanding course is always full—and not just with engineering and science students!

What's in a name? When Japanese sports cars first came into the United States, Datsun (now called Nissan) imported and named its contender Fair Lady. This was a bad choice, a very bad choice. It had to compete with European cars that had "racy" sounding names, such as MG, TR-6, BMW, and JAG. And, at the time, the United States was offering muscle cars with names such as GTO, Barracuda, and BOSS Mustang. What chance did a sports car called Fair Lady have? Not much. What's in a name? A lot!

CRAFTING A TITLE

On the more serious side of the topic of crafting a presentation title, here are some suggestions for getting people to flock to your presentation.

- Promise benefits

  Title: *Projecting Enthusiasm and Using the Acting/Performance Skills Presented in This Book Will Make You a More Dynamic Presenter*

  You're thinking: I know that I am enthusiastic about what I present. I feel it *inside*. I probably should show it more on the *outside*. Perhaps these acting and performance skills can help me.

- Promise a story

  Title: *Why Is It That Sea Turtles Seem to Have No Fun: A Story in Itself?*

  You're thinking: I don't really think all that often about sea turtles, but it does seem a shame that they don't have any fun. I wonder why that is the case?

- Put a number at the front

  Title: *What Are the Three Most Effective Pain Reliever Treatments?*

  You're thinking: I know the subject fairly well, but I probably should check out what others believe are the three *most* important treatments. What's the harm?

- Provoke curiosity

  Title: *Praise: It Beats Getting Hit in the Eye with a Stick. Maybe!*

  You're thinking: How could praise possibly be so savagely attacked? I want to hear what this guy says! I think that he is full of "ka gee, gee" beads (term for full of you know what).

- Arouse concern

  Title: *Are you Using Outdated Diabetes Medications for Your Patients?*

  You're thinking: Just maybe the medications or treatments that I am currently using may not be the best for my patients. I'll attend and find out for sure.

FOR THE LOVE OF THREE

Humans seem to have a love of "three" of anything, even three of the same words as in the three most important words in real estate—*location, location, location.* Consider "the three little pigs," "the three wise men," "Goldilocks and the three bears," "the good, the bad, and the ugly," "blood, sweat, and tears," "lights, camera, action," "that's the truth, the whole truth, and nothing but the truth," "reading, writing, and arithmetic," "stop, look, and listen," "friends, Romans, countrymen," and "government of the people, by the people, for the people."

For some reason three, not two or four or five, is the magic number. Knowing this, presenters could include the magic number three in presentation titles to help get people in the door, and then insert three-word sequences within their presentation, itself, to better hold the audience's attention. These sequences of three become a powerful entrance "hook."

ENTRANCE RITUALS

The presenter's entrance to his or her venue is no less important than that of the actor's entrance onto the stage (Greenberg and Miller 1991). Both signal, or at least should signal, that it is time for something to happen. A performance is to begin, a presentation is to commence, or a meeting is to start. When starting a meeting, one of my deans would walk to the front of the room, remove his watch, and place it on the lectern in front of him. Given that every room on campus had a large wall clock, why did he need to place his watch in front of him? He used it to signal to faculty that it was time to start the meeting. We got the message.

For those who must meet with the same audience over and over, a consistent entrance (opening line or routine) may be recommended. It certainly worked for Mister Rogers. What ritualistic entrances or opening lines do you use? Which, with your creative hat on, could you use?

One educator I know, saving his voice, rings a musical triangle to signal the starting of class. Its tinkling sound travels to all corners of the room. In the theater, lights are dimmed to signal it is time to begin. According to Greenberg and Miller, "if the entrance does not get the audience's attention, it should be reassessed" (1991, 435). Note, the use of a normal entrance (or exit) routine does not discount the need to insert *wow*-generating "hooks." There is room for both.

ENTRANCE PAGEANTRY

Recall the grand beginnings so carefully crafted for the Olympic Games of the modern era. The pageantry, the torch lighting, the parades of athletes all are coordinated to draw in the viewer and heighten his or her expectations of the events to come. The same effect is created by the dramatic arrival of the stars at a movie premiere, the sweeping searchlight openings of a Chicago Bulls home game and the trumpet blasts announcing the play's beginning at the Stratford Festival in Canada. The audience is virtually on the edge of their seats, ready to receive an exciting performance!

The raising of a curtain in the theater is an attention-getter; it is a signal that one's focus should be directed toward the stage. It signals something is about to happen; something is about to be revealed! Perhaps presenters could duplicate the positive effects of raising a curtain.

One math teacher brings his daughter's toy plastic stage (about 18″ by 18″)—complete with a curtain that can be opened and closed. We are told that his daughter makes him "rent it" from her. With the curtain closed, he places the plastic stage on the edge of his desk prompting a bit of "suspense" in the audience's mind. When it is time to start class, with a bit of exaggerated fanfare, he raises the curtain, the presentation's title is revealed, and the festivities begin. Corny? Yes, but it works.

Presenters should consider using the elements of suspense and surprise when they enter. What successful entertainer would simply, without fanfare, walk onto a stage? Rock stars have their accompanying fireworks and smoke, live theater has its dimming of the house lights and the raising of the stage curtain, and *SNL* television has its "Live from New York, it's Saturday Night!"

Although it is usually preferable for presenters to arrive well before its official starting time, an occasional variance from such expected promptness can be surprising and suspense-building. What could the presenter be up to? It is almost time to start.

A presenter might also work on varying how he or she enters the room. Whereas predictability breeds contentment, the unexpected breeds attentiveness. One could burst into the room and, while rapidly walking to the front, begin presenting. Consider varying exits, too.

A PRESENTER'S MARQUEE

The classroom should be an entrance into the world,
not an escape from it.
—John Ciardi

Most clubs, theaters, and cinemas like to boldly advertise. The advertisement is meant to capture the attention of passersby and act as an invitation to enter. Their most visible form of advertisement often is their marquee.

Why shouldn't presenters use a marquee—advertising to audiences a bit of what they are in store for? A presenter could place a manageable-sized homemade marquee, made from poster board or cardboard, on the entrance door. It could be painted; it could have a "slot" to insert presenter-prepared and regularly changed messages (e.g., snappy title for the day's presentation). If the idea will not work for every presenter, it does not mean that it can't work for some of them.

For those marquees designed to permit the words to be regularly changed, audiences can experience a sense of anticipation and wonder each time they see the marquee and the messages displayed on it. What does Dr. Knouse's marquee mean by the words, "Shakespeare on rye served today?" What does Mr. Bennett mean when he advertises, "Roaches: Man's best friend!" What does Ms. Specht mean by her marquee that says, "Lincoln: What did he really keep under his stove top hat?" What does Attorney Hogg mean by saying, "In a showdown, who would win, Ben Matlock or Perry Mason?" Audiences don't know for sure what these marquee messages mean, but they want to step inside and find out. This idea, like many of the attention-getting ideas in the book, are a form of put-ons, but put-ons for a purpose. They grab the audience's attention and run with it!

ENDING ON A HIGH NOTE

Every exit is an entrance somewhere else.
—Tom Stoppard

According to Henry Wadsworth Longfellow, "great is the art of beginning, but greater is the art of ending." When it comes to ending each concert, who can forget the way that Elvis Presley did it? After his last song and despite raucous applause demanding still more, over the loud speaker it is announced, "Elvis has left the building!"

Creative and purposeful presenter exits are just as important as their entrance counterparts. Yet, according to Maier and Panitz (1996), in their article "End on a High Note," the pedagogical literature is surprisingly sparse on the topic of presentation endings. Two decades later, the situation has not improved. Fortunately, creative presenters, equipped with the acting and performance skills highlighted in this text, can strike out on their own to fill this ending or exit void.

The etiquette of ending a class, meeting, or presentation should be discussed, even negotiated. As the presenter you, too, would be expected to abide by the ending "rules"—such as ending on time. Knowing that the session is coming to a close, you can plan for it. You should avoid trying to "cram" still more information in at the last moment. No one will be listening. It would be better to summarize (you or the audience) what was presented today or what is still confusing. This is also a great time to provide a "hook" for your next presentation.

Presenters may want to avoid the commonly delivered closing statement, "Now, in conclusion . . ." This signals to some audience members that at that very moment class is over. Notebooks begin to close, one after another, filling the last moments of class with a shuffling sound. One professor anticipates this audience behavior and instructs them, in unison, to "slam their books closed." Once the books have closed—taking just a second or two—the remainder of the time is available for the presenter's concluding remarks. The ending ideas can be endless. Planning your entrances and exits is just as important as planning the lesson sandwiched in between.

STAGE FRIGHT

It's all right to have butterflies in your stomach.
Just get them to fly in formation.
—Rob Gilbert

Before you step onto your version of a stage, remember Mark Twain's admonition, "There are only two types of speakers in the world. 1. The nervous type and, 2. Liars!" I take it that you are not the latter; therefore, along with most of the world, you must be the former.

Presenting on the edge can be edgy. There will never be a dull moment. Presenters, even with the best planned lessons, must improvise from day to day because no two days, or two audiences, are ever the same. Too often presenters essentially attempt to follow a script. Yet, in practice life is often spontaneous. One must be prepared to go off-script. Thinking on one's feet is often required.

For new teachers and presenters, dealing with subject matter that is fresh to them where, quite literally, they may be just one step ahead of the learners, can be both daunting and exciting (Showalter 2003). A case of stage fright can occur. Technically it is called "aphonia" or the inability to speak. There is, of course, a medical definition of it, but if it happens to us, we know it, we don't need a definition.

Some presenters find even walking into a presentation venue anxiety laden. One professor reports that quickened and shallow breathing and a headache often accompanied him through the door. Still another professor—actually, me—recalls having bad dreams where he forgot to go to his class or that he arrived at class completely unprepared. A first-grade teacher in a private school dreams that she is in front of the class in her underwear. She realizes that something is not right, but she doesn't know what it is.

A cartoon viewed recently shows a dad apparently trying to get, what we think is his child, out from under the bed on the first day of school. He is saying "Come on, come on, honey." You can hear the "child" screaming, "I won't go. You can't make me!" The dad soothingly exclaims, "Now honey [actually it is his wife under the bed] you are the teacher and you have to go to school."

This stress is not unique to presenters. Sometimes called "performance anxiety," it also is shared with athletes, entertainers, and other speakers. Bill Russell, perhaps the greatest basketball player ever, regularly threw up before a game. It got to the point where it was a "good luck charm," and the team would not leave the locker room until the event occurred. Hall of Fame quarterback, Jim Kelly, often threw up before a game. Rihanna, Adele, and Jennifer Lawrence have experienced stage fright. You can add Cher, Brian Wilson, and Barbra Streisand, who avoided live performances for years.

How do people describe their stage fright? Probably they describe it much the same way that you do. They use "feeling" words such as:

> Jitters, apprehension, terror!, absolute terror!, anxious, dry mouth, racing pulse, butterflies, sweaty palms, ill-prepared, fear of messing up, will they accept me?, about to throw up!, shallowness of breath, digestive system goes berserk, breathing becomes rapid, soaked armpits, everyone will see me as a phony, knees like rubber, "Please God, let me get through this!" or "I should have become a monk!"

It does little good to tell such anxious people to "relax," "calm down," "don't worry," or "take it easy." What is needed, and what I have tried to do in this book, is to offer readers proven delivery strategies that can help them to enter the classroom or other presentation venue with greater confidence. These skills, along with knowing one's subject matter, should help ameliorate stage fright concerns.

As you take these first steps along the path toward great presenting, whether you are or are not enthusiastic, *act* that way! The skills presented in Part II of this book hopefully helped you to convincingly *act* that way. A philosophical question arises, "Which came first, actions or enthusiasm?" William James says that you will discover, "I don't *act* this way because I'm enthusiastic; I'm enthusiastic because I *act* that way." Either way, just make it happen. Don't waste time sitting and waiting to be inspired. Newman (n.d.) notes, "The great composer does not set to work because he is inspired but becomes inspired because he is working." Get ready for the ride of your life as you begin your work in the preparation and delivery of dynamic presentations.

SHOWTIME!

> *I have stage fright every single concert I've done. I have at least four or five minutes of it. It's absolute living hell.*
> —Brian Wilson

Walk on stage with a purpose, a presence, a positive posture, and confidence. Smile, establish eye contact with a couple people in the audience, stand tall. If necessary, "fake it until you make it." This is your opportunity to mimic, in fact exaggerate, those characteristics of successful presenters. Audiences consciously—or not—absorb the demeanor of the presenter as well as aspects of delivery, such as his or her tone of voice and attitude (Wright 2010). Establish a positive presence.

Consider skipping the normally uttered, "Good morning. Today we are going to do such-and-such." Simply get straight into your presentation, immediately launching your audience-capturing "entrance" or "hook" to grab their attention. Once you start your presentation, especially if you have prepared well and have opened with an attention-getting hook, you will calm down. Athletes calm down after that first tackle, that first pitch, or that drive toward hole number 1. Actors and other performers, too, calm down after the show begins. In each case, being well prepared helps carry the day.

Because we have been "speaking" all of our lives, it seems strange that so many of us experience "stage fright" which, at its basis, is all about speaking. Yet, a colleague recently wrote in an email, "Public speaking is not one of my natural talents." The uplifting part of the email came at the end when, after formally examining some of the strategies successful presenters use, he said, "I'm (now) motivated to use some of the presentation strategies that we discussed."

And, if you still are nervous, be truthful. Tell the audience, in a matter of fact fashion, that you are a bit nervous. Just mention it, don't dwell on it. You are not looking for pity, but for compassion. The audience knows how scary public speaking can be. Audiences like underdogs and will cut you some slack.

Don't feel too sorry for yourself if public speaking triggers a bout of stage fright. Take solace in the fact that some of the very people in the audience are experiencing the same feeling. More than one of them is sitting out there praying that you do not call on them, not because they don't know the material, but because their response would be a form of public speaking (Fish 2012).

You are about to finish reading this book. Now, carefully consider just how you might better incorporate the specific acting and presentation skills from Part II into your presenting. Hopefully, you are "chomping at the bit" to get in there and put them to use. Your thoughts will be, "Move aside stage fright, I'm coming through!

SUMMARY

As a tribute to *Mister Rogers' Neighborhood*, I will ask Fred Rogers to exit this chapter as he did each episode of his show. "You make each day a special day. You know why? By just being you. There's no person in the world like you; and I like you just the way you are."

Let us tell you a brief story about Mr. Rogers. One day he parked his older Chevy on a street close to the PBS studio in Pittsburgh. After a day's taping, he came out to find the car gone. He filed a police report, and the story was picked up by the news media. Within two days, his car was returned to the exact spot where it had been stolen with a note on the dash, "If we'd known it was yours, we never would have taken it."

We thank you, Fred, for sharing your life with us. We are better for it. You made us feel important and special. Your entrances & exits were gracious, calming, and welcoming. They set the stage for all the great stuff that you squeezed in between. We hope we can all model for others what you modeled for us!

16

Behind the Scenes

INTRODUCTION

> *Take the first step in faith. You don't have to see the whole staircase, just take the first step.*
> —Martin Luther King Jr.

An actor is vividly aware that the performance seen by the audience is a mere fraction of the work involved in staging a play. It is an *important* fraction, but still a fraction. The bulk of the work happens "behind the scenes" out of sight—just like the bulk of an iceberg is out of sight underwater. That is the reminder for presenters: most of the work that makes a presentation come alive happens behind the scenes. Some of this "behind the scenes" work is physical and some of it is mental. Both are necessary to take that all-important step of crossing the presentation threshold—day after day.

WORK BEHIND THE SCENES

For an actor, the behind the scenes category includes endless hours of personal preparation. In most trades, the rule-of-thumb is measure twice and cut once. Once a mistake is made, it is difficult or impossible to undo. Whereas the carpenter might be able to spackle or glue to repair, as a presenter you cannot get back those wasted minutes (and the audience's first impressions of you) due to a lack of preparation.

When one thinks of preparation about presenting, content mastery is probably what comes to mind. Content mastery certainly is vital, but this book focuses on the *projected* enthusiastic delivery of that content. In this instance, preparation refers to preparing for the *act* of presenting, not preparing the subject matter per se. Such preparation requires attention to the presenter's "spirit," if you will. It is the presenter's task to create the motivation that allows his or her *passion* and *enthusiasm* for the subject matter and the act of presenting to be evident.

Capturing that passion is what internal preparation is all about. Like actors, presenters must feel a commitment to express themselves before going on their version of a stage. That commitment is what gives presenters self-confidence. Amid the many pressures that accompany presenting—too little time, too little training, too many other duties—presenters must remind themselves *why* they got into their chosen field. It is the magic of learning, the challenge to make a difference, the wonder of knowledge. Do these reasons sound familiar? Every presenter who can capture that passion within is prepared to handle the tools and techniques of successful presenting.

BEHIND THE SCENES SUGGESTIONS

Confidence is preparation. Everything else is beyond your control.
—Richard Kline

The time behind the scene is your own. Given institution or company restraints, what you do with that time is up to you. Here are some suggestions.

- Review this book. Try to recapture your thoughts while reviewing each chapter.

- Realize that you have something to offer the audience. You don't have to know it *all*.

- You do not need to eliminate *all* fear, nervousness, and anxiety. A bit of fear is actually a terrific desire to do well! Presenters need to make that nervous energy an ally rather than an enemy.

- Good preparation is one of the best antidotes to feelings of anxiety—do not leave the preparation until the last minute. Get your presentation down pat.

- Check out the venue where you will present. Are the needed materials there—chalk, overhead, PowerPoint projector, screen darkening blinds? What is your "plan B" if the resources you expected to be present are not there?

- Form an argument to defend the use of acting and performance skills in your presentations. By forming your own argument (e.g., pedagogical reasons) you not only will better convince yourself, you will be in a better position to respond to others who might try to dismiss the value of you using these skills.

- Seriously consider taking an Introduction to Acting 101 course at your own or at a nearby college or university. Working with a community theater, too, may be helpful. Use the buddy system—enroll with a friend! You will have a blast! Such a modest investment of your time and energy will reap endless pedagogical benefits throughout your entire career.

- Practice, practice, practice—it is supposed to make perfect. No actor would go on stage without having first rehearsed his or her lines and delivery. Why would you? If presenting is a significant part of your career, launch it successfully. Do all that you can do to succeed the first few times because "nothing breeds success like success!"

- With colleagues, review the annoying habits that previous presenters of yours may have had. Because everyone has a history of having had some bad presenters or those with distracting habits, everyone in the group should have something to contribute. Soon, colleagues will be starting out their turn by saying, "Gee! You think that your presenter was bad. Just wait until you hear about my example."

- Get together with a few colleagues and take turns presenting a brief presentation or informal talk to each other on a topic representing your subject area or other area of interest. Five minutes or so presentations should be enough. Critique each other's presentation—not for what they said, but for *how* they said it—how they used, or could have used, one or more of the dynamic presentation skills in this text. Start off your critique with, "Have you considered using . . . ," "I wonder how effective it would have been if you had . . . "?

- With colleagues, discuss the often-delivered advice to new, anxious, presenters, "Just go in there and be yourself." Now that you have read this text, do you find this advice useful? If so, why? If not, why not?

Remember, even the best presenters make mistakes. The world will not stop spinning—I guarantee it. If you pick up and continue, so will the audience.

Have you noticed that most, if not all, of these suggestions are designed to loosen you up and are fun to do? After all, learning is *fun*(damental)! These suggestions are especially fun to do when you can do them with others. When you get to use what you have practiced, their benefit can be fun—fun for you and fun for your audience.

SUMMARY

Presenting is harder than it looks! Don't let anyone tell you otherwise. Stepping across that presentation threshold takes courage. And to take this action as a professional, it also requires knowledge, preparation, and practice. Perhaps the Boy Scouts said it best when they tell their members, "Be Prepared." This is good advice for all of us to follow. I hope that the knowledge and skills presented in this text will help in your preparation.

PART III

Engage Master Presenters

Assuming one knows his or her content, the *key* to dynamic presenting is being enthusiastic on the inside and projecting it on the outside! You have read this statement several times. I keep repeating it because it is true.

Now that you know the importance of projected presenter enthusiasm, and you know the variety of skills that dynamic presenters use to convey that enthusiasm, you are well prepared to engage master presenters—both by talking with them and by watching them in action. At this stage, you know better what to listen and look for. You also are prepared to ask pertinent pedagogically oriented follow-up and clarifying questions of them.

17

Engage the Masters: Learn from Them

INTRODUCTION

> *Asking for help does not mean that we are weak or incompetent.*
> *It usually indicates an advanced level of honesty and intelligence.*
> —Anne Wilson Schaef

"Exercise power over me. Please! Keep doing it. It feels so good!" Now it may be true that most people claim they do not like it when power is exerted over them, but they are wrong. It depends upon the type of power being wielded. The explanation follows.

French and Raven (Tauber 1985) identified five social bases of power that each of us either wield on others or allow others to wield on us. They include coercive (ability to supply or remove pain), reward (ability to supply or remove pleasure), legitimate (flows from one's position), referent (personal power), and expert (recognition of other's special knowledge or skills). Coercive and reward power reflect authoritarian (e.g., B. F. Skinner) views. The goal is to control. Referent and expert power represent more humanistic (e.g., Carl R. Rogers) views. Their goal is to influence.

Most people, if given a choice, resist the attempted control of coercive and reward powers. Sometimes they fight back, sometimes they try to escape, but the most debilitating of all, sometimes they just sit and take it. None of these responses are healthy or conducive to learning. Coercive and reward powers, in other words, control, work only so long. At some point, most healthy people move beyond the grasp of the controller. A common example can be found in the homes of those who have children, where, at a neighborhood outing, a parent can be heard to lament, "I don't know what happened. Johnny used to listen to me. Now, I may as well be talking to the wall. I've lost control!"

On the other hand, people are willing to let themselves be influenced by referent and expert power. In fact, people love it when these two power bases are wielded on them! Referent power, the most powerful of the five power bases, works because the other person identifies, personally, with the power wielder. He or she respects the power wielder as a person and wants to emulate him or her. A sense of oneness exists. I had Mr. John Sabol as my high school physics teacher. He was demanding, fair, gave no special favors to cheerleaders or athletes, was enthusiastic about his subject matter, and conveyed to us that we had it in us to succeed. I wanted to be just like him—hence, I majored in physics. I greatly appreciated Mr. Sabol's wielding of referent power.

With respect to expert power, people, including me, actively seek out those with expert skills or unique knowledge that they wish to acquire. Want to learn the ins and outs of playing pickleball? Take Pickleball 101 from one of the masters. Want to seek truth or understand the meaning of life? Sit at the feet of a mountaintop guru. Want to start a small business? Seek out experts in that area. You get the idea. We simply love it when wanted expert power is wielded on us.

As presenters, you are in a unique position to capitalize upon both referent and expert power. More than likely your audience identifies with you because of your shared interest in a subject area and because they want to acquire as much of your expertise as they can. Being enthusiastic about what you are presenting (and projecting it) will have an audience wanting to be more like you, as a person, and will have them appreciative of the knowledge, skills, and expertise you can impart.

NO SERIOUS CHALLENGE TO THIS BOOK'S PREMISE

Be smart enough to know when you need help, and
brave enough to ask for it.
—Anonymous

I have yet to meet an effective presenter who seriously challenges the argument that a parallel exists between acting, teaching, and presenting. Further, most presenters agree that they could become more engaging and dynamic presenters by using more acting and performance skills. The question now becomes, where are presenters to go to learn these skills? Hopefully, this book has helped.

KNOCK ON THEIR DOORS; PICK UP YOUR PHONE

Courage is doing what you're afraid to do. There can be no courage unless you're scared.
—Edward Vernon Rick

The point is that there are recognized expert presenters out there, and we need to knock on their doors. Some experts are nearby, some further afield. Some are at our own institution, some at other institutions. Some are in our own specialty, some in unrelated fields. We need to watch them, watch them with a more discerning eye now that we have read this book, learned the power of enthusiasm and the acting and performance skills that can be used to project that enthusiasm. Now that you are knowledgeable of these skills, you are very likely to see them.

We need to approach these experts and engage them in a conversation about dynamic presentation practices, specifically what do they do that engages and holds the attention of an audience. We need to sit in on their presentations, classes, or other oratory venues so that we can see for ourselves what they do that is so captivating. We can take from discussions with, and observations of, these "dynamic presenters" what we think would be useful in further developing our presenter-self, our *dynamic* presenter persona.

Once you have located presenting "experts," read samplings of their work, use a phone call to learn firsthand still more information, and, if possible, schedule a time to meet with them. At a minimum, you are establishing "an old boys' (or girls') network" that you can turn to over and over throughout your career. Once these more widespread contacts have been made, many professional opportunities can emerge besides having met new colleagues—perhaps shared publications, invites to conferences, sources of new ideas, sites for sabbaticals, and so on.

THEY HAVE WALKED IN YOUR SHOES

We stand on the shoulders of those who came before us.
—Gerald J. Popek

Clearly, one of the best ways to become an amazing presenter is to observe presenters who have excellent delivery reputations (Mack, Bloom, and Foster 2017). These "experts" have walked in your shoes. Few, if any, of them entered their respective profession knowing the importance of *projecting* enthusiasm and having mastered the dynamic delivery skills presented in earlier chapters. We could, through trial-and-error, without turning to expert presenters for guidance, learn the hard way what does and does not work in our deliveries. But, starting from a Locke's tabula rasa, or "blank slate," and doing it all ourselves is neither sensible nor efficient. It is like inventing the wheel, which has long since been invented! You should be looking for ways to incorporate the dynamic delivery skills into your presentations.

HUMILITY AND CURIOUSNESS

Life is a long lesson in humility.
—James M. Barrie

Approaching colleagues or others who are recognized as expert presenters can be a bit humbling. You might find it hard to acknowledge that you could use some help. Some see asking for help as a sign of weakness. Yet, seeking help regarding presenting is a sign of both humility and curiousness. Both are virtues. It's that very quality of humility that keeps you grounded when your head begins to swell. It is that very quality of curiousness that probably prompted you to pursue your current career. You have everything to gain from learning from others. Approach them. Ask for their help. Most will be flattered that you asked. You learned most of what you know of your craft from others; you can learn much of what you need to know about dynamic presenting from others, too.

"OBJECTION, YOUR HONOR"

What you are interested in you will see, and you will see it everywhere. It was there before, but now you are tuned into it. If you are interested in how one engages and captivates an audience, you need look no further than a politician stumping for votes, a preacher delivering a spirited sermon, actors and actresses on stage at a play, or a courtroom lawyer scene with *Perry Mason, Matlock,* or most recently *Bull.* You will see body language, gestures, selective eye contact, raised eyebrows, suspense, surprise, a little storytelling, humor, use of props, and entrances and exits, if only shown by the lawyer leaving the witness stand saying in an exaggerated utterance, "I have nothing more for *this* witness!" He walks away, and for the jury's benefit, shakes his head in disgust. It is all an *"act"* performed for the jury!

STOP SPINNING YOUR WHEELS

William Glasser, in his book *Choice Theory* (1999), tells the reader to try something else if what you are doing is not working—don't just keep doing the same unproductive thing over and over. He is amazed how committed some people are to repeating actions that have not proved fruitful. He describes a person stuck in the snow with his tires beginning to spin. The driver tries to extricate himself by pushing the gas pedal down a little further. What happens—the tires spin more. Undaunted, and convinced that what isn't working now will somehow magically start working, the driver pushes the gas pedal clear to the floor. You know the outcome. The wheels really spin making that "wonderfully" satisfying whine and the car settles in the snow and is "stuck."

It is time to stop doing what isn't working or isn't working well. Time to call the *AAA*. Time for a pedagogical Plan "B."

WHAT ELSE CAN YOU DO? LOTS!

> *He who does not research has nothing to teach.*
> —Proverbs

You have already made a move in the right direction by reading this book. You now are better prepared to profit from the suggestions that follow. You know what to look and listen for as you watch master presenters in action.

Think of the sage advice offered to young investors. "Time is your friend. Start a savings or investment plan now, contribute to it regularly, and over time it will pay off." Professionals who are called upon to present should follow the same advice. Start making an investment in your dynamic presenting skills early. It will not only pay off later, but unlike an IRA, you will not have to wait until you are seventy-and-a-half to collect. As soon as you learn what contributes to dynamic presenting, you can put it to use immediately and for years to come. Why wait?

- Get together with fellow presenters to brainstorm ideas for projecting enthusiasm and for the better engagement of an audience. Surely with all the talent among your professional community, some great ideas would be generated.

- Ask someone from the theater department of a local university to work with you, individually, or to present a hands-on workshop on how what is learned and practiced in the world of drama could assist you in your presenting. It would be well worth paying for a lunch or two.

- Invite someone from a speech department to offer training in effective public speaking. What was overlooked in one's public speaking college course could be mastered now—it is never too late. Be ready to spring for more lunches.

- On an individual basis, as mentioned earlier under the two acting skills, animation in body and animation in voice, consider video-taping or audio-taping your presentations. View or listen to the tapes with a more targeted vision and more acute hearing for where you did well, and where some improvement might be needed. Call upon a colleague to offer his or her feedback.

- Although most people you ask for help will agree and will feel flattered, make it easy for them to say "no." You don't want someone helping you who doesn't really want to."

- Go to the theater, watch movies, watch television using your now more critical "eye" to the actions that performers use to engage their audience. What could you incorporate into your enthusiastic, dynamic presentations?

- View numerous TED talks. These are always well done (e.g., enthusiastic and informative) and are powerfully delivered. Again, using your now critical "eye," extract from their delivery techniques those that you can use.

- Approach your institution for their support—time and money—to bring in other presentation experts. Invite folks from across the institution or company. You are all in this together.

- Have the administration establish and reserve a place where those of you who are interested in great presenting regularly can meet-and-discuss. Snacks and drinks would be appreciated.

- Start a professional library of articles, books, and videos focusing upon the importance of presenter enthusiasm and the use of the various acting and performance skills highlighted in this book. When you locate a great resource, send out an email sharing the discovery. Later, during the meet-and-discuss time, explore the application of what the article presents.

- Become a contributor—yes, a contributor—to the shared goal of using acting and performance skills to deliver dynamic presentations. When you do something that seems to interest and engage an audience, consider writing up what you have done and submitting it for delivery at a professional conference or for publication in a journal. I would like to receive a copy, too.

- Do not overlook one of your greatest resources—audiences themselves. Ask them to critique your dynamic delivery methods. Tell them that although a critique is helpful, it should be presented with some ideas of their own as to how the subject matter could have been better delivered. Remind them that they may soon be in your position—the presenter. It is best that they start now to prepare for that part of their career. This would be a real advantage to them, an advantage that I suspect many of you wished you had had.

- It may be scary for new presenters to learn and begin to incorporate these acting skills into their presentations. It can be downright frightening for seasoned presenters to do the same thing. But, "true teaching takes courage because we must constantly be reinventing ourselves . . . we must change, else how can we ask students to change" (Searle 2001, 6). Palmer (2007) explores this same idea in his book, *The Courage to Teach*. Shouldn't teachers lead by example?

- If your institution is serious about effective presenting, then they must formally recognize the importance of the ongoing process of becoming trained to present well. Great presenting must be recognized as an important part of one's job description.

18

Conclusion

(Actually, this may just be the beginning!)

Knowledge is of no value unless you put it into practice.
—Anton Chekhov

INTRODUCTION

For a final time, let us emphasize that as noted in the Preface, the purpose of this book is to identify and defend that one major characteristic (e.g., enthusiasm) most often cited of great presenters, and then to offer a set of acting and performance skills that you can use to *project* that important characteristic. The bottom line is, these skills work! Audiences testify to their success and award-winning presenters sing their praise. I hope that my attempt has been successful.

Constructive feedback would be welcome. Send such feedback to:

Robert T. Tauber, PhD
Professor Emeritus
Pennsylvania State University
rtt1453@comcast.net

WILLINGNESS AND COURAGE

What I am asking presenters to undertake may be challenging, but the payoff for both presenters and audiences is worth it. It takes willingness, perhaps even courage, to step into the shoes of thespians and use their proven delivery skills of animation in body, animation in voice, humor, suspense and surprise, role-playing, use of props, space utilization, and creative entrances and exits.

You apparently had what it takes to master your subject matter. At times I am sure that that task, too, was daunting. But you succeeded. Now that you have digested this book's message on how to better *project* enthusiasm, there is no doubt that you also will excel as a more dynamic presenter. Yes, this takes courage; it takes heart! Go for it.

A PRESENTER'S MANNER AND METHOD

As the author of this book, I want to acknowledge that teaching is taken very seriously at my institution. Merit pay, tenure, and promotion all are influenced by these results. Our sense of accomplishment, too, is influenced by these results. When audiences report, in anecdotal form, that "he or she was able to make an otherwise boring subject interesting," we are torn between competing reactions. One part of us wants to grab the respondents, shake them, and announce in no uncertain terms that all subject matter is inherently interesting. Another side of us recognizes that perhaps we have accomplished just what we have set out to do—we have begun to engage, inform, and motivate them. Time will tell.

"When we look back on our schooling, we remember teachers rather than courses—we remember their manner and method, their enthusiasm and intellectual excitement, and their capacity to arouse delight in, or curiosity about, the subject taught" (Hook 1981, 24). This manner and method reflect many of the acting strategies presented in this book that can, and should, be used by presenters. If you display enthusiasm and energy in the delivery, your audience will be convinced that you are a someone who is in command of not only your subject matter but also your presenting.

Of all dramatic elements, says Klein and Fitch (1990), characters and their dramatic actions are recalled more strongly and frequently than dialogue. We remember more about what people do than what they say. Audiences may forget the details presented in their courses, but few forget the enthusiasm and passion with which inspirational teachers present day after day. "Even more so than an actor, a teacher is a sculptor in snow"

(Hook 1981, 24). Like the snow sculpture that will melt in the warming sun, the memories of a great teacher are preserved only by those who have *seen* him or her in action.

I hope that by reading this book you will develop your own stage presence by performing, performing, performing—in the very best pedagogical sense. I hope you will begin developing your unique, yet effective, "manner and method" dynamic presentation skills.

THE CURTAIN COMES DOWN

Theater audiences do not expect to be bored, unmoved, and sorry they came. Other audiences, too, feel the same way. Let's not disappoint them. Good presenting practice is out there. As I have argued throughout this book, part and parcel of this "good practice" is making better use of acting and performance skills. "Even the dullest of subjects can be taught in a way that intrigues the learner" (Rubin 1985, 100). But how is this sense of intrigue generated? It's likely that the presenter used "something dramatic, imaginative, and bewitching" (Wells 1979, 53). Yes, these are two dated references, but they are as true today as when they were written.

FERRIS BUELLER'S DAY OFF

> *Remember, before you can be great, you've got to be good.*
> *Before you can be good, you've got to be bad. But before you can*
> *even be bad, you've got to try.*
> —A. L. Williams

Now that you have read this book and are ready to put what you have learned into practice, it is time for you to leave and get on with it. Thank you for reading this book!

Why haven't you left yet?

Recall what Mathew Broderick, in his housecoat, said at the end of the 1986 film *Ferris Bueller's Day Off*. He turned and faced the movie audience directly as if he were there with them live, and said, "You're still here? It's over, go home. Go."

APPENDIX

Enthusiasm Rating Chart

CATEGORIES	LOW	MEDIUM	HIGH
1. Vocal Delivery	Monotone, minimum inflections, little variation in speech; poor articulation.	Pleasant variations in pitch, volume, and speed; good articulation.	Great and sudden changes from rapid, excited speech to a whisper; varied tone and pitch.
2. Eyes	Looked dull or bored; seldom opened eyes wide or raised eyebrows; avoids eye contact; often maintains a blank stare.	Appeared interested; occasionally lighting up, shining, opening wide.	Characterized as dancing, snapping, shining, lighting up, opening wide, eyebrows raised; maintains eye contact.
3. Gestures	Seldom moved arms out toward person or object; never used sweeping movements; kept arms at side or folded, rigid.	Often pointed; occasional sweeping motion using body, head, arms, hands, and face; maintained steady pace of gesturing.	Quick and demonstrative movements of body, head, arms, hands, and face.
4. Body Movements	Seldom moved from one spot, or from sitting to standing position; sometimes "paces" nervously.	Moved freely, slowly, and steadily.	Large body movements, swung around, walked rapidly, changed pace; unpredictable and energetic; natural body movements.
5. Facial Expression	Appeared deadpan, expressionless or frowned; little smiling; lips closed.	Agreeable; smiled frequently; looked pleased, happy, or sad if situation called for.	Appeared vibrant, demonstrative; showed many expressions; broad smile; quick changes in expression.
6. Word Selection	Mostly nouns, few adjectives; simple or trite expressions.	Some descriptors or adjectives or repetition of the same ones.	Highly descriptive, many adjectives, great variety.
7. Acceptance of Ideas and Feelings	Little indication of acceptance or encouragement; may ignore students' feelings or ideas.	Accepted ideas and feelings; praised or clarified; some variations in response.	Quick to accept, praise, encourage, or clarify; many variations in response.
8. Overall Energy Level	Lethargic; appears inactive, dull or sluggish.	Appeared energetic and demonstrative sometimes, but mostly maintained an even level.	Exuberant; high degree of energy and vitality; highly demonstrative.

SOURCE: Chart courtesy of Mary Lynn Collins (adapted from *Practical Applications of Research*, *PHI DELTA KAPPA Newsletter*, June 1981)

References

Akechi, H., et al. 2013. Attention to eye contact in the West and East: Autonomic responses and evaluative ratings. *PLoS One* 8(3):1–58.

Ambady, N., and Rosenthal, R. 1993. Half a minute: Predicting teacher evaluations from thin slices of nonverbal behavior and physical attractiveness. *Journal of Personality and Social Psychology* 64(3):431–441.

Aring, C. D. 1971. A sense of humor. *JAMA* 215(13):2099.

Bain, K. 2004. *What the best college teachers do.* Cambridge, MA: Harvard University Press.

Bandura, A. 1986. *Social foundations of thought and action.* Englewood, NJ: Prentice Hall.

Baral, S. 2016. Can't quit saying "um" and "ah"? Just learn to use them better. *Qz.com.* July 25.

Bariso, J. J. 2016. This 10-minute TED Talk will teach you everything you need to know about presenting. *Inc.* May 4.

Baughman, M. D. 1979. Teaching with humor: A performing art. *Contemporary Education* 51(1):26–30.

Berk, R. A. 2007. Humor as an instructional defibrillator. *Journal of Health Administration Education* 24(2):97–116.

Bligh, D. A. 2000. *What's the use of lectures?* San Francisco: Jossey-Bass.

Boerman-Cornell, W. 1999. The five humors. *English Journal* 88(4):66–69.

Borins, M. 2003. Are you suffering from a laugh deficiency disorder? *Canadian Family Medicine* 49:723–724, 730–732.

Boyd, S. 2003. Using your tone of voice. *Public Speaking Tips.* January 31.

Boyd, S. 2010. The wow factor! *Public Speaking Tips.* April 6.

Braithwaite, L. 2013. Public speaking: Making eye contact with your audience. *Businessknowhow.com.* August 19.

Brookfield, S. D., and Preskill, S. 1999. *Discussion as a way of teaching: Tools and techniques for democratic classrooms.* San Francisco: Jossey-Bass.

Bruner, J. S. 1960. *The process of education.* Cambridge, MA: Harvard University Press.

Brunvand, J. H. 1991. More on the trained professors. *FOAFTale News* 24:2–6.

Bunny, M. 2017. Want more attention? Whisper your voice over. *Bunny Inc.* December 26.

Burns, M. U., and Woods, P. S. 1992. *Teacher as actor.* Dubuque, IA: Kendall/Hunt.

Caldwell, M. 2007. *Blink: The power of thinking without thinking.* New York: Back Bay Books.

Calman, K. 2001. A study of storytelling, humour and learning in medicine. *Clinical Medicine* 1(3):227–229.

Carroll, J. 2002. Getting good teaching evaluations without stand-up comedy. *Chronicle of Higher Education: Chronicle Careers.* April 15.

Cavanagh, S. R. 2017. All the classroom's a stage. *Chronicle of Higher Education.* June 27.

Charles, M. 2015. Elaine Showalter's *Teaching Literature. Higher Education and Theory Network.* September 7.

Coenen, D. T. 2011. Four essentials of effective teaching. *Chalk Talk.* fyo.uga.edu.

Collins, M. L. 1981. *PHI DELTA KAPPAN Newsletter.* June.

Colmenares, C. 2005. No joke: Study finds laughing can burn calories. REPORTER (Vanderbilt University Medical Center). June 10.

Dabell, J. 2017. Supply teaching: The element of surprise. *SecEd.* sec.ed.co.uk. November 1.

Day, C. 2004. *A passion for teaching.* New York: RoutledgeFalmer.

Deiter, R. 2000. The use of humor as a teaching tool in the college classroom. *NACTA Journal.* June:20–28.

Dembo, M. H. 1988. *Applying educational psychology in the classroom.* New York: Longman.

Dlugan, A. 2013. Simple secrets to improve your eye contact. *Six Minutes.* July 8.

Donovan, B. 2017. Master list of facial expressions for writers! *Thepbsblog.com.* December 6.

Drury, E. 2013. Memorable history lessons: Dress up, role play and personal stories. *The Guardian.* April 29.

Dubrow, H., and Wilkinson, J. 1984. The theory and practice of lectures, in *The art and craft of teaching,* ed. M. Gullette (p. 25). Cambridge, MA: Harvard University Press.

Dudas, R. A., and Bannister, S. L. 2014. It's not just what you know: The non-cognitive attributes of great clinical teachers. *Pediatrics* 134(5):852–854.

Eble, K. E. 1988. *The craft of teaching.* 2nd ed. San Francisco: Jossey-Bass.

Estes, A. C. 2005. Shock and awe in the civil engineering classroom. *Journal of Professional Issues in Engineering Education and Practice* January:1–5.

Felman, J. L. 2001. *Never a dull moment: Teaching and the art of performance.* New York: Routledge.

Finckel, J. 2014. The silent professor. *The Teaching Professor* 28(6):1, 4.

Finkelstein, S. 2018. The best leaders are great teachers. Harvard Business School. *Hbr.org.*

Fish, B. 2012. Glossophobia. *Counseling Services Newsletter.*

Gelatt, H. B. 2015. Ignorance is bliss. *hbgelatt.wordpress.com.* October 11.

Genard, G. 2015. Acting skills for business: The art of persuasion. *genardmethod.com.* March 8.

Genard, G. 2016. How to begin a presentation: The critical first 60 seconds. *genardmethod.com.* March 6.

Glasser, W. 1998. *Choice theory in the classroom.* New York: HarperCollins.

Glasser, W. 1999. *Choice theory: A new psychology of personal freedom.* New York: HarperCollins.

Gordon, T. 2001. *Leadership effectiveness training: L.E.T.* New York: TarcherPerigee.

Gorman, C. K. 2010. Great leaders talk with their hands. *Forbes.* September 21.

Gorman, C. K. 2012. Seven tips for effective body language on stage. *Forbes.com.* February 13.

Goulden, N. R. 1991. Improving instructors' speaking skills. *IDEA PAPER 24.* Center for Faculty Evaluation and Development, Kansas State University, Manhattan. January.

Graham, P. 1999. Roundtable discussion: Strengthening the schools. *Harvard Magazine.*

Graham, P. 2005. Personal communication with author. December 19.

Green, M. C. 2004. Storytelling in teaching. *aps Observer.* April.

Green, M. C. 2007. Storytelling is teaching, in *Teaching at the University of Manitoba: A Handbook* (pp. 3.55–3.62). Winnipeg, Manitoba: University Teaching Services.

Greenberg, E., and Miller, P. 1991. The player and the professor: Theatrical techniques in teaching. *Journal of Management Education* 15(4):428–446.

Greengross, G., and Miller, G. F. 2008. Dissing oneself versus dissing rivals: Effects of status, personality, and sex on the short-term and long-term attractiveness of self-depreciating and other-deprecating humor. *Evolutionary Psychology* 6(3):393–408.

Gregoire, C. 2016. The fascinating science behind "talking" with your hands. *Science.* February 4.

Hanning, R. W. 1984. The classroom as theater of self: Some observations for beginning teachers. *ADE Bulletin* 77(Spring):33–37.

Hanning, R. W. 2005. Personal communication with author. September 23.

Hansbury, M. 2009. *The law of attraction.* New Delhi: Epitome Books.

Harbinger, A. 2015. 7 things everyone should know about the power of eye contact. *Art of charm.* May 14.

Havener, K. B. 2005. Method acting for lawyers. *GPSolo Magazine* 31(4):1–3.

Herbert, P. J. 1991. *Humor in the classroom: Theories, functions, and guidelines.* Paper presented at the Annual Meeting of the Central States Communication Association, Chicago. April.

Herrell, H. 2016. The physician as teacher. *Howardisms.* April 22.

Holmes, J. 2016. *Nonsense: The power of not knowing.* New York: Broadway Books.

Hooda, M., and Annu, D. 2017. Determinates of teacher enthusiasm. *International Journal of Research in Engineering, IT, and Social Sciences* 7(8):1–3.

Hook, S. 1981. Morris R. Cohen—Fifty years later, in *Masters: Portraits of great teachers*, ed. J. Epstein Jr. (p. 24). New York: Basic Books.

Hunsaker, J. S. 1988. It's no joke: Using humor in the classroom. *The Clearing House* 61(6):285.

Jordan, J. R. 1982. The professor as communicator. *Improving College and University Teaching* 30(3):120–124.

Jose, P. E., and Brewer, W. F. 1990. Early grade school children's liking of script and suspense story structures. *Journal of Reading Behavior* 22(4):355–372.

Keane, B. 2005. Family circus. *Times.* December 14, 7D.

Keller, M. M., Neumann, K., and Fischer, H. E. 2013. Teacher enthusiasm and student achievement, in *International guide to student achievement*, ed. J. Hattie and E. M. Andermann (pp. 247–250). New York: Routledge.

Kher, N. M., Molstad, S., and Donahue, R. 1999. Using humor in the college classroom to enhance teaching effectiveness in "dread courses." *College Student Journal* 33(3):400–406.

King, A. 1993. From sage on the stage to guide on the side. *College Teaching* 4(1):30–35.

Klein, J., and Fitch, M. 1990. First grade children's comprehension of "noodle doodle box." *Youth Theatre Journal* 5(2):7–13.

Kolowich, L. 2015. The science of a great TED Talk: What makes a speech go viral. *Hubspot.com.*

Kottler, J. A., Zehm, S. J., and Kottler, E. 2005. *On being a teacher: The human dimension.* Thousand Oaks, CA: Corwin Press.

Krathwohl, D. R., Bloom, B. S., and Masia, B. B. 1956. *Taxonomy of educational objectives: Handbook II affective domain.* New York: David McKay.

Landrum, M. 2009. Speaking eye to eye: A meeting of the eyes denotes a meeting of the minds. *Toastmasters International.* December.

Leblanc, R. W. 2010. Good teaching: The top 10 requirements. *Faculty Focus, Magna Publications.* August 11.

Lewis, D. L. 2018. Personal email communication. May 28.

Low, G. T. 1990. Humour in the classroom. *Teaching and Learning* 11(1):3–14.

Lundberg, E. M., and Thurstone, C. M. 2002. *If they're laughing, they might just be listening.* Fort Collins, CO: Cottonwood Press.

Mack, O., Bloom, K., and Foster, T. 2017. Teaching 101 for lawyers: Basic preparation for attorneys-turned-teachers. *Accdocket.com.*

Maclean, N. F. 1975. On changing neckties: A few remarks on the art of teaching. *Perspectives in Biology and Medicine* 18(2):227–237.

Maier, M. H., and Panitz, T. 1996. End on a high note: Better endings for classes and courses. *College Teaching* 44(4):145–148.

Marshall, L. B. 2009. Combating speech disfluencies . . . in *Chemistry.* September/October.

McCrory, P. 2018. Personal communication. January 23.

McKay, J. 2000. *Generation of idiom-based witticisms to aid second language learning.* Edinburgh: University of Edinburgh.

McTaggart, J. 2003. *From the teacher's desk.* Bangor, ME: Booklocker.

Medley, M. 2017. 7 distracting mannerisms: Learning what not to do in public speaking. *Black Speakers. Network.* June 9.

Menon, P. R., et al. 2013. Laughing at life's lessons: The role of humour in medical teaching—An interactive assessment among medical faculty in Southeast Asia. *Education in Medical Journal* 5(3):100–107.

Merys, G. 2014. Teaching without talking. *Teaching Today' Students: Tips on Teaching.* August 6.

Mortimer, C. 2018. Graduate loses bid to sue Oxford University over failure to get a first. *Independent.* February.

Mozes, A. 2007. Theatre classes help docs' bedside manner. *HealthDay News.* September 7.

Napoli, J. 2018. Surprise or suspense? *Creative Screenwriting.* March 11.

Newman, E. n.d. AZ Quotes.

Norris, E. M. 2012. The constructive use of images in medical teaching: A literature review. *JRSM Short Reports* 3(5):33.

Notas, N. 2012. How to develop a confident, attractive voice. *Nicknotas .com*. December 29.

O'Donnell, M. 2005. Doctors as performance artists. *Journal of Rural Social Medicine* 98(7):323–324.

Oldenburg, D. 2005. Laugh yourself skinny. *Washington Post*. Sunday, May 1.

Oleniczak, J. 2015. 7 things students can learn from acting classes. *Noodle .com*. October 28.

Osler, W. 1913. *A way of life*. London: Constable.

Palmer, P. J. 2007. *The courage to teach: Exploring the inner landscapes of a teacher's life*. San Francisco: Jossey-Bass.

Peterson, K. 2017. The 3 qualities of an exceptional professor. *College: Study Break*. July 27.

Pickering, S. 2004. *Letters to a teacher*. New York: Atlantic Monthly Press.

Pitman, M. 2011. Saving the most valuable teaching tool—Teachers' voices. *HuffPost*. September 16.

Poirier, T. I., and Wilhelm, M. 2014. Use of humor to enhance learning: Bull's eye or off the mark. *American Journal of Pharmaceutical Education* 78(2):27.

Princeton Language Institute, and Laskowski, L. 2001. *10 days to more confident public speaking*. New York: Warner Books.

Ramani, S. 2006. Twelve tips to promote excellence in medical teaching. *Medical Teacher* 28(1):19–23.

Ramesh, N., et al. 2011. Use of humor in orthopedic teaching. *Journal of Clinical and Diagnostic Research* 5(8):1618–1623.

Ramsell, B. 1978. The poetic experience of surprise and the art of teaching. *English Journal* 67(5):22–25.

Rivas, C. 2017. The way you smile, according to science, determines if people think you are smart or stupid. *Rebel Circus.com*. July 27.

Ross, E. 2005. A good laugh may help shed extra weight. *Associated Press*. June 4.

Rossetti, J., and Fox, P. G. 2009. Factors related to successful teaching by outstanding professors: An interpretive study. *Journal of Nursing Education* 48(1):11–16.

Rubin, L. J. 1985. *Artistry in teaching*. New York: Random House.

Schwartz, K. 2013. Why teachers should be trained like actors. *MIND/ SHIFT*. July 1.

Searle, B. 2001. The spirit of teaching. *NEFDC Exchange* 12(2):6.

Shields, H. M. 2010. *A medical teacher's manual for success*. Baltimore: Johns Hopkins University Press.

Shipman, S. 2017. How to reduce "ums," "ahs" and filler words. *Stacyshipman.com*. October 26.

Showalter, E. 2003. *Teaching literature*. Malden, MA: Blackwell.

Simerjit, S., Pai, D. R., Sinha, N. K., Kaur, A., Soe, H. H. K., and Barua, A. 2013. Qualities of an effective teacher: What do medical teachers think? *BMC Medical Education* 13(1):128.

Skinner, B. F. 1948. *Walden two.* Indianapolis: Hackett.

Smith, J. 2014. 10 public speaking habits to avoid at all costs. *Business Insider.com.* June 9.

Spangler, A. 2000. She who laughs, lasts! January 2.

Spooner, J. J. 2014. In response to "Use of humor to enhance learning: Bull's eye or off the mark." *American Journal of Pharmaceutical Education* 78(4):84.

Starratt, R. J. 2012. *The drama of schooling: The schooling of drama.* London: Routledge.

Stevenson, S. 2012. There's magic in your smile. *Psychology Today.* June 25.

Stone, G. H. 2010. Teachers as actors. *Gentlyhewstone.com.* September 20.

Strang, T. 2014. What in an instructor's most valuable trait? *Cengage.com.* April 14.

Sultanoff, S. M. 2002. Integrating humor into psychotherapy, in *Play therapy with adults*, ed. Charles Schaefer (pp. 107–143). New York: Wiley.

Sutkin, G., Wagner, E., Harris, I., and Schiffer, R. 2008. What makes a good clinical teacher in medicine? A review of the literature. *Academic Medicine* 83(5):452–466.

Tauber, R. T. 1985. French and Raven's power bases: A focus for educational researchers and practitioners. *Australian Journal of Education* 30(3):256–265.

Tauber, R. T. 1988. Overcoming misunderstanding about the concept of negative reinforcement. *Teaching of Psychology* 15(3):152–153.

Tauber, R. T., and Mester, C. S. 2007. *Acting lessons for teachers: Using performance skills in the classroom.* Westport, CT: Praeger.

Taylor, R. B. 2007. *Academic medicine: A guide for clinicians.* New York: Springer Science-Business Media.

The Telegraph. 2012. Why making finger quotes marks may cost your credibility. July 5.

Tompkins, J. 1990. Pedagogy of the distressed. *College English* 52(6):653–660.

Torok, S. E., McMorris, R. F., and Lin, W. 2004. Is humor an appreciated teaching tool? Perceptions of professors' teaching styles and use of humor. *College Teaching* 52(1):14–20.

Toth, E. 1997. *Ms. Mentor's impeccable advice for women in academia.* Philadelphia: University of Pennsylvania Press.

Turner, T. L., Palazzi, D. L., and Ward, M. W. 2008. The clinician-educator's handbook. *MedEdPORTAL Publications.*

250 Funny Reasons You Know You're a Nurse. 2015. *NurseBuff.com*. November 21.

Urban, H. 2008. *Lessons from the classroom: 20 things good teachers do*. Redwood, CA: Great Lessons Press.

Urbanowicz, C. F. 2000. Teaching as theatre: Some classroom ideas specifically those concerning Charles R. Darwin (1809–1882). *csuchico .edu*.

Urbanowicz, C. F. 2003. Teaching as theatre once again: Darwin in the classroom (and beyond). *csuchico.edu*.

Van Edwards, V. 2015. 20 hand gestures you should be using. *HuffPost*. August 25.

Villarroel, G. 2015. How passion can make a difference in the classroom. *Masters Teacher Program*. West Point, NY.

Vozzella, L. 2010. Vocal cords and classrooms: Overuse of the voice can leave some teachers perpetually hoarse. *Baltimore Sun*. December 20.

Waja, M. 2015. Public speaking & the power of a smile. *Linkedin.com*. July 17.

Walthausen, A. 2013. Don't give up on the lecture. *The Atlantic*. November 21.

Wandersee, J. H. 1982. Humor as a teaching strategy. *American Biology Teacher* 44(4):212–218.

Webster's Seventh New Collegiate Dictionary. 1972. Springfield, MA: G. & C. Merriam.

Wells, E. F. 1979. Bewitched, dazzled, and delighted. *Teacher* 96(9):53–54.

Wenk, G. L. 2011. Addicted to smiling. *Psychology Today*. December 27.

Williams, W., and Ceci, S. 1997. "How'm I doing?" Problems with student ratings of instructors and courses. *Change* 29(5):12–23.

Witte, M. H. 2017. Handbook for teachers: Curriculum for translating translation and scientific questioning. *Medicalignorance.org /resources/Teacher*. January.

Wright, L. 2010. Enthusiasm: It's catching. *Clinical Teacher* 7(4):227–229.

Wyeth, S. 2014. 10 reasons eye contact is everything in public speaking. *Inc .com*.

Zhang, Q. 2014. Instructor's corner #3: Teaching with enthusiasm: Engaging students, sparking curiosity, and jumpstarting motivation. *National Communication Association*. February 14.

Zubrzcki, J. 2015. How teachers are like opera singers: Everything depends upon a clear voice. *Chalkbeat*. January 13.

Index

Acting, 27–31, 33–34, 36–39, 42, 44–46, 49, 51, 55, 71, 82–83, 92–93, 97, 103–105, 112–113, 115, 121, 134, 137, 152, 157, 161, 164, 167, 172–173, 176–180
Adler, Stella, 44
Akechi, Hironori, 59
Allen, Gracie, 104
Allen, Steve, 115
Ambady, Nalini, 53
Animation in body, 29, 36, 47, 50–54, 67, 69, 76, 78–79, 102–103, 115, 125, 137, 176, 179; do nothing, but do it well, 54–55, 76; eye contact, 28, 54, 59–61, 68, 144–145, 149, 163, 174; facial expression, 49, 51, 58–62, 121; gestures, 30, 42, 49, 51, 53–58, 62, 69, 78, 86, 140, 174; plan where you step, 55; smiling, 20, 54, 58, 61–62, 101
Animation in voice, 29, 36, 47, 51, 66, 69, 73, 78–79, 103, 115, 148–149, 176, 179; cadence/inflection, 15, 28, 71, 76–77; pauses, 6, 73, 76–77; pitch, 6, 47, 53, 67, 71, 75; projection, 70, 72; quality, 47, 72, 75, 77, 97; rate, 47, 67, 71, 73, 77; tone, 32, 67, 73–75, 83, 163; variations, 70, 71, 72, 74–75, 77; volume, 47, 71–73; whispering, 72–73, 78, 104
Annu, Devi, 20
Archimedes, 100, 122
Aring, Charles D., 81

Aristotle, 66
Aykroyd, Dan, 123

Bain, Ken, 46
Bandura, Albert, 35
Bannister, Susan L., 21
Baral, Susmita, 77
Bariso, Justin J., 66
Barrie, James M., 174
Behind the scenes, 165–166
Bell, Alexander Graham, 135
Bennett, Bo, 30
Benny, Jack, 76
Berk, Ronald A., 82
Blazing Saddles, 63
Bligh, Donald A., 14
Blink: The Power of Thinking without Thinking (Caldwell), 53
Blocking, 142, 144, 146
Bloom, Benjamin S., 35
The Bob Newhart Show, 138
Boerman-Cornell, William, 85
Bon Jovi, Jon, 24
Borge, Victor, 82
Borins, Mel, 80
Bowell, John, 90
Boyd, Stephen, 74, 149
Bradbury, Malcolm, 14
Braithwaite, Lisa, 59
Brewer, William F., 110
Bronte, Charlotte, 25

Brookfield, Stephen D., 24
Brown, Charlie, 107
Browning, Elizabeth Barrett, 5
Bruner, Jerome S., 35
Brynner, Yul, 42
Bunny, M., 73
Burns, Morris U., 42, 46, 81

Caine Mutiny, 64
Caldwell, Malcolm, 53
Calman, Kenneth, 81
Cameron, George, 12
Cameron, Julia, 103
Carnegie, Dale, 49
Carroll, Jill, 30, 45
Carroll, Virginia Schaefer, 36
Carson, Johnny, 151
Cartoons, 10, 90–92, 135
Cavanagh, Sara Rose, 33
Ceci, Stephen J., 52
Charles, Mathew, 3
Chekhov, Anton, 178
Chester, Henry, 31
Choice Theory (Glasser), 174
Christie, Agatha, 103
Churchill, Winston, 67, 76, 113
Ciardi, John, 160
Clarke, John Hendrik, 41
Coaching, 6, 86
Coenen, Dan T., 87
Collins, Mary Lynn, 48, 182
Colmenares, Clinton, 94
Competent and confident, 80–81
The Courage to Teach (Palmer), 177
Craftspersons, 43, 45–46, 69
Creating characters, 77, 114, 118

Dabell, John, 97, 130
Daniels, Anthony, 54
Day, Christopher, 23
Dead Poets Society, 52, 83, 114, 139, 143, 145
de Bergerac, Cyrano, 74
Deiter, Ron, 95
Del Toro, Benicio, 130
Dembo, Myron H., 35

Dewey, John, 99
Disney, Walt, 80
Dlugan, Andrew, 60
Donahue, Roberta, 94
Donovan, Bryn, 60
Dragnet, 67
Drama, xv, 32, 38, 45, 99, 102, 106, 124, 175
Dramatic, xvi, 13, 26, 29, 32, 35, 45, 60, 76, 98, 102, 115, 117, 128, 131, 159, 179–180
Dreaded "Ums," 77
Droke, Steve, 45
Drury, Emma, 114
Dubrow, Heather, 13, 17
Dudas, Robert A., 21
Dunham, Jeff, 131

Eakin, Richard M., 111–112
Eble, Kenneth E., 26, 28–29, 43
Edwards, Tryon, 20
Einstein, Albert, 35–36, 69, 132
Eisenhower, Dwight D., 93
Eison, James, 111
Eliot, Charles, 13
Eliot, T. S., 88
Emeril (Lagasse), 23
Emerson, Ralph Waldo, 19
Engage the masters, 171
Enthusiasm, 18–31, 34, 37, 39, 41, 43–45, 48–49, 51, 53, 55, 58–59, 62, 65, 71, 73, 95, 97, 125, 149, 157, 163, 166, 169, 173, 175–176, 178–179
Enthusiasm (projecting), xvi, 16, 21, 27, 43–44, 157, 173, 175
Enthusiasm Rating Chart, 48–49, 182
Entrances, 29, 33, 47, 49, 54, 105, 115, 123–126, 128, 135, 147–148, 150–151, 153–155, 159, 161, 164, 174, 179
Escalante, Jamie, 130
Estes, Allen C., 97, 108
Exits, 29, 33, 47, 49, 54, 105, 115, 123–126, 128, 135, 147–148, 153–154, 160–161, 164, 174, 179
Expectations, 11, 13, 30–31, 42, 75, 98, 159

Felman, Jyl Lynn, 29
Ferris Bueller's Day Off, 25, 85, 180
Finkelstein, Sydney, xvi
Fischer, Hans E., 22
Fish, Barbara, 164
Fitch, Marguerite, 179
Forbes, Malcolm, 23
Foster, Troy, 173
Fox, Patricia G., 21
French, John, 171
Fripp, Patricia, 52
Fun, xvi, 10, 68, 74, 80, 82–83, 101, 114, 125, 130, 134, 137, 150, 157, 167–168
Fun(damental), 10, 167
Furnham, Adrian, 22

Gelatt, H. B., 100
Gelbart, Larry, 92
Genard, Gary, 27, 148
Gershwin, George, 14
Gilbert, Rob, 161
Glasser, William, 10, 82, 101, 174
Godwin, Gail, 7
Gorbachev, Mikhail, 32, 67
Gordon, Thomas, 107
Gorman, Carol Kinsey, 56, 150
Goulden, Nancy R., 18, 138
Graham, Patricia, 25
Great orators, 67
Green, Melanie C., 100–101
Greenberg, Ellen, 158–159
Greengross, Gil, 87
Gregg, Alan, 37
Gregoire, Carolyn, 55
Grimnes, Karin A., 37
Guide on the side, 15

Hamlet, 76, 122–123
Hanh, Thich Nhat, 61
Hanning, Robert W., 21, 38, 45, 113
Hansbury, Michael, 23
Harbinger, Andrew J., 60
Harris, Irene, 20, 28
Harrison, Carol L., 37
Herbert, Patrick J., 79, 82, 95
Herrell, Howard, 5

Highet, Gilbert, 83
Hippocrates, 89
Holmes, Jamie, 99, 103
Hooda, Madhuri, 20
Hook, Sidney, 180
Hooks, 36, 54, 98, 105, 116, 123, 128, 148–153, 156, 158–159, 161, 163
Hope, Bob, 10
Howard, Ron, 16, 153
Humor, 29, 42, 43, 47, 49, 58, 76–77, 79–90, 92–95, 100, 103, 115, 125–126, 131, 133, 135, 137, 140, 148, 156, 174, 179; anecdotes, 85, 100, 135, 145; benefits, 79, 81, 93; cartoons, 10, 90–92, 135; deadpan, 85; doodles, 86; funny story, 85; humorous comment, 85; humorous titles, 86; irony, 86; joke, 49, 79–80, 83–84, 86, 90, 92–93, 131; knock-knock, 86; limerick, 85; Murphy's Law, 85, 135; oxymoron, 84; parody, 85; pun, 10, 49, 84, 92, 112, 128; riddle, 49, 84, 92; self-deprecating humor, 86–87; slapstick, 86
Humor Is an Instructional Defibrillator (Berk), 82
Hunsaker, Johanna S., 80
Hurl your words, 68

Iacocca, Lee, 34
If They're Laughing, They Might Just Be Listening (Lundberg and Thurstone), 80
Ignorance 101, 99–100
Imagine, 105, 126–128
Irwin, Steve, 22

James, William, 163
Jeopardy, 125
Jordan, James R., 21
Jose, Paul E., 110
Joubert, Joseph, 4

Keane, Bill, 94
Keane, Glen, 51
Keating, John, 83, 115, 139, 143
Keller, Melanie M., 22

Kennedy, John F., 67, 80, 102
Kher, Neelam M., 94
King, Alison, 15
King, Martin Luther, Jr., 67, 88, 149, 165
Kingsley, Charles, 30
Klein, Jeanne, 179
Kline, Richard, 166
Kolowich, Lindsay, 56
Kottler, Ellen, 80
Kottler, Jeffrey A., 80
Kramer, Cosmo, 147
Krathwohl, David R., 35
Kulik, James A., 67

Landrum, Michael, 60
Laryngitis and sore throats, 78, 104
Laskowski, Larry, 55
Laugh Yourself Skinny (Oldenburg), 94
Leblanc, Richard W., 10
Lectern lingering, 140
Lecture, 12–13, 15–17, 26, 36, 41, 59, 60–61, 108, 133, 143, 151, 153, 156
Lennon, John, 105, 126, 128
Letterman, David, 87
Lewis, Dara Lee, 6
Lewis, Sinclair, 15
Light, Douglas, 37
Lin, Wen-Chi, 83
Lombardi, Vince, 18–19
Longfellow, Henry Wadsworth, 161
Low, Guat Tin, 79
Lundberg, Elaine M., 80, 84

Mack, Olga, 173
Maclean, Norman, 38
Mahoney, William M., 37
Maier, Mark H., 161
Manner and method, 25, 179–180
Manogue, Michael, 12
Marquee, 156, 160
Marshall, Lisa B., 77
Masia, Bertram B., 35
McCrory, Paul, 29
McKay, Justin, 84
McKeachie, William J., 67
McMorris, Robert F., 83

McTaggart, Jacquie, 23
Medley, Marc, 140
Menon, P. Ramesh, 81
Merys, Gina, 78
Mester, Cathy Sargent, 36–37, 72
Mickey Mouse, xvi, 80
Migrant Mother, 114, 123
Miller, Geoffrey F., 87, 158–159
Mime, 54, 121
Molstad, Susan, 94
Mortimer, Caroline, 26
Mozes, Alan, 28
Mr. Rogers' Neighborhood, 131, 147, 154–155, 164
Murder on the Orient Express, 103
Musical chairs, xvi, 107–108, 149–150

Napoli, James, 98
Neumann, Knut, 22
Newman, Ernest, 163
Nonverbal, 51, 64, 70, 141
Norris, Elizabeth M., 90
Notas, Nick, 76

O'Donnell, Michaem, 30
Oldenburg, Don, 94
Oleniczak, Jennifer, 14
Osler, William, 19

Palmer, Parker, 177
Panitz, Ted, 161
Paralanguage, 70–71
Passion, 5, 19, 22–26, 30, 44, 154, 166, 179
Pasternak, Boris, 97
Peale, Norman Vincent, 18
Pedagogy, 3–4, 17, 20, 69, 80, 139
Performance skills, 28, 36, 39, 42, 44, 97, 103–104, 115, 157, 161, 167, 172–173, 176, 178, 180
Peterson, Kaitlyn, 23
Pickering, Samuel F., 139
Pierce, Charles Sanders, 96
Pitman, Michael J., 69
Plitnik, George, 157
Poe, Edgar Allan, 75–76, 128
Poirier, Therese I., 81

Popek, Gerald J., 173
Posture, 51, 55, 62–63, 83, 113, 120, 151, 163
PowerPoint, 70, 91, 137–138, 143
Presenter-self, 44–45, 105
Preskill, Stephen, 24
The Princeton Language Institute, 55
The Process of Education (Bruner), 35
Props, 29, 32, 36, 47, 49, 93, 96, 103, 105, 109, 112–115, 117–118, 120, 122–126, 128–138, 148, 150, 154, 156–157, 174, 179
Proverbs, 94, 175
Proxemics, 141, 146
Puppets, 131–132
Putting it all together!, 48

Rabin, Susan, 21
Ramani, Subha, 45
Ramesh, Narula, 81
Ramis, Harold, 134
Ramsell, Barbara, 97
The Raven (Poe), 75–76, 128
Reagan, Ronald, 32, 67, 86
Rees, Roger, 50
Rick, Edward Vernon, 173
Rivas, Christine, 62
Robins, Spencer, 44
Rogers, Carl R., 55, 105, 118–120, 171
Rogers, Fred, 92, 131, 147, 154–155, 159, 164
Rogers, Martha, 37
Rogers, Will, 88–89
Role-playing, 29, 36, 47, 49, 77, 83, 105, 111–117, 119–121, 123, 125–126, 134, 148, 179
Roosevelt, Franklin D., 13, 85, 115
Rosenthal, Robert, 53
Ross, Emma, 94
Rossetti, Jeanette, 21
Rubin, Louis J., 45, 107, 180
Ryan, Meg, 136

Sage on the stage, 15–16
Sarcasm, 56, 86
Saturday Night Live (SNL), 28, 85, 159

Schaef, Anne Wilson, 171
Schiffer, Randolph, 20, 28
Schulman, Tommy, 139
Schultz, Charles, 34
Schwartz, Katrina, 28
Searle, Barbara, 177
Sea turtles, 16, 101, 157
Seinfeld, 8, 125, 147
Shakespeare, William, 8, 17, 33, 46, 68, 76, 85, 122, 160
Sheeran, Ed, 129
She Who Laughs, Lasts (Spangler), 95
Shields, Helen M., 5, 19, 32, 67
Shipman, Stacey, 77
Showalter, Elaine, 26, 37–38, 45, 162
Simerjit, Singh, 21
Sivarajah, Rebecca T., xvii, xix, 35–36, 64, 66, 88, 102, 126, 128, 132, 153–154, 156
Skinner, Burrhus Frederic, 13, 55, 105, 118–120, 151, 171
Smith, Jacquelyn, 63
Sommer, Robert, 139
Space utilization, 29, 36, 38, 47, 115, 133, 139, 141–142, 146, 148, 179
Spandex, 129–130
Spangler, Ann, 95
Spooner, Joshua J., 93, 95
Stage fright, 44, 63, 161–164
Stand and Deliver, 130
Starratt, Robert J., 83
Steuernagel, Trudy, 35, 37
Stevenson, Sarah, 61
Stone, Gently Hew, 29
Stoppard, Tom, 160
Storytelling, 36, 47, 96–97, 100, 102–103, 115–116, 120, 174
Strang, Tami, 21
Sultanoff, Steven M., 86
Surprise, 9–10, 15, 29, 36, 42, 44, 47, 49, 59, 71, 73, 76, 78, 80, 83, 96–110, 115–116, 124–126, 131, 134, 137, 139, 143, 148, 152, 159, 174, 179
Suspense, 9, 10, 15, 29, 47, 49, 76, 78, 96–110, 115–116, 124–126, 136–137, 143, 148, 159–160, 174, 179

Sutkin, Gary, 20
Synonyms, 8, 19–20, 109

Tauber, Robert T., 36–37, 152, 171
Taylor, Robert B., 13
Teacher-self, 45
TED Talks, 6, 16–17, 53, 56, 100, 176
The Telegraph, 56
Thurston, Cheryl Miller, 80, 84
Tompkins, Jane, 3, 37
Torok, Sarah E., 83
Toth, Emily, 17
Tracy, Spencer, 140
Trebek, Alex, 125–126
250 funny reasons you know you're a
    nurse, 87

Ueshiba, Morihei, 62
Urban, Hal, 20, 101
Urbanowicz, Charles F., 27, 112

Van Edwards, Vanessa, 53, 56–57
Van Gogh, Vincent, 27
Venue, xvi, xvii, 5, 15, 29, 30–31, 45,
    62, 72, 82, 104, 137, 142, 158,
    162–163, 166
Venue seating, 143
Villarroel, German, 23
Voltaire, 80
Vozzella, Laura, 78

Wagner, Elizabeth, 20, 28
Wait time, 131
Waja, Mo, 61
Walthausen, Abigail, 16
Wandersee, James H., 84
*Webster's Seventh New Collegiate
    Dictionary*, 86
Wells, Elaine F., 180
Wells, H. G., 35
Wenk, Gary L., 61
Wilde, Oscar, 109
Wilkinson, James, 13, 17
Williams, Art L., 180
Williams, Robin, 52, 83, 95, 114–115,
    139, 145–146
Williams, Tennessee, 26
Williams, Wendy M., 52
Wilson, Brian, 163
Winfrey, Oprah, 4
Witte, Marlys H., 99–100
The Wonder Years, 93
Woods, Porter S., 42, 46, 81
Work the crowd, 36
Wright, Lucie, 163
Wyeth, Sims, 59

Youngman, Henny, 81

Zehm, Stanley J., 80
Zhang, Qin, 20

About the Author

Robert T. Tauber, PhD, is professor emeritus, Penn State Behrend, The Pennsylvania State University. He is the author of nine texts, including *Self-Fulfilling Prophecy, Acting Lessons for Teachers,* and *Classroom Management: Sound Theory and Effective Practice.* He has authored numerous journal articles and has delivered many presentations. Dr. Tauber has served academic sabbaticals at Durham University, England, and the University of Melbourne, Australia. After retiring, he taught as an adjunct professor in the Graduate School at the University of Florida and at Gannon University.